The Ultimate Sales Training Workshop

The Ultimate Sales Training Workshop

A HANDS-ON GUIDE
FOR MANAGERS

Gerhard Gschwandtner

Founder and Publisher of *Selling Power*

McGRAW-HILL

NEW YORK | CHICAGO | SAN FRANCISCO | LISBON | LONDON | MADRID | MEXICO CITY
MILAN | NEW DELHI | SAN JUAN | SEOUL | SINGAPORE | SYDNEY | TORONTO

The **McGraw·Hill** Companies

1 2 3 4 5 6 7 8 9 0   DOC/DOC 0 9 87 6

ISBN-13: 978-0-07-147603-4
ISBN-10: 0-07-147603-2

McGraw-Hill books are available at special quantity discounts to use as premiums and sales promotions, or for use in corporate training programs. For more information, please write to the Director of Special Sales, Professional Publishing, McGraw-Hill, Two Penn Plaza, New York, NY 10121-2298. Or contact your local bookstore.

DISCLAIMER OF LIABILITY

Selling Power and Gerhard Gschwandtner hereby state that the training material in this book is being presented for illustrative and training purposes only. No liability is assumed or taken for any use or misuse of these articles and training guides. Do not use any guides or training contained in this book without prior approval of your management or legal department. Never say anything that is not true for your company or for your products or services.

CONTENTS

In each chapter you will find a Sales Manager's Meeting Guide and Additional Reading for Sales Reps.

INTRODUCTION

TRAIN TO WIN

The profession of selling is constantly changing. What doesn't change is the need for sales managers to train their salespeople. For the past 150 years, leaders of successful companies have trained, educated, and motivated their sales teams to reach greater levels of success.

In 1859, it was Henry Baldwin Hyde, the founder of the Equitable Life Assurance Society of the United States, who wrote and published a little book titled *Hints for Agents*. This sales bible contained persuasive arguments that salespeople could use to help prospects make a favorable decision. Hyde believed that good salespeople followed a system, once saying, "My rule in everything that is to be done, from writing a letter, to planning an important business, is to use my best skill, regardless of time, engagements, and everything else." Hyde focused on product knowledge and selling skills to create the leading life insurance company in America.

> **"Knowledge will forever govern ignorance; and a people who mean to be their own governors, must arm themselves with the power which knowledge gives."—James Madison**

In 1887, John Henry Patterson, the founder of NCR, realized at a trade show in Chicago that his salespeople had little product knowledge and none of them followed a consistent sales process. He immediately started a training program and hired an elocutionist to teach salespeople to deliver stellar presentations. Patterson soon discovered that the top salespeople used more effective techniques, so he sent his brother-in-law Joseph Crane to travel with the top producers and record their best practices. Soon NCR salespeople received the *Primer*, a detailed book of best-practice instructions on how to sell the cash register. The *Primer* contained tested ways for getting prospects away from their place of business into a nearby hotel meeting room where they could deliver a planned presentation without interruptions. Salespeople would learn about what customer objections they could expect, and for each objection, the *Primer* would offer several field-tested responses. The book also contained the best ways for closing the sale, such as adding benefits and calculating the savings and the financial gains achieved from investing in a cash register.

In the 1920s, Alfred C. Fuller created the Fuller Brush company. His motto was, "Make it work, make it last, guarantee it no matter what." Fuller Brush salespeople had to know the product, follow a systematic presentation, and ask for the order. Fuller educated his salespeople in the fine art of door-to-door selling. Fuller Brush salespeople had to ring the doorbell, and when the homemaker opened the door, the salesman was trained to take a step back and smile. The nonverbal message and differentiable competitive fact was that a Fuller Brush salesman was not the typical foot-in-the-door salesman.

While sales techniques change, the need for sales training remains the same. As in the old days of the Equitable Life Assurance Society, NCR, and the Fuller Brush Company, every company has its own personality or branding. Successful companies train their salespeople to deliver a branded sales experience. Good sales training can enhance the buying experience, while the absence of sales training can quickly destroy it. Good sales training is an extension of a company's mission, a reflection of a company's values, and a pleasing expression of a company's personality.

The best sales training contains a blended approach that comprises the right mix between creative guidelines for telling the company's story and successful blueprints for engaging customers in a productive and creative dialogue. Sales training must be constantly adapted to help salespeople earn the coveted trusted-adviser status. Ideally, the trusted adviser is a relationship expert, a business-efficiency consultant and a team leader capable of delivering innovative solutions that help customers experience a measurable, positive, and profitable transformation.

HOW TO GET THE MOST OUT OF THIS BOOK

Please Read This Section Carefully

The purpose of *The Ultimate Sales Training Workshop* is to help you train your salespeople more effectively so that they will be able to do the following:

- ☑ Create better relationships
- ☑ Generate more sales leads
- ☑ Deliver better presentations
- ☑ Create more effective proposals
- ☑ Handle customer objections more easily
- ☑ Understand customers better

☑ Close more sales

☑ Stay motivated and focused on success

> **"Who dares to teach must never cease to learn."**
> **—John Cotton Dana**

This book contains 15 complete sales training workshops that sales managers can deliver in one hour or less. Each chapter contains a step-by-step guide that sales managers can follow to conduct the training session. At the end of each chapter, you will find additional reading material for sales professionals.

This book has been created for the busy sales manager who wants to use fresh content for a weekly or monthly sales meeting. Using this book will save you time and energy. The tested sales training material in this book will help you become a stronger leader of your sales team. Since every sales training session requires lively interactions with your salespeople, you will quickly uncover the fact that your salespeople are in greater need of professional training than you originally assumed.

Remember that sales professionals have a short attention span, they don't like to be lectured to, and they learn best by doing. That's why each training session follows an interactive format in which salespeople can share their best practices, discuss new techniques, learn tested ideas, and role-play new skills.

To Get the Most Out of This Book, Follow This Simple Five-Step Plan:

1. Go to the section topic that has the most appeal to you, and read the hands-on guide for sales managers and the additional reading material for your salespeople. (Max. 20 min.)

2. Follow the preparation steps outlined in the Sales Manager's Meeting Guide (you will find this step-by-step guide in every section). It will take you less than one hour to prepare for your meeting.

3. Conduct your sales meeting, and always insist on active participation. Remember the formula for a successful training session: participation after presentation = progress activation. At the conclusion of each meeting ask each salesperson to apply the new skills every day.

4. To reinforce learning, share additional reading material with your salespeople in small doses as a follow-up (for example, one short article per day).

5. Conduct a follow-up meeting, and ask your salespeople to share examples of how they have used the new skills in the field. Recognize and celebrate your salespeople's

successful experiences. Remember that success celebration leads to progress acceleration.

The best way to ensure the success of each training session is to share your own challenges with learning, changing, and growing. It is a good idea to remind your team that with every growth step comes a little pain, which will quickly fade. Without growing, the pain will never abate.

ABOUT THE SALES TRAINING EXPERTS

Each training session has been written based on extensive interviews with some of America's most respected and most successful sales trainers. Many of these experts have written best-selling books and have created award-winning training courses. While some of the trainers conduct public workshops, others focus on customized training, and all of them offer consulting services.

> **"Learning is a race without a finish line."—Anonymous**

The great advantage of *The Ultimate Sales Training Workshop* is that it allows you to expose your team to the tested techniques of the best sales trainers in America. Each chapter will help your salespeople round out their experience and improve their skills. If your salespeople want to further expand their knowledge, you may want to invest in purchasing some of the books authored by these leading sales trainers.

If you want your company to become a market leader, it is inevitable that you will need to create your own customized sales training program. That's where the sales training experts featured in this book can help with innovative solutions. You can find their contact information at the end of each article. Check their Web sites, and contact these experts for a consultation. I can recommend every one of these trainers without reservation. They are the best in their field, and they've earned the highest honors in my book.

Gerhard Gschwandtner
Founder and Publisher
Selling Power Magazine

Prospecting

A HANDS-ON GUIDE FOR MANAGERS

TRAINING GUIDE TIME REQUIRED: 45 MINUTES

HOW TO EARN CUSTOMER REFERRALS

The Definition of a Referral

Referrals are report cards. They tell you how well you are doing at building business relationships and friendships with your customers.

Most salespeople wrongly believe that a referral happens when some customer is nice enough to give you the name of another potential customer. But that's not a referral; it's a fantasy.

In fact, referrals have nothing to do with being nice. Referrals are all about risk and trust. A referral means that your customer is willing to risk his or her friendship or relationship with others in order to give them to you as a business lead. When customers refer friends or business contacts, they trust you to deliver top-notch products and services.

In short, referrals are never just given—they are earned.

> **Most salespeople wrongly believe that a referral happens when some customer is nice enough to give you the name of another potential customer.**

Earning Referrals

The key to earning a referral is gaining the customer's trust while reducing the customer's risk. There are five ways to do this.

1. **BECOME FRIENDS WITH YOUR CUSTOMERS.** Meet them socially, at business networking events, on the golf course, at informal lunches, or anything else that's not strictly business. Customers who are your friends naturally want to put you in touch with their own friends.

2. **PROVIDE INCREDIBLE SERVICE.** Be certain that you and your company provide the absolutely highest level of service in your industry. The resulting credibility greatly reduces the risk of doing business with you.

3. **BE PROACTIVE ABOUT THEIR NEEDS.** Anticipate what they're likely to want and arrange ahead of time to have it taken care of. For example, Lexus will pick up and drop off your car at your office, leaving you a rental in case you need to drive somewhere during the day.

4. **BE A PROVIDER OF EXTRA VALUE.** Find something that you can do for the customer that's in addition to the expected products and services. For example, write an e-mail newsletter providing inside information about your customer's industry.

5. **GIVE REFERRALS TO YOUR CUSTOMERS.** Show your customers where they might be able to get new business. But do it in a way that lets them know that you don't necessarily expect anything in return. If you try to do referrals tit for tat, you'll end up looking manipulative.

Types of Referrals

All referrals are not equal; some are more valuable than others. In the order of least valuable to most valuable, here are the three types of referrals:

A. **SOLICITED.** You request and receive a referral from an existing customer. This does not mean that you "asked" for the referral. When it comes to referrals, the trick is to "ask without asking." Two ways to do this are described later in this chapter.

B. **PROACTIVE.** Without your asking, your existing customer calls you and gives you the name of a potential new customer. This is superior to a solicited referral because it indicates that you have built a trusting, risk-free relationship with the customer.

C. **UNSOLICITED.** An entirely new prospect calls you because one of your existing customers gave you a good recommendation. This is the best kind of referral, because it indicates that you have earned so much trust that your existing customers have become your sales representatives! Making a sale from an unsolicited referral is usually much easier than other sales situations, because most of your job has already been done for you—by your existing customers!

QUICK TIPS FOR YOUR NEXT SALES MEETING

In a nutshell, here's how to get more referrals:

- ☑ Have a sales philosophy that emphasizes relationship building.
- ☑ Value the relationship more than you do making your quota.
- ☑ Consider yourself and your firm as the best at what you do.
- ☑ Achieve a perfect job of delivering what you promised.
- ☑ Provide absolutely impeccable service after the sale.
- ☑ Help the customer build the customer's own business.
- ☑ Think end-of-time friendships not end-of-month totals.

Soliciting Referrals at the Point of Sale

Most salespeople are told to ask for referrals whenever they close a sale. That seldom works, though, because you haven't yet earned the customer's trust. At the point of sale, the customer has shown a willingness to do business with you, but that's all. The customer is already taking a risk by buying from you. Why would the customer want to compound that risk by recommending you to friends and contacts?

In the best case, asking for referrals at the point of sale will make the customer feel awkward; worst case, the customer will think you're greedy. If you follow up a day or two later with a telephone call saying, "Hey, how about those referrals I asked you about?" you'll ruin what's left of the relationship.

Rather than ask for a referral at the point of sale, you should use a postclosing conversation describing the actions that you will be taking in order to earn the trust that would naturally result in a referral. Compare the following two conversations.

INEFFECTIVE:

Customer: OK, we'll buy.

Salesperson: Great! Gee, do you know anybody else who might buy?

EFFECTIVE:

Customer: OK, we'll buy.

Salesperson: Great! Thank you so very much for being my customer. We're going to perform for you so phenomenally that you're going to be completely amazed and delighted. But here's what I want you to do for me. I want you to be thinking of a few people who you think should be doing business with us, if we are as incredible as we say we are. And after I know that you know we're the absolute best, I'm going to remind you of this request; but before you give me any names, I'm going to bring you a new customer for your own business. Is that fair enough?

Soliciting Referrals in an Ongoing Relationship

If your company already has a relationship with the customer and you believe that you have earned the customer's trust, a good way to solicit a referral is to ask for a testimonial. Tell the customer that you'd like to share his or her opinions and perceptions with prospective customers. If the customer agrees, ask such questions as:

- ☑ What could we be doing better?
- ☑ What have we done right for you so far?
- ☑ What would it take for you to refer other people to us?

Needless to say, you should listen very carefully to the responses and write down any comments that might prove valuable in your sales materials. But you are also looking for the series of green-light answers that indicates you've built up enough trust so that it's fair to expect some referrals. When this is the case, you can solicit referrals by asking (with a smile), "So, who are you thinking of referring to us?" Chances are that the customer will laugh and then give you a few names. Of course, if the customer launches into a set of complaints, you know that you're not in a position to solicit referrals.

Obtaining Proactive and Unsolicited Referrals

Proactive and unsolicited referrals are the result of building a strong personal relationship with the customer, combined with superlative products and services. That having been said, there are several things you can do to make it easier for your delighted customers to take action that will bring customers to you.

A good way to make it easy for the customer is to provide the customer with an excuse to talk about you when other people visit his or her office. Don't bother with such overused "spifs" as coffee mugs, though. Instead, give the customer a personalized gift that will become an office conversational item. For example, if a customer is a big baseball fan,

FREQUENTLY
ASKED
QUESTIONS

SALES REPS' FREQUENTLY ASKED QUESTIONS

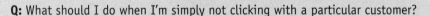

Q: How can I avoid misconceptions while becoming friends with a customer of the opposite sex?

A: A certain amount of sexual tension is inevitable between friends of the opposite sex, but that doesn't mean that the subject need ever come out into the open. Be friendly without being flirtatious. If there's any question about how your actions will be perceived, err on the conservative side.

Q: What should I do when I'm simply not clicking with a particular customer?

A: If you want referrals, you're going to have to get them from a different customer! There are some situations where your personalities simply aren't going to mesh. Rather than waste time on a friendship that isn't going to happen, find a customer with whom you're more personally compatible.

Q: How can I get referrals if my company isn't the best in the business?

A: You probably can't. Companies that don't provide superlative products and post-sales support always have lukewarm customers, at best. Realistically, if you want to get referrals, you'll need to work with the other departments in your firm to improve overall quality.

you might take a baseball, have everybody on your team autograph it, and then present it to the customer, with a stand, labeled "Thanks for Helping Our Team."

While the specific approach will vary from customer to customer, use your personal relationship and friendship-building skills to devise a personalized gift that will remain on display and continue to generate positive comments.

JEFFREY GITOMER was interviewed for this article. He is author of the business best seller *The Sales Bible* (Wiley) and founder of TrainOne, a Charlotte, NC-based firm that delivers a wide variety of online sales training. Gitomer also delivers seminars and runs annual sales meetings, and his customers include Coca-Cola, Caterpillar, BMW, AmeriPride, DR Horton, Enterprise Rent-A-Car, and NCR. TrainOne and Buy Gitomer are located at 310 Arlington Ave., Loft 329, Charlotte, NC 28203. Telephone: 704-333-1112. Web: www.TrainOne.com and www.gitomer.com.

SALES MANAGER'S MEETING GUIDE

Below are 14 practical steps to help your sales team get more referrals.
This sales meeting should take about 45 minutes.

1. One week prior to the meeting, e-mail your team and ask members to make a list of all the customer decision makers with whom they are in regular contact. Ask them to bring the completed list to the meeting.

2. Prior to the meeting, prepare a slide listing the five key ways to earn referrals from this article.

3. Open the meeting by saying that the purpose of the meeting is to work on increasing the number and quality of referrals that come from existing and new customers.

4. Tell the team to categorize their customer contacts into three groups:
   a) buddies who will always take a call
   b) friends with whom they have something in common
   c) acquaintances

5. Tell the team to put a mark next to the name of each contact for each referral that the contact has provided.

6. Ask the team members whether they see a pattern. They will probably observe that nearly all of their referrals come from categories A and B and that a disproportionate number come from category A.

7. Show the slide summarizing the key ways that salespeople can earn referrals. Go through each point briefly. You should now be 10 minutes into the meeting.

8. Lead a discussion of the first key way ("Become friends with your customers") in detail. Explain that the best way to get more referrals is to use those techniques to raise their contacts from level Cs and B to level A. Draw from your own experience or ask team members for suggestions for accomplishing this. Spend approximately 10 minutes on this.

9. Lead a discussion of the second, third, and fourth key ways in the context of your team's and your company's ability to deliver as promised. Brainstorm any ideas to improve performance in these areas. Spend approximately 10 minutes on this.

10. Have the team members identify a customer contact who has not yet given them a referral, and have them identify somebody whom they could bring to that contact as a referral for the customer's business.

11. Ask for a volunteer to be a customer contact. Go through the two dialogues in "Soliciting Referrals at the Point of Sale." Ask the team which approach is likely to prove more effective.

12. Break the team into groups of two and have them practice the effective approach, alternating the role of the customer.

13. Make it clear that over time you intend to grade their sales performance, not just on making quotas, but on the number and quality of the referrals that they receive.

14. Thank the team members for their participation and close the meeting.

QUICK TIPS

QUICK
TIP

☑ For a dramatic, pointed opening to the training session, prepare three slides. The first has the question "What are we doing to get more referrals?" The second has the answer "Not enough." The third has the single word "Yet."

☑ Your training session may include experienced team members who have great customer contacts. If appropriate, ask the experienced members to share their techniques for getting past administrative assistants and voice mail in order to get to the customer contact directly. If the experienced team member is a particularly confident performer, have him or her actually make a demonstration call on a cell phone during the meeting.

☑ Here's a great rule of thumb: the two best ways to get referrals are (1) to earn one and (2) to give one. These are little-used techniques in selling, because they require hard work on the part of the salesperson, and many salespeople are not willing to do the hard work it takes to make selling easy.

ADDITIONAL READING

If you're looking for ways to manage your territory so that you get a full day each week in front of new prospects, here's a road map. But it's up to you to implement, implement, implement. No magic bullet here.

Just solid, sensible strategy.

No matter how often you tell yourself you're going to start setting aside time for prospecting, no matter how many planners and time management programs you buy, you always seem to end up with too few hours in the day. And it's always the hours you set aside to make cold calls and meet with new prospects that get short shrift.

If you're not following through on the prospecting commitments you've made to yourself, the problem may not be lack of time but something else entirely: you haven't devised a strategy for prospecting, and you've failed to quantify your prospecting activities' value for you as a salesperson. "Prospecting gets dropped, not because of lack of time, but because it's harder," says Tom Jordan, managing director for MBIA Municipal Investor Service Corporation in Armonk, NY.

The first step in developing a successful prospecting strategy is to identify potential customers in your territory. "Territory management begins with a careful analysis of what accounts are there and who has the potential to reward you for your efforts," says Max Tyrrell, senior sales representative for laboratory supplies company VWR in Knoxville, TN.

> "Territory management begins with a careful analysis of what accounts are there and who has the potential to reward you for your efforts."

"Whether you receive leads from your marketing department, get referrals from existing clients, or generate your own prospects, you need to organize these targets," says Jordan. He arranges prospects in a comprehensive yet simple manner, classifying his prospective customers—municipalities and government agencies with funds to invest—by their potential and projected sales volume.

"While you may be tempted to go after the 'big dogs,' instead," says Jordan, "focus on the 'sweet spot'—the customers who'll give the highest return for your investment." Instead of targeting the largest organizations with the biggest investment potential, Jordan has his salespeople go down a level to the midsize agencies. Why? The largest cities gain a lot of attention and tend to be more volatile, while the smaller organizations tend to be too small to justify the time investment. "We send our salespeople where they're going to get the most production for their activity. We're looking for the steady investor who needs our services," he says. That's not to say MBIA would turn away a larger investor—or a smaller one. But his salespeople spend their time cultivating the customers who are most likely to represent a significant account.

The next step is to keep track of and manage your activities in a way that makes sense for you. Don't assume you must invest in the latest digital technology if you're more comfortable with a paper planner and careful notes. "The key is to make the system useful," says Tyrrell, who uses a combination of a database management system and paper calendar.

Each of Jordan's salespeople—they are expected to spend about a third of their time cold prospecting—has about 100 to 125 "sweet spot" targets at a time, ranked from 0 to 5 based on their participation and interest level (5 means no physical sales call has been conducted, while 0 means the prospect has become a customer). Regular reports to management and reminder e-mail messages to salespeople keep everyone focused on the prime targets.

If this level of detail isn't your cup of tea, adapt the process to fit your personality. Tyrrell relies on a whiteboard divided into a grid, hanging on his office wall. A "Hot Deals" column denotes orders expected to close within the next month; "Targets" lists his top prospects for the quarter; "Longer-Term Deals" is for farther-out opportunities; and "Needs a Sales Call" highlights his top priorities. "Every morning I come down here, I turn around and see what I have to do," he says. "That whiteboard has made more difference to me than anything else." It's so useful that Tyrrell regularly photographs the board and e-mails a picture to his manager.

Once you've developed a workable tracking mechanism, you'll be able to quantify exactly how much time you've put into each sale—and into each nonproductive lead. You'll know what percentage of sales you get from each type of customer, and you'll be able to define how much each prospect is worth to you. "You can almost manage your success back to your goal or quota," says Jordan. For instance, if your quota is $100 million in new business, and your average "sweet spot" client is worth $2 million in orders, you need to bring in 50 new clients. And if you know you close about a third of your deals, you'll need to call on 150 new prospects.

This knowledge will easily allow you to set appropriate goals for the week, month, and quarter—and will help you determine why you're not as successful as you'd like to be, even though you're working as hard as you can. "The most effective sales reps are the ones who know how to focus on the big payoffs," says Jordan. If you're running as hard as you can just to stay even, you're probably working on the wrong things.

When you know your activity is more likely to yield dividends, it's easier to make prospecting a priority. At the same time, though, keep your perspective. "You don't have to sell everything the first time you meet the prospect," reminds Tyrrell. The journey from target to actual customer is a progression. "Most people don't put all their cards on the table right away," he says. Instead, think of the initial sales call as a fact-finding mission where you can gather and update your information on the account and begin to determine how to best position your product, your company, and yourself.

QUICK
TIP

GET THE MOST OUT OF YOUR TERRITORY

Every sales territory is a potential gold mine, but whether you strike it rich depends on targeting your efforts to tap into the richest vein of customers. The best way to accomplish this is to plan your days, weeks, and months to keep your territory delivering maximum sales. Here are a few suggestions.

START BIG, THEN NARROW. Begin with your goals for the next month, and then plot them out. From there, develop your weekly plans and, from those, your daily schedule. At the end of each day revise as necessary so that you are concentrating on the most productive accounts in the most efficient manner possible.

DO YOUR HOMEWORK. Existing customers and hot prospects should be your top priority, of course. Prospects won't just volunteer their heart index, however, so before setting your appointments, do some research to help gauge each prospect's temperature. Information gathered ahead of time will also give you a sense of how long a prospective call should take.

RESIST TEMPTATIONS. The attraction of a big customer or opportunity that's well out of your way can be enticing, but don't give in. If the opportunity evaporates upon your arrival, you may have wasted half a day or more chasing a red herring. Instead, find a day in the future when you can make that prospect fit your schedule and not throw you off your plan.

GO FAR TO NEAR. Whenever possible, try to schedule the appointments that are farthest from your office first, and then work your way back through the rest of your calls. As the day draws to a close, you can race toward the finish like a thoroughbred on the home stretch.

EXPERT ADVICE: THE PROSPECTING HABIT

EXPERT ADVICE

While some super-successful salespeople make it seem as if new customers bloom overnight, fully formed and ready to buy, the truth is that prospecting takes a lot of time and effort. "You need to build it on a continual basis. Build that momentum, and make that a way of life for you," recommends Alan McAnally, president of Commonwealth Sales Consulting.

In other words, prospecting must become something you do, day in and day out, in good times and in slumps. And in the bad times, you can't rely on the same old tricks as every other salesperson if you're hoping to grow good, solid new customers out of an overworked, recession-stricken territory. Instead, says McAnally, by bringing variety to your approaches, you'll be more likely to develop new contacts—and maximize your productivity.

For instance, try setting up meetings before or after business hours. "Most people who you want to talk to, who have some power, are usually in before the secretaries," and stay later, says McAnally. "The hours between 7:00 and 8:30 in the morning and 5:00 and 6:30 in the evening can be surprisingly productive."

Also, make such "barriers" as voice mail work for you. "It costs you very little to dial that number seven times in a day," says McAnally. And the beauty of automated systems is that you don't have to leave a message every time—you can keep calling until you get the person you want to speak with.

Be prepared to use "found" time. Make follow-up calls or check in with your manager while traveling to and from meetings. If you have a half-hour on your hands because of a no-show or late appointment, bond with the receptionist or catch up on your paperwork. Or drive around an unfamiliar office park to see which companies are expanding and which have vanished. "Wasting time is in your mind. It's not a reality," McAnally says. "An effective person can use their time wisely, no matter what the situation. It's an attitude."

ADDITIONAL READING

You can't sell them if you can't tell them. And you can't tell them if you can't see them.

Getting in to see prospects has always been a salesperson's number one challenge.

While getting a foot in the door was always a sales challenge, face-to-face visits with prospects have become a matter of wits, timing, and preparation— not to mention outright schmoozing.

Steve Skaggs, general sales manager of the Nickel Ads advertising shopper in Portland, OR, runs into prospect access issues every day. Since most of his staff make cold calls in person, he emphasizes the image his salespeople project. "How the prospect perceives you when you walk in the door of a business is very important," he says. "You need to be confident, friendly, and have an attitude that makes everyone want to know you and be part of your team."

Skaggs adds, "Salespeople have to know how to read prospects and realize not everybody is ready to buy when you want to sell. Sometimes it's in your best interest to tell prospects to hide their checkbook because all you're doing today is finding out what's happening with their business and what their needs are. Once they know it's not going to cost them anything, they're more likely to take the time to see you.

"I encourage my salespeople to try to make a friend, no matter where they go, and not to prejudge people, because you never know who the real influencer is. From the moment you hit that auto showroom floor, start talking to sales reps. It doesn't hurt to get as many people on your side as you can, and they might be able to help you set up a meeting with the decision maker."

Although it's obvious sales logic, Skaggs encourages salespeople to qualify their prospects, and he makes sure they can adequately probe for and answer questions. "Even though it's basic, salespeople have to identify and qualify decision makers," he explains. "Sometimes it's easier to just walk into a business and ask to see the owner, but it's much more professional to call in advance and find out whom you need to talk to and get background information. That way, when you walk in and demonstrate you're on top of your game, the chances of seeing that person are better.

"I coach all of my sales reps to make sure they know how to ask the proper questions and, on the flip side, know how to answer the prospects' questions. If you're trying to convince prospects to take time away from their business to meet with you, you better appear businesslike and organized."

EXPERT ADVICE: WINNING STRATEGIES FOR MEETING PROSPECTS

EXPERT ADVICE

Successfully meeting with prospects requires salespeople to be prepared, be quick on their feet, and project a strong, benefit-oriented sales message.

"Voice mail is a real hindrance to today's salesperson," says sales trainer and consultant Linda Richardson. "You have to learn how to leave a positive, short-but-compelling message with the most important ingredient being what you can do for the prospect. It has to make the prospect want to call you back."

"Do your research to find out about the prospect and develop a purpose for the call, linked to a potential client benefit," advises Richardson. "You need to engage the prospect as quickly as you can to find out if you're in the right place and pew."

Richardson believes that salespeople should pay special attention to how they sound on the phone and not work off scripts.

"Pick up the phone at the office and leave a voice mail for yourself at home," says Richardson. "When you listen to it, ask yourself, 'What type of impression am I making, and do I sound like someone I'd want to call back?'"

"Stay away from scripts because scripts defy a dialogue and defy engagement. Unless you're as talented as Sir Laurence Olivier, you won't be able to bring it to life. Define a purpose for your call, have a list of benefits, and practice responses to objections, but don't use a script."

If salespeople are dealing with gatekeepers, Richardson advises them to start building relationships with them from the get-go. "Be ready and willing to talk to gatekeepers," she urges. "Be respectful and treat them as intelligent, valuable members of the prospect's team. Once you get to know gatekeepers and build rapport, they are a terrific source of information and can open all kinds of doors for you."

Richardson feels that utilizing referrals is the best way to get into the prospect's door. "Ask everyone you know for referrals, and explore all potential sources of leads," she says. "Go after the low-hanging fruit first, and remember that a warm call gets through to a prospect a lot quicker than a cold one."

"Ask a current customer to pave the way for you by making a phone call to a prospect. It gives you automatic credibility and eliminates a sales threat."

Know what you want to accomplish, but don't go overboard. "Salespeople need to keep in mind the objective of the phone call to get an appointment and be careful not to overextend," Richardson advises. "Monitor yourself so you don't talk yourself out of a meeting."

"Take notes of what prospects are saying and circle any key words that you can incorporate into what you say back to them. Use a checklist and ask for feedback to keep the dialogue going until you get closure on an appointment."

Linda Richardson is president of The Richardson Company, specializing in sales training and consulting. For information call 215-935-9255, or visit www.richardsonco.com.

Enthusiasm and passion for the product go a long way in convincing a prospect to meet with you. "Our salespeople have to convey to prospects that they have a good reason for being there and are excited and passionate about the fact that our paper is a good fit," says Skaggs. "The tone and the excitement will carry through to the prospects."

According to Teammates Commercial Interiors president and chief salesperson Michael Berkery, research, e-mail, and referrals are the most effective tools in getting to see new prospects. "Once we learn about a prospect, we try to get an introduction to that prospect from another source," he observes. "We try to find someone we've worked with in the past, one of our customers or even somebody we know in a related field, to write a letter or make a call on our behalf."

"If we're not lucky enough to know anybody, we start doing research, checking out Web sites, and reading press releases. If we can find the prospect's e-mail, we'll send a little note or postcard electronically, with a link to the Teammates Web site. That way they can click on us and learn what we're all about and respond. It's a nonthreatening way to make a prospect contact."

"If we're making an in-person cold call," Berkery adds, "we don't try to see or sell anybody the first time. We look around to get a feel of what the prospect might need and try to get such information as an annual report or collateral material. We talk to the receptionist and start building rapport. We find that most receptionists really do want to help and give you honest feedback when you ask them what is the best way to get an appointment with a decision maker. In many cases, they become one of your champions."

> **"The ability to relate benefits to needs is what separates the good salespeople from the ones who just leave brochures at the front desk. You become a resource that the prospect didn't know about, and that makes getting a legitimate meeting easier."**

"If you do have an opportunity on a cold call to talk to a decision maker," Berkery says, "your opening statement is critical and is what separates you from the rest of the pack." "Instead of saying, 'we sell office furniture and cubicles,' we say, 'I'm sure you never have a problem with loud noises and distractions and your employees probably never miss a day of work because their backs hurt,'" he explains. "You need to talk to the point where it gets emotional and they have a pain that you can fix. The ability to relate benefits to needs is what separates the good salespeople from the ones who just leave brochures at the front desk. You become a resource that the prospect didn't know about, and that makes getting a legitimate meeting easier."

When push comes to shove, Berkery feels that persistence, combined with a valid reason to meet with the prospect, often wins the day. "You have to have perseverance to be a good salesperson," he says. "Sometimes when I'm working really hard trying to chase a prospect down, I just set in my mind that I'm going to meet with this person if it's the last thing I do. It's kind of a game. I'll call and leave a message saying, 'Call me back and let me know how many messages I have to leave before you call me back.'"

"As the president of a company, I get calls every day from people wanting to sell me things, and I don't get back to them unless I see a clear-cut reason and benefit to me for doing so. If they have something decent to talk about, I'll return their calls. But if I think they're just going down their calls sheets, forget it."

When it comes to prospecting, you have to look beyond the obvious. You need to seek out leads where no one else is looking, and one of the best spots to find information on current and prospective customers is through regional newspapers and magazines.

Many salespeople make reading the newspaper a part of their daily routine, but you have to think beyond *The Wall Street Journal*, *USA Today,* and your major metropolitan daily, says K. C. Frew, sales representative with high-vacuum technology company Varian Inc., in Knoxville, TN. In fact, Frew says the usefulness of the periodical is inversely proportional to its size: the larger papers, he's found, are the least useful when looking for leads.

Frew, who covers Kentucky, Tennessee, and Arkansas, says the first thing he does when he comes to town is stop at a grocery store. He moves right past the metropolitan and national papers and heads for the smallest paper he can find—typically a county or town paper put out on a weekly basis. "My competitors usually cover a larger territory than I do, and I'm guessing they don't read these little dinky papers. But they're just oozing with good stuff," says Frew.

That "good stuff" is Frew's lifeline to communities that he may visit only a few times a year. News about new construction, business deals, and other sales opportunities shows up on the pages of the *Oak Ridger* long before it hits the pages of the *Knoxville News Sentinel*. Frew gives the example of the proposal to build a nuclear plant in one of the smallest counties in the state. This was a huge opportunity for Frew's company. "I saw it in the Nashville paper two days ago," he says. But he's been following the proposal for months, ever since reading about it in the county's weekly paper a year and a half ago. "Now I've got the jump on the competitor," he says.

"If the areas you cover don't have small papers, larger metropolitan dailies and weekly regional business journals can serve the same purpose," he says. The key is to get as close to the community as possible, looking for leads that wouldn't appear in periodicals with a larger focus. The periodicals he avoids, though, are the industry journals. They're too national in scope, too dated, and too accessible to competitors to make them worth his while.

Once you've amassed mounds of papers from cities and towns in your territory, you need a plan for dealing with the information. Mike Frotten, the southeast group manager and senior vice president for Interfirst Wholesale Mortgage Lending in Orlando, FL, knows that for his company certain sections present more viable opportunities than others. "In the Sunday real estate section will be several leads," he says. Depending on your business, you may be interested in news in technology, finance, or even sports.

HOW TO QUALIFY LEADS

QUICK
TIP

As you probably know, all leads are not created equal. Your goal, when a new lead comes in, should be to qualify or disqualify it as soon as possible so you'll know whether to pursue it. Essentially, you want to do some quick research to determine four things.

1. **WANT AND NEEDS.** Is there a good match between the customer's needs and what you have to offer? Get information up front about this prospect's unique business challenges to pinpoint how well you match up.

2. **WHERE'S THE BUDGET?** Customers who desperately need your product or service immediately are only hot prospects if they have the financial resources to be able to buy.

3. **THE POWER OF YES.** During your investigation, be sure to confirm that your potential contact is the decision maker. If he or she is not, do a little more digging to see how difficult it would be to get to the individual who is.

4. **CHECK THE CALENDAR.** Rather than frustrate yourself by pursuing a lead only to find out the customer won't be ready to buy for another nine months, be sure to establish that the prospect is hot now—not slowly warming over a prolonged period of time.

Certain sections are worth perusing, regardless of your industry. Look for construction news and new business deals in the news section. New construction, investment dollars, or large deals—as in the case of the power plant—mean a company has money to spend, and the time to make the contact is before everyone else hears about it.

The business section always includes a "People on the Move" column, with lists of promotions, awards, and new employees. "Even if someone has received a promotion, it's an opportunity to prospect," says Frotten.

"Another source of valuable information is the want ads," says Frew. "Just as with new construction, a hiring push is a signal to pay closer attention. Whether it's an existing customer or a company you've never heard of, 'They're spending money, and they're hiring. Something's going on,'" Frew says. "And if they're hiring for a position directly involved in purchasing your product, 'That's a guy I need to meet when he's hired,'" says Frew.

After scavenging the paper, your next step depends on the type of information you've discovered. "For announcements of new hires, promotions, and awards, make a call or

> **The business section always includes a "People on the Move" column, with lists of promotions, awards, and new employees.**

write a note and include a clipping of the article," says Frotten. He remembers when, as a brand-new loan officer, he read about a real estate agent receiving a large piece of business. He phoned the agent, saying, "I'm also new, and maybe we could help each other out," Frotten recalls. The agent laughed and agreed to a lunch meeting, and the two ended up referring business to each other for years.

While Frew doesn't typically write congratulatory notes, he does make note of awards and patents received by current customers in order to mention their success the next time they meet. And if an unknown person is working on something that might be relevant to Frew's business, "My antenna is really up," he says. He'll then place a quick call to the person to get additional information about the projects.

If the information gleaned from the paper isn't immediately actionable, Frew says he tucks it away in a "tickler" file to be reviewed later. Then he'll check in with the appropriate contact or company to see how things are progressing.

In any case, the information is absolutely worthless unless you follow up on it. And when you do follow up—whether it be in person, by phone, or on paper— remember that you're establishing a contact, nothing more. "People try to do too much. That's why there's sales reluctance," explains Frotten. "Your first challenge is merely to arrange a meeting and determine if you can help each other. And, if you truly believe you can help someone else, why are you nervous about it?" he asks.

HOW TO MAKE LEAD GENERATION A STANDARD PART OF YOUR SALES DAY

ADDITIONAL READING

If you want to grow, prosper, and set sales records, it's up to you and your sales team to find new customers. You need to reach out and touch more potential customers in new markets and bring them into the fold. However, what is the best way to generate new leads? Pick one of the following: (a) talk to truck drivers, (b) get referrals, (c) go through old files, (d) attend trade shows, (e) use direct mail. And the answer?

Well, it's a toss-up. Using any one of these methods can produce potentially lucrative sales leads—not tire kickers, but real, live, legitimate prospects.

CIRCLE OF REFERRALS

For qualified sales leads, it's hard to beat referrals. Knowing someone who knows someone automatically gets your foot at least part of the way in the door. And the best place to get referrals is in your own marketplace. Jennifer Reimer is the inside sales manager, eastern division, for Essilor Laboratories, a major supplier of prescription safety eyeglasses. She advises her sales reps to spend time researching their respective markets to find companies that may have a need for their product. "If a prospect has big machines and/or conveyer belts, that means there's the potential for flying objects," she notes. "If that's the case, there's a good possibility that safety glasses are needed. We use manufacturers' guides to get a feel for what kind of business a company does, and if it looks like a fit for prescription safety glasses, we take it a step further and research it on the Internet. If it still looks viable, we make phone calls to find out who the appropriate person is to talk to and arrange an appointment."

Reimer has a system that creates a win-win situation for all concerned. "We get a lot of referrals from our eye-care provider network, which are local doctors who do the eye exams, fitting and measuring for the glasses," she explains. "Since not every optometrist (OD) or eye-care provider wants to do safety glasses, we've developed a network of recommended dispensers who are interested in doing safety glasses. We give a list of them to our customers."

"We have ODs calling us and saying, 'Here's a local company that needs prescription safety glasses but doesn't know where to go to get them.' By our referring business to them, they in turn refer business back to us, that we then can refer back to them. It's like a big referral circle," says Reimer.

No business is an island, so Reimer makes sure her referral circle is as encompassing as possible. "We get referrals from companies we do business with, their 'sister' companies in other areas and companies that recently purchased one of our customers," she notes. "We might do safety glasses for a small shop that just got purchased by a larger organization, and they refer us. In each case they say, 'These people did a great job for us. Give them a shot.'"

"Another source of referrals comes from networking with safety equipment distributors. They sell hard hats, boots, earplugs, and they sometimes get asked if they provide prescription safety glasses. If they don't, they refer the customer to us."

"Referrals are our number one source for leads, and a lot of it has to do with building rapport," says Candace Munson, account manager for Killington Wood Products, a division of Carris-Reels in Rutland, VT. "They come from customers and even competitors that we have a good relationship with. Even though we do a variety of pallets, there are certain specialty items we can do better than anyone else, and we have competitors actually on our side."

"Salespeople shouldn't just look at getting referrals from existing customers. Instead, they should make asking for them an integral part of every cold call," says sales trainer and consultant Bill Truax, president of Trufield Enterprises Inc., in Chagrin Falls, OH. "Salespeople should continuously seek referrals from existing customers, friends, and even prospects they're talking to for the first time," he advises. "Don't fall into the trap of thinking that you can only ask for referrals from people whom you know or are already doing business with."

"At the same time, it's imperative for salespeople to know how to ask for referrals. On a first-time call, if I asked you to think, off the top of your head, of anybody else who could use our widgets, you'd probably say no," Truax points out. "But if I asked you to give me the names of three people you know who are in positions similar to yours, who could also use my product, and whom I can call on, you could probably come up with those three names."

ON WITH THE SHOW

Never overlook the value of trade shows when looking for qualified leads. "We do a lot of trade shows that are targeted toward safety directors, human resource managers, nurses—anybody who is involved with the safety of employees," says Reimer. "We notify current customers and prospects to whom we've been trying to sell that we're going to be there and invite them to stop by our booth."

Trade shows present an excellent opportunity for networking. "Our parent company, Carris Reels, attends trade shows, and we do get some feedback from them," says Killington Wood's Munson. "It's a way of connecting with the customer you already have, and hopefully your good name and good service will filter through that trade show to the people who don't know who you are."

"In our industry, we have a number of customers who feed from each other, and trade shows are a good way to network. For example, maybe three booths down from your booth is a chemical company that will feed a plastic company that supplies their plastic materials to a wire and cable company that then buys reels from Carris Reels and pallets from us."

Truax also believes trade or consumer shows can be effective lead generators. "Trade shows actually give salespeople the opportunity to make the first sales call right there at the booth. And the great thing is that the prospects come up to them," says Truax. "If done correctly, trade shows are a wonderful selling tool."

However, trade shows require special skills that many salespeople need to acquire before setting foot on the show floor. "Salespeople need to be trained ahead of time how to ask the questions that are relevant at a show," Truax notes. "The companies that do it well have salespeople with gentle personalities, not coming on hard, asking a few qualifying questions and finding out who the right person to talk to is and then following up in a timely fashion."

IT'S IN THE MAIL

"If used correctly, direct mail can be your private sales force in the field to prospect for new business," says Lois Geller, president of Geller & Mason, a direct mail/marketing agency. "But before you can do that, you need to work the numbers and calculate an 'allowable.'"

According to Geller, an "allowable" is how much money you can spend to get one order and break even, or get one order and make a predetermined profit. "Determine what the gross revenue per order is," she explains, "and subtract the cost for that order, including the cost of the mailing, the cost of sending out a salesperson, and any of the additional costs of closing the sale. That gives you your breakeven or 'allowable.'"

When considering using direct mail as a lead generator, Geller also takes into consideration the lifetime value of a customer. "Ask yourself how much potential revenue that lead could produce over the course of time," she says. "For example, if you're selling cars, don't just calculate the allowable based on the sale of one fully loaded new car. Take into consideration whether that customer is going to trade it in every three years, based on customer sales history."

"Once you get all the numbers down, it makes it more scientific and gives you a picture of what type of response you need to be successful."

Direct mail is not a hit-or-miss operation. "Once you have the numbers crunched and know what you can afford to spend on acquiring a lead, make sure your mailing is targeted, builds rapport quickly, and contains a compelling offer to generate a quick response—what we call a 'quick call to action,'" says Geller.

How do you get prospects to open your letter? "Create a 'willing suspension of disbelief,'" Geller explains. "Even though prospects may know it's a form letter, they still want to believe that it came from a real person. Sign your name in blue, put a Post-it note on it, mail it out first class or write your name over the company name on the outer envelope."

Dennis Poulos, an agent for New York Life in Flint, MI, is a true believer in utilizing direct mail to get qualified leads. He sends out more than 100,000 pieces of mail annually, promoting the 16 retirement and estate-planning workshops he conducts each year through local community education departments.

"On an average, we get approximately 25 people attending each of our workshops. And we have a sign-up ratio between 70 and 80 percent of follow-up visits at our office," says Poulos. "We'll eventually do business with about 25 percent of them.

"Because of the workshop format, our initial contact with prospects is nonthreatening, and we don't get into any specific products at all. They come to a workshop, then a follow-up visit 6 to 12 months down the road, and then we end up working with them on their retirement and estate plans."

Once prospects express a need, Poulos partners with attorneys, CPAs and, if a business is involved, business appraisers. That means additional referrals for Poulos. "We want customers to come to our office, and then we'll find the appropriate professional for them," says Poulos. "We do a tremendous amount of referral work for other professionals, and we get a decent amount of referrals back from them. It just naturally happens. And because of it, we've done some very nice cases over the years."

> "We do a tremendous amount of referral work for other professionals, and we get a decent amount of referrals back from them. It just naturally happens."

"We've tried advertising in other media but found that nothing works nearly as well as direct mail. You have to send out large quantities to an identifiable target audience over a long period of time and have the right mix and blend in terms of what you offer. But it does work."

LOOK OUTSIDE THE BOX

Truax stresses that salespeople should be constantly aware of opportunities to get new leads. "Just use your head as you're driving along. Be aware and talk to people," he advises. "My dad used to call it 'smokestack prospecting.' If you see a truck stopped at an intersection with the name of a company on it that you're not aware of, make a note of it and do some research. Talk, ask questions, and listen to people. Leads are all around you, but you have to have the mind-set to recognize, acknowledge, and take advantage of them."

Killington Woods' Munson receives a significant number of leads from her company's truck drivers. "Our truck drivers are a huge source of information and leads for us," she says. "A lot of times our drivers are dropping off pallets in industrial parks and jot down the names of companies."

"They talk to customer receiving and shipping people who fill them in on who is a good prospect in the area for us. Sometimes they even tell our drivers to use their names as referrals. We follow up with a phone call, send a package of information, and set up an appointment."

Many salespeople don't realize that an excellent source of leads is right beneath their fingertips: old company files. "Never throw away your old files. Archive them," Munson advises. "I have found a number of people from companies that we haven't done business with for years because we didn't have the right equipment at that time and something has since changed. It's time to go back and talk to them."

"Keep an open mind," urges Essilor Laboratories' Reimer. "The place where you least expect a lead is where you're going to get it. For instance, we got a lead on a company that made pet food. I never in my wildest dreams thought that they would need safety glasses. But when you think of how pet food is made, with machines and conveyer belts, it makes sense."

Sales Process

A HANDS-ON GUIDE FOR MANAGERS

TRAINING GUIDE TIME REQUIRED: 50 MINUTES

WHAT IS SALES PROCESS?

There are two ways of thinking about sales: as a set of goals or as a process. Goal-oriented selling focuses on predetermined milestones, starting with the initial introduction to the client and finishing with the closing of the sale. While many sales reps find this motivating, focusing exclusively on goals blinds the sales rep to the process by which opportunities evolve into sales.

As an analogy, compare the performance of weekend athletes with that of Olympic athletes. The weekend basketball player thinks about shooting the ball into a basket, the last 10 misses, the last 3 successful baskets, what the ultimate score is, and even how stupid another miss might look. By contrast, an Olympic athlete scouts the competition, knows the style of play, senses the position of the ball, the presence of the other players, and the exact movement needed to move the ball closer to the basket and effectively score.

In other words, for the weekend athlete the goal largely blots out the process, making success a hit-or-miss proposition. For the Olympic athlete, the process leads naturally and progressively toward the goal. The same is true in sales.

QUICK TIPS

QUICK
TIP

☑ Sales process is the study of a lifetime; don't expect to grasp the concept or master the techniques immediately. Focus on a few basics to begin.

☑ Engaged listening is a valuable tool that weaves you into the conversation; that shows you care and creates an environment to foster a good human relationship, even outside of the work environment.

☑ Body language and engaged listening are interrelated. When the customer is talking, you'll be more interested, and seem more interested, if your expression and posture indicate interest.

Goal-oriented sales reps often feel more comfortable aggressively pushing their solution in search of a problem, despite the fact that the customer is likely to feel railroaded. Even consultative sales techniques can seem harsh and awkward in the hands of a goal-obsessed sales rep. Suppose, for example, the sales rep has been trained to ask probing questions to discover customer needs. If the sales rep is focused exclusively on the goal of making a sale, the customer will quickly realize that the point of the questioning is simply to manipulate the customer's answers to lead inexorably toward a close.

Process-oriented sales reps, by contrast, don't focus much on the day-to-day routine of closing and quotas. Instead, they try to build long-term, collaborative customer relationships in which the customer actively brings up business and opportunities. This kind of relationship can only develop through the building of trust, credibility, and rapport, which always evolve naturally from the sales process and never from the achievement of a short-term sales goal.

Nearly every business journal talks about the lifetime value of a customer and how customer loyalty is the key to long-term profitability. Extensive studies have been completed that show it is eight times easier to earn new business from existing customers than from new prospects. Many companies have incorporated the lingo of being "customer-centric" but find customer loyalty difficult to achieve, because the sales team is not trained in how to manage the sales process so it builds long-term collaborative customer relationships.

As a result, salespeople who master sales process are in extremely high demand, because the end result is that the sales rep's firm becomes the customers' preferred provider. By contrast, "product hawks" tend to quickly move their companies from a preferred to a negative position, leaving their firm vulnerable.

Becoming Process-Oriented

The challenge to becoming more process-oriented is that every sales rep has a chattering internal voice that is full of fears and expectations:

- ☑ "If I don't make my quota for the month, my boss is gonna kill me."

- ☑ "My kid's tuition is due, and if I don't make this sale, I won't be able to pay the school."

- ☑ "I hope this guy doesn't tell a boring story, because I've got to get to the airport in two hours."

This constant mental noise creates an enormous distraction, and the odds are 2:1 that this internal monologue frantically pulls the attention of the sales rep away from the customer and toward the sales rep's own priorities and goals.

To counteract this, the sales rep must create "breaks" in the internal dialogue in order to focus on the process. The best way to do this is through a four-step process that starts with engaged listening, followed by active acknowledgment, followed by thoughtful

SALES REPS' FREQUENTLY ASKED QUESTIONS

FREQUENTLY ASKED QUESTIONS

Q: I'm successful as a salesperson because of my outgoing, goal-driven personality. How can I focus on sales process without seeming phony?

A: Think of the sales process as setting up a set of boundaries that delineate appropriate behavior at customer meetings. Those boundaries create a frame for your unique personality, channeling your dynamism into creating trust, credibility, and rapport.

Q: What if the customer short-circuits the questioning with such a remark as, "Everything's fine and we don't need anything"?

A: Approach the subject obliquely. Ask the customer how things have gotten better and what parts of the business are running the most smoothly. Through questioning, determine whether there is some as-yet-undiscovered way for your firm to add value.

Q: How can I be certain that I can add value to the discussion?

A: The key factor is research and preparation. Before making a customer call, be certain that you learn everything you can about the company, its mission, its goals, and, most importantly, its customers. The most powerful way to add value is to help your customer do a good job serving your customer's customers.

exploratory questions that confirm understanding, and finally a well-thought-through response.

1. **ENGAGED LISTENING.** Hear what the customer has to say, without trying to frame what you're going to say next or interrupting during the discussion. Your goal is to try to see the situation through the customer's frame of reference or "operating reality," without automatically trying to create a sales opportunity.

2. **ACTIVE ACKNOWLEDGMENT.** Redescribe and characterize what the customer said to you in a way that confirms that you were really listening to the customer (and not your internal dialogue) and that you understood what the customer was telling you. Active acknowledgment can be both verbal and nonverbal. This acknowledgment makes sure you earn the extra credit from your customer for listening and helps create the "break" in the internal dialogue.

3. **EXPLORATORY QUESTIONS.** Add value to the conversation by asking questions that help the customer clarify his or her own thoughts and ideas. In this step you are not mining for information. You are using your experience and your ability to ask perceptive questions to ensure that you truly understand the customer's position, while minimizing interference from your own operating reality, adding a deeper

TRAINING QUICK TIPS

The three most common errors that occur when sales reps
first try to focus on sales process are as follows:

1. **CONFUSING A SALES CALL WITH A SOCIAL CALL.** Some sales reps keep conversations at a superficial level in the mistaken belief that chatting will build a relationship. This makes the sales rep look like a visitor rather than a valued professional, which makes it more difficult to build trust, credibility, and rapport.

2. **CONFUSING QUESTIONING WITH THERAPY.** Some sales reps get so into questioning that they become passive and unengaged listeners. The customer provides relevant and irrelevant data that result in no action. A content-free sales call becomes the norm, and the sales rep never contributes any substance, thus failing to build credibility.

3. **CONFUSING QUESTIONING WITH INTERROGATION.** Some sales reps become so aggressive in their quest to uncover information about the customer that they seem more like police investigators than people who care about the customer. This does not build either trust or rapport.

understanding of the customer's issues and ensuring that you respond in a way that has meaning for your customer.

4. **RESPONDING.** All sales reps know how to respond. In fact, one of the big problems with goal-focused reps is that they skip listening and move quickly to the response. By listening, acknowledging, exploring, and then responding, you are more likely to have a clear response that matches the customer's operating reality. This builds credibility, which is a key component of a collaborative relationship.

Using these techniques benefit both the customer and the sales rep. The customer gets to draw on the sales rep's expertise and perspective, while the sales rep comes to a deeper understanding of the customer and the customer's needs. At the same time, the process builds the trust, credibility, and rapport from which a successful sale will naturally emerge.

Sales Process and Presentation

Focusing on process does not mean that you never present to the customer. However, a process-oriented approach changes the way sales reps prepare and give presentations.

Most sales reps—even if they use questioning as a sales technique—have a canned presentation, usually in PowerPoint, that they want to show the customer. In many cases, the presentation is full of product details, solution details, case studies, diagrams, and so forth. Such presentations are counterproductive when they can't be customized to match whatever has emerged from the sales process. Sales reps who try to use canned presentations are essentially saying to the customer, "All the stuff you told me is interesting, but here's what I wanted to talk about, regardless of what you think you need."

By contrast, process-oriented sales reps tend to use both generic and customized presentations.

1. GENERIC. The highly generic presentation is used when the customer meeting evolves to the point where it's appropriate to talk about what the sales rep's firm can offer the customer. The sales rep has learned what the customer needs and now improvises on the spot to create a solution, based on the rep's company's capabilities, that matches those needs. Because the solution will be highly dependent upon what the salesperson has learned, a canned, detailed presentation would be off base. Instead, the presentation slides should only provide a framework rather than actually describe the solution.

> **Sales reps who try to use canned presentations are essentially saying to the customer, "All the stuff you told me is interesting, but here's what I wanted to talk about, regardless of what you think you need."**

Such a presentation consists of a few slides with high-level labels, such as "Introduction," "Requirements," and so forth—but without specific product details. Instead, the content comes from the sales rep's perspective on how his or her firm can help the customer.

2. CUSTOMIZED. The customized presentation is appropriate when there is a break between the customer meeting and the presentation. The sales rep collects or creates slides that specifically address the customer's needs as they emerged from the previous meeting. The two techniques can also be combined, with the customized presentation providing additional details and confirmation of the content that was improvised during the generic presentation.

What's important here is balance. When you focus on process, you need to sense the flow of the conversation and where the customer is going, listening actively and adding value when appropriate. When done correctly, a sales process naturally leads toward a fruitful presentation and a successful, almost effortless, close.

JEFFREY SEELEY was interviewed for this article. He is president and CEO of Carew International Inc., a leading sales-training firm whose workshops use case studies, customized role-plays, and structured experiences to simulate sales calls. Carew's customers include Coca-Cola International, Grainger, Accenture, First Data, and International Paper. Carew International is located at 3805 Edwards Road, Fourth Floor, Cincinnati, OH 45209-1940. Telephone: 513-621-0229. Web: www.carew.com.

SALES MANAGER'S MEETING GUIDE

Below are 12 practical steps to improve your team's ability to focus on sales process. This sales meeting should take about 50 minutes.

1. Open the meeting with enthusiasm and explain that the sales team is going to work on a set of skills that will help members not only build better customer relationships but also interact more effectively with virtually everybody with whom they communicate.

2. Have the team members write down every thought that comes into their minds for two minutes, starting with, "I wonder why I have to do this." Emphasize that they are to record even such random thoughts as, "I wish I had a burrito . . ." After two minutes, have everyone stop writing. Ask team members to count the number of thoughts that they recorded.

3. Have three team members read their thoughts aloud. Point out that all three people had wildly different thoughts, even though they were experiencing exactly the same situation and that those thoughts represent their "internal dialogue"—a constant mental chatter that is unique to each individual.

4. Tell the team members that you're going to tell them a story and that you want them to write down their thoughts, same as before. Then, in a complete monotone, read the following story: "Things sometimes get confused here at XYZ Industries. Fred, who was our VP, moved over to head up the other engineering group, which before had been headed by James, and which also employed his wife, who left the company later, but when Sally, the HR VP, tried to change over the engineers that went with them, she also transferred, on paper, some of the product and service purchasing responsibility so that we're not exactly sure whether the responsibility lies with HR or with the other engineering group, especially since James left the company. So we can't buy anything without the approval of the HR VP."

5. When you've finished, ask the team members the following question: "What is the first name of the vice president of human resources?" Chances are that nobody will be able to answer this.

6. Admit to the team members that you tricked them, but explain that you're trying to make them aware of how internal dialogue gets in the way of sales process.

7. Explain the four-step process of engaged listening, followed by active acknowledgment, followed by thoughtful exploratory questions that confirm understanding, and finally a well-thought-through response. Explain how this process creates trust, credibility, and rapport.

8. Now explain that you're going to tell them the same story, but that you want them to stop listening to their internal dialogue and instead try to listen as carefully as possible. Read the story again.

9. When you've finished, ask the team members to write a brief statement that would indicate to the customer that the team member heard and understood what was said. Ask some team members to share their remarks. Give feedback on whether those remarks would provide the confirmation that builds trust and rapport.

10. Ask the team members to pretend that you're a customer and they need to understand what you're talking about in order to make a sale. Ask the team to share some of the questions. Provide feedback on whether those questions would help build the team member's credibility.

11. Select the best confirmation and follow-up question. Select a team member to be the salesperson, then read the story a final time, and have a team member role-play the conversation. (Be sure to be an engaged listener.) Ask the team members to provide feedback as to whether that conversation would be more likely to lead to a sale than something like, "Uh, who did you say the VP of HR was?"

12. Break the team into groups of two, so that they can practice engaged listening. Suggest to the team members that they focus on this process during their future sales calls. Offer to work one-on-one with sales reps who would like to hone this skill.

ADDITIONAL READING

Here are some practical, put-'em-to-work-now ideas for building sales.

1. **KEEP SURPRISING YOUR CUSTOMERS.** Be dramatic. For example, one insurance agency offered to buy small contractors "the biggest steak dinner" in town if its company's policies couldn't save them money on their business insurance.

2. **GET TO THE RIGHT PERSON.** Addressing mail to "Facilities Manager" or "Office Equipment Buyer" is weak. Hitting the target is the name of today's game, and the bull's-eye is coming in contact with the precise individual you want to do business with. Also remember that you may be selling to only one individual today, but others in the same firm may be prospective users or buyers.

3. **BE CREATIVE.** Just getting the mail to the mail room isn't the goal! Will anyone be intrigued enough to read your mailer or newsletter before tossing it in the wastebasket? Today, it takes a highly creative approach to be distinctive and compelling. Yes, creativity costs money. But if people read your ad, your newsletter, and your mailer, you have a much better chance to do business with them.

4. **FOCUS ON WHAT YOUR CUSTOMERS CARE ABOUT.** No one cares about pictures of your staff or that you think you're the best, the oldest, or the biggest. Figuring out precisely what the customer wants, needs, and expects is what works. When this is your message, your product or service will be in demand.

5. **LET PEOPLE KNOW WHAT THEY SHOULD THINK OF YOUR COMPANY.** They draw conclusions by making comparisons. Ratings make a big difference to consumers. After several life insurance companies fell by the wayside, customers began asking about "company strength." The J. D. Powers' customer satisfaction surveys of cars and personal computers influence buying behavior. Wise companies spend time and effort consciously influencing the way they are perceived by customers and prospects (and stockholders, too).

6. **MAKE YOUR OFFER A GOOD ONE.** Customers are cautious. They don't like being put on the spot, because no one wants to make a mistake. This is why offers are so important.
   ☑ "Try it out. There's no obligation."
   ☑ "Use it for 30 days."
   ☑ "Your satisfaction guaranteed."

☑ "We'll buy you the biggest steak dinner in town if we don't save you money on your insurance."

☑ "Use it risk-free."

Pull the customer to you. All this is another way to extend your hand, put people at ease, and create confidence in your company and your product.

7. **BE IN THE RIGHT PLACE AT THE RIGHT TIME.** "I wish I had thought of you last week, when we bought the new . . ." Some salespeople shrug off such comments: "Oh, well. No one can be everywhere at once." Wrong! The job today is to be in front of the customer when the need arises.

8. **NAME YOUR PRODUCT OR SERVICE.** One way to stand out from the crowd is to give your product or service a distinctive name. "We provide 24-hour ComfortCare service." Not just plain old service, but "ComfortCare" service. Give the ordinary a new meaning to separate your company from others in the business. Make sure, however, that the name appeals to your customers and not just to you!

9. **BE RELENTLESS.** In marketing and sales, persistence is power. Too many firms never stay with anything long enough to produce results. They never develop a consistent marketing momentum. This all adds up to wasted money, time, and effort.

10. **IDENTIFY NEW PROSPECTS.** The single most important daily activity in any business is prospect identification. By making this a continuous process, companies have a steady flow of new sales leads. Keep asking the question, "Whom do we want to do business with if we have the chance?" To cultivate them over time, add prospects to a database.

11. **WRITE CUSTOMER-CENTERED LETTERS.** "As per our conversation . . ." "Pursuant to our agreement . . ." When was the last time you heard someone talk this way? Yet, put many people behind a pen and they become stilted, cold, and ineffective. Letters should be warm, friendly, interesting, and customer-centered.

12. **FOCUS ON THE QUESTION.** Why should anyone want to do business with us? What makes us different from others in the same business? Why do we deserve to be in business? Once companies begin asking these questions, they uncover the real reasons why customers should want to do business with them.

13. **TELL ONLY PART OF THE STORY AT ONE TIME.** There's a tendency to try to jam everything we know into one brochure, one ad, one newsletter. We don't want to leave anything out! The really difficult job is to pull it all apart, break ideas into component parts, and then develop an ongoing campaign.

14. **PERSONALIZE EVERYTHING.** The day of "Dear Friend," "Dear Customer," and particularly "Dear Valued Customer" is gone. Don't bother mailing a letter that isn't personalized with a name. Use the power in personalization.

15. **TAKE ADVANTAGE OF TESTIMONIALS.** Your credibility increases if you let a satisfied customer blow your horn for you. People are sometimes reluctant to provide a testimonial because they are not sure they're saying the right words or are afraid that you will be disappointed with their comments. A better way is to interview them, hear what they are saying, and then prepare comments for their approval. This way you reassure them and get testimonials that will work best for you.

16. **MAKE MARKETING YOUR MISSION.** Too many companies turn to marketing only when they need to increase their sales. This "shotgun" approach simply won't work! Communicating your company's message in new and interesting ways is an ongoing process. Getting customers and prospects to believe in your product or service is the best way to attract and keep them.

   It isn't good enough to produce the best produce or service. The final goal is to get the customer to want what you sell. That's where these 16 down-to-earth suggestions can make a big difference to your sales.

"Customers are becoming more demanding," says Dr. Michael Hammer, president of Hammer and Company, Cambridge, MA. "More products are becoming like commodities. If you want to distinguish your company from competitors, you need to differentiate through your sales process."

"Technology also has a lot to do with change, if it is used right," Hammer adds.

"The old rule, 'automating a mess gives you a mess,' still applies. Throwing technology at something doesn't help. Just putting up a Web site doesn't change much. There is a potential to do things really differently if you go through a fundamental rethink."

Old, familiar problems are growing less tolerable in fast-shifting markets. "There is the lack of an efficient integration of the parts," Hammer notes. "In some companies, to put together a quote, you must have a million cooks—the reps, the finance department, someone from engineering to configure it and from logistics to deliver it."

"The pure number of kitchen helpers can lead to miscommunication, misunderstanding, and inconsistencies. So, 'You have to integrate the process better,'" Hammer states. "That means fewer people doing it or at least doing it more consistently. Very frequently, you just need fewer people. If you use technology right, you can integrate a lot of backroom work into the rep's laptop."

> **"If you want to distinguish your company from competitors, you need to differentiate through your sales process."**

Delay is the big cost of overgrown sales bureaucracies. "By integrating the process, you can shorten the sales cycle enormously," Hammer urges. "That's critical because we now have shorter product life cycles. Some products live for only a few months. Getting from the first sign of customer interest to closing the sale always speeds up cash flow. In many cases, it may significantly extend the product's life on the market."

Where do you start fixing all this? The rest of this reading shows what top consultants and sales execs are doing. Here are four different angles from which to approach—or think about—improving the sales process.

THINK ABOUT TIME

"People ought to be thinking first of what can they do to create more selling time," emphasizes Gil Cargill, president of Cargill Consulting Group Inc. of Culver City, CA. "A lot of salespeople confuse what you do on a sales call with the sales process. The process is also what you do before and after the call."

REPS SHOULD BE ASKING DIFFERENT QUESTIONS

Reps, as well as managers and consultants, must think outside the box to restructure sales processes. "One way to get out of the box is simply to ask different questions," says Paul Selden of Performance Management.

1. **MONEY:** Instead of, "How much money can I make off this deal?" ask, "What is the lifetime value of this customer?"

2. **TIME:** Instead of, "How can I close quickly?" ask, "How can I satisfy my customer to ensure we get that lifetime value?"

3. **SELLING TECHNIQUE:** Instead of, "How do my company's top-revenue reps sell?" ask, "How can I use technology and imagination to sell better than any other reps now sell?"

4. **CONTACT:** Instead of, "How can I increase 'face-time' with my customers?" ask, "How can I blend all my communication tools together to satisfy my customers most economically?"

5. **TEAM:** Instead of, "Who signs my checks?" ask, "Whom do I need to work with in my company to sell better?"

Cargill estimates that the average salesperson spends only 20 to 29 percent of the day pursuing revenue from prospects or customers. The biggest nonsales element, consuming 34 percent of sales force time, is administration. What really annoys Cargill is that, "60 percent of this time is spent on correcting someone else's mistakes. So you spend two hours a day correcting errors."

Reducing administrative burdens or simply eliminating mistakes could lead to a significant increase in selling time and revenue.

What leads to unnecessary administrative burdens? Cargill lists several causes.

1. **INADEQUATE AUTOMATION OR AUTOMATION TRAINING.** Bad systems suck up sales time. Badly understood systems drive frustrated salespeople to keep double records: one on the system for management, another on old-fashioned paper for their own use.

2. **INADEQUATE SUPPORT.** Cargill recalls his early days at IBM, when there was one experienced sales secretary for every four or five reps. Modern word processors reduce the burden of doing letters, reports, proposals, and quotes, but you cannot automate away these jobs completely. Some companies have thrown the whole administrative burden onto their reps and the reps' laptops. "As a result," says Cargill, "The administrative work doesn't get done, or done well, and the salesperson wastes selling time."

3. **TRANSPORTATION.** Simply getting there can be a frustrating time vacuum and not just for long trips. One of Cargill's clients had high-performing reps who were spending

three hours a day in traffic searching for parking when they visited their Washington, DC, customers from their office across the Potomac. Cargill reckoned the lost selling time might have made it cost-effective to have the reps chauffeured to their calls.

Confusion about technology also blocks improvements. "In the first 10 years of sales automation, there were a lot of computer glitches," Cargill says. "So they now define a successful system as all the laptops glowing when we push the buttons. But they should be asking, 'are we selling more?'"

The Internet is creating a revolution in sales. However, Cargill points out, "Sometimes the Internet dilutes the issue. You can't tell whether your salespeople are selling more or if it is coming from the Internet."

That sort of confusion is what really bothers sales productivity experts like Cargill. "To improve any process, you first need to define it, then measure it, and control it," he urges. "If you can define and control the sales process, you can control results. Every other business function has a set of documented processes that, when followed, produces predicted results," Cargill emphasizes. "Sales usually does not. There is nothing written down."

> "If you can define and control the sales process, you can control results. Every other business function has a set of documented processes that, when followed, produces predicted results."

The solution is definition of responsibilities. You have got to say who does each job, how it is to be done, and how it will be measured. You have got to put all this down on paper first and then ask, "Do these jobs work together?" A very good question, as Delta Air Lines discovered.

THINK ABOUT THE PEOPLE WHO HAVE TO MAKE IT WORK

In some businesses, process changes must work through skilled support staff who simply cannot be replaced. The trick here is to educate, persuade, and motivate. Often, the best incentive is not money but just understanding supporting players' jobs. Delta Air Lines faced this challenge as it prepared to provide much more personalized service for the nine percent of its customers that accounted for about one-third of the airline's revenue.

Delta installed an expensive new computer system that could flag these top flyers as they hit airport ticket counters and check-in gates. "The ticket agent will hit a couple of keys, and up pops a profile of the passenger, what he or she likes to eat or drink, and where they like to sit," explained Vince Caminiti, Delta's senior vice president of Sales and Distribution. "It will even show if, God forbid, we have ever lost their luggage."

The new tool is quite useful in letting special travelers know they are appreciated and thus keeping their business. Delta made a major commitment, $300 million in new hardware costs alone, but some very time-pressured employees, the agents who get late arriving passengers onboard fast, had to be able to use the tool.

Caminiti knew he couldn't just dump a new PC screen on a pressured employee. "We had to get the message out that the new system will also help them do their current jobs better," he said. "It will help our agents expedite things, avoid assigning duplicate seats, know where the connecting passengers are, and so forth. It will help them better balance the decision on when to close the door. If I can show them it will do all that, they will see the system as a positive support, not as an intrusion. That is the key to making it work."

THINK LIKE A START-UP

Sometimes, a sales process is so inefficient that inspecting it for little time wasters or motivational challenges is no solution. In Hammer's view, "Often, things are so messed up that just tinkering around the margins won't work. You must break all the rules and think creatively. You need to start with a clean sheet and ask, 'How should it be done?'"

"That is one reason," Hammer notes, "that it can be easier for a start-up company to get the process right than for an established firm to reform successfully. Start-ups do not have as much as to unlearn. In process reform, everybody has to change, people need to work with shared accountability and interactions. Salespeople need to work with backroom people. There is the messiness of emotions. Frequently, you must dump managers who don't get it. Sometimes, you must dump whole departments."

Hammer has heard two reactions again and again from the "victims" of process overhaul: "They all say that the transition to the new process was 'the worst experience of their lives.' And then they say, 'Now, I would never consider going back to the old way.'" He draws a simple lesson. To minimize the misery, "Don't drag it out. It is a very bad idea to make it gradual. It will be more painful if you slow it down."

Hammer knows top salespeople have special qualities that must be preserved throughout change. "You don't want to break their spirits. We are not talking about creating automations. Salespeople must retain their independence and creativity, but they must learn how to work in the context of a team."

Making sure it is truly a team is the toughest part. One key to making it real is what Hammer calls Process Ownership. "One person must be accountable for the whole process from beginning to end, not just sales but the support work as well," he argues. "We are not talking about an individual sale or account, but about the whole activity of sales, crossing the boundaries of business units or divisions."

The process owner must usually be a senior executive, the CEO, a very senior sales executive, or someone else responsible for sales, marketing, and distribution.

THINK ABOUT YOUR CUSTOMER'S CUSTOMERS

Some process changes are driven by new market opportunities, new technologies, or both. Selling is going to change—there is no choice about that—but the company does choose how fast, how completely, and how well it will adapt its selling methods. The boom in Internet sales has brought an accompanying boom in the express cargo business. UPS shipped about 60 percent of Internet-ordered packages, a nice position to be in. The veteran shipper also led the business-to-business shipping market, helping Internet selling companies keep their shelves full of components and inventories for fast order fulfillment.

The package business is fiercely competitive, and there are new, hungry rivals for UPS's dominant position. How does UPS distinguish itself from the new entrants? UPS had long known that "information moves with every single package, and the information is just as valuable as the package," explains Jordan Colletta, vice president of Electronic Commerce Sales. "A business customer of UPS wants reliable delivery, of course, but the customer also wants to know where packages are and when they will get there, so it can run its own operations efficiently."

"UPS developed a suite of powerful computer tools for managing its business. Why not let customers use them to track this vital part of their own businesses? The new rule is, if you want to sell to a customer, think of the customer's customer. It applies with special force to business-to-business shipping."

"Access to UPS's own tracking tools helps business shippers in several important ways," Colletta argues. "First, think of their customer service departments. Think how powerful it is, when they are taking orders, if they have all the current information on their inventory shipments."

"Second, UPS's major customers have their own Web sites that their customers can visit. UPS can arrange a link from that Web site to its own shipping tracking site, allowing the customer's customer to view the shipping status as well. 'This adds tremendous value to the customer's Web site,' Colletta notes. The UPS tools also improve management of the customer's account receivables and return operations."

"It puts information about shipments at the customer's fingertips," Colletta summarizes. "It saves money, improves image, and improves service."

All this is easy enough to see in principle. Making it work in practice required major efforts. UPS invested about $1 billion each year on technology, far more than it spent on trucks. More than 15,000 customers had downloaded at least some UPS Internet tools from the company's Web site, but were they getting the full value of all the tools? What about the rest of the 1.6 million UPS customers that receive daily pickup service?

For both the customers and UPS to get the full value out of the e-commerce tools, these tools had to be explained and sold to each business shipper. UPS realized in March 1998 that

RETHINK THE SALES PROCESS

1. Create a vision of what the new process should be.

2. Communicate it to your people.

3. Make people understand it is necessary and inevitable.

4. Provide incentive for them to do it. When the customer is talking, you'll be more interested, and seem more interested, if your expression and posture indicate interest.

its 2,500 regular reps and 200+ national account managers could not do that alone. It decided to create a special unit, an electronic commerce sales force of 40 reps, to do this job better.

The E-C reps were chosen from UPS managers based on education, prior training, and proven ability to do consultative selling. Selection and e-commerce training took about four months.

Every E-C rep was trained in the value of all the online tools UPS had developed. "We wanted to make sure the entire solution set was available to every customer," Colletta says. "In this new world of information, you need to understand the whole picture. You cannot do it piecemeal."

The reps trained interactively with all the E-C tools. They used them every day during training in a simulated sales contact with a business customer. Colletta explains: "The team sat down afterward and asked, 'What did we learn about the customer? What do they need? What's the solution set? What is the best fit?'"

> **Technology had changed what the shipping business could be. That business first became selling information, then selling use and control over the information to improve each customer's own business.**

Training finished up with a final sales call and recommendation to the customer. The E-C teams competed for making the best recommendation to each of their simulated customers.

By spring, UPS was ready to roll with both its tools and its reps. Technology had changed what the shipping business could be. That business first became selling information, then selling use and control over the information to improve each customer's own business.

In short, better technology demands different and better selling. In Colletta's business, "At some point, it becomes the price of admission."

Strategic Accounts

A HANDS-ON GUIDE FOR MANAGERS

TRAINING GUIDE TIME REQUIRED: 55 MINUTES

BUILD RELATIONSHIPS WITH STRATEGIC ACCOUNTS

What Is a Strategic Account?

An account is strategic if (and only if) the success of both firms is intimately tied to the health of the relationship. Because there are two firms involved, there are two criteria that must be met:

1. The account must view the relationship as critical to its ongoing, long-term success. Ideally, your firm should be involved in the development of business and organizational strategy within the account. By contrast, if the account merely views you as a commodity supplier that can easily be replaced and plays you off against your competition in order to push your prices down, the relationship is not yet strategic—even if the account is a major purchaser of your goods and services.

2. Your firm must view the relationship as critical to the ongoing, long-term success of your firm. For example, if the account is responsible for so much revenue that the loss of that revenue would significantly affect your firm's finances, the account is strategic. Similarly, if your business plans hinge upon future sales to that account, the account is strategic. Finally, if the relationship with that account is necessary to maintain your firm's credibility in the marketplace (e.g., a software reseller's relationship with Microsoft), the account is strategic. In short, if losing the account would significantly hurt your firm's business, the account is (or should be) strategic.

Note that both criteria must be met for an account to be strategic. If your firm considers the account strategic but the account views your firm as replaceable, the account is not yet strategic. Similarly, if the account views you as strategic, but the loss of the account would have no impact on your firm's business, the account is not strategic.

QUICK TIP

QUICK TIPS

Have your strategic account managers assess their current ability to develop a strategic account by asking themselves the following questions:

☑ Does the account consider me a strategic resource?

☑ Do my account contacts regard me as crucial to their own success?

☑ Am I truly adding value to the account?

☑ Do I have expertise outside my own firm's products and services?

☑ Do I have sufficient sales skills to close business when required?

☑ Do I have clear and measurable goals for my strategic accounts?

Selecting Strategic Accounts

The first step to developing and strengthening strategic accounts is to obtain consensus inside your own firm on which accounts are (or should be) strategic. This cannot be done by the sales group alone. It requires the participation of every group that directly contributes to the operation of the company, including marketing, engineering, finance, support, manufacturing, and so forth. This is essential because strategic accounts often require specialized support from organizations outside the sales group.

For example, suppose a strategic account requires a specialized piece of equipment that would be uneconomical for your firm to manufacture but represents an opportunity for your firm to become embedded in the account's business plans. Unless your firm's engineering and manufacturing groups are onboard with the idea that the account is truly strategic, they're likely to balk when asked to manufacture the specialized equipment. By contrast, if engineering and manufacturing both understand the importance of the account, they're more likely to support the logic of taking a short-term tactical loss in order to win a long-term strategic gain.

There are Four Steps to Achieving Consensus about Strategic Accounts

1. **BUILD A PROFILE.** Define the kind of account that might be strategic. For example, a start-up company that's selling innovative technology but lacks market credibility might seek a strategic account that has an easily recognizable brand name and a reputation for successfully implementing new technology.

2. **IDENTIFY CANDIDATE ACCOUNTS.** Using the profile, look for accounts or potential accounts that meet the profile. Pay particular attention to accounts to which your firm can add unique value, helping the account achieve a goal, avoid a problem, or fulfill a need.

3. **SET GOALS AND LIMITS.** For each candidate account, set specific revenue goals and timelines for achieving them. In addition, set limits on the amount of resources (financial and human) that your firm is willing to expend in order to develop and maintain the account. This is important, because it prevents strategic account spending from spiraling out of control.

4. **MONITOR PROGRESS.** Consensus is an ongoing process. Every group that's needed for the support of strategic accounts should be constantly informed about the measurable success (or failure) of the strategic account effort.

Becoming a Strategic Vendor

In many cases, the challenge is to transform a run-of-the-mill account into a strategic account. In order to do this, you must embed your firm's products and services deep inside the account's own strategic plans. There are generally two keys to accomplishing this: uniqueness and account penetration.

1. **UNIQUENESS.** Your firm's products or services must be unique in order to differentiate your firm from the competition. The three most common types of uniqueness are:

   a. **DE FACTO MONOPOLY.** If your firm is in the fortunate position of offering an essential product or service that no other company can provide, then you can forge a strategic relationship with virtually any company that needs that product or service. A prime example of this is Microsoft, which uses its de facto monopoly of desktop operating systems in order to penetrate other software categories. This type of uniqueness is rare and precious.

   b. **BEING BEST-IN-CLASS.** Whatever your firm does better than other firms can potentially drive a strategic relationship. Note that this kind of uniqueness need not be tied directly to your actual product or service as offered to the rest of the (nonstrategic) world. For example, a company that sells a replaceable commodity product might have world-class expertise in volume

> Ideally, you want your firm represented at any internal meeting inside the account that offers the potential for additional sales of your firm's offerings.

FREQUENTLY ASKED QUESTIONS

Q: What's the difference between a major account and a strategic account?

A: An account is "major" if it is responsible for a large amount of revenue. However, if the major account treats your products and services as commodities, the account is not strategic. An account is strategic only if the relationship has a business purpose beyond generating revenue.

Q: What's the difference between a regular account manager and a strategic account manager?

A: A strategic account manager has a broader focus and must be fully versed in general business issues and industry-specific issues. Rather than seeking the immediate gratification of making a sale, a strategic account manager values building long-term relationships in the firm belief that they will eventually generate revenue.

Q: How do I know when I'm making progress?

A: Progress results from a deepening of the relationship between your company and the strategic account. Even if you lose a big sale, you are making progress if the sales process opens new contacts inside new departments, gives you access to higher management, or leads to your inclusion in strategic planning meetings.

manufacturing. That expertise could presumably be lent to a strategic account in order to reduce its manufacturing costs.

c. **HIGH COST OF REPLACEMENT.** If it would cost the account a prohibitive amount to replace your firm's products and services, you have a strong potential to build a strategic relationship. However, this type of uniqueness is useful only after a sale has been made, because prior to the sale, the account is likely to see it as a liability rather than an asset.

2. **PENETRATION.** You must obtain access to the inner workings of the account so that your firm is involved in the account's strategic planning. Ideally, you want your firm represented at any internal meeting inside the account that offers the potential for additional sales of your firm's offerings.

In order to accomplish this, the mere presence of the account team inside the account must add value to the account. The account team must learn everything it can about the account's goals, problems, and needs and then be able to articulate clearly how your firm's unique offerings can help. Beyond this, the account team must be able to bring additional

QUICK TIPS

The purpose of the meeting is to draw upon the combined expertise of your sales organization to help build plans that can lead to better, stronger strategic relationships.

Make it clear during the brainstorming, that there are no bad ideas. However, at the end of each brainstorming, put a star next to the ideas that you (or the team) believe have the most promise.

After the meeting, ask the strategic account managers for written plans to raise the strategic level of their account relationships based upon input from the meeting.

If your firm has more than six strategic accounts, you may want to schedule a longer training session or break the training session into two parts.

If you've got an account that's at level five, be sure to ask the strategic account manager questions that will help the team visualize how to approach other accounts. For example, what exactly did the account manager do? What were the exact results? What were the biggest challenges?

expertise to the table, such as a broader industry perspective, additional contacts that might prove useful to the account, and expertise that doesn't involve the sale of your firm's offerings.

For example, IBM sometimes assigns an employee as a general information technology (IT) consultant inside Fortune 100 firms. In addition to being a sales representative, that employee is mandated to act as an independent IT resource that the account would otherwise have to hire separately as a consultant. In addition to helping the account implement and support its IT systems, the employee acts as a clearinghouse for any problems that occur and a source of information about IBM's offerings.

In many cases, these strategic account managers add so much value that the account actually gives them an office at the account's own facility. As a result, IBM often has a presence during strategy and planning meetings that results in the firm getting the inside sales track for large, strategic, and potentially profitable projects.

SAM REESE was interviewed for this article. His prolific and dynamic career in sales and marketing management provides a foundation that has made him an ideal leader for Miller Heiman. His ongoing tenure at Miller Heiman has led to expanded product offerings, valuable e-learning initiatives, and significant advancement within the industry. Reese's previous background of managing large sales forces for three different Fortune 500 companies provides him with a unique perspective on how to truly drive sales effectiveness throughout an entire organization. Miller Heiman is headquartered at 10509 Professional Circle, Suite 100, Reno, NV 89521. Telephone: 1-877-678-3380. Web: www.millerheiman.com.

SALES MANAGER'S MEETING GUIDE

SALES MANAGER'S MEETING GUIDE

Below are 10 practical steps to improve your team's ability to develop strategic accounts. This sales meeting should take about 55 minutes.

1. One week prior to the sales meeting, e-mail your strategic account managers and ask for a brief summary of the status of their accounts. Review this material the day before the meeting.

2. Prior to the meeting, set up a flip chart with colored pens, and write the name of each strategic account, in alphabetical order, at the top of a page. On a whiteboard, write the following:
Level 1: You are a commodity supplier.
Level 2: You provide good products and/or services.
Level 3: You provide good service and support.
Level 4: You contribute to their business issues.
Level 5: You contribute to their organizational issues.

3. Open the meeting. Explain that this is going to be a brainstorming session to help develop strategic account plans, and will require the full participation of every sales representative on the team, even those who are not strategic account managers.

4. Summarize the concept of a strategic account, and explain that there are five levels of account relationships, with level five being the most strategic. Explain that the goal of this session is to identify current relationship levels and brainstorm ways to move strategic account relationships to a higher level.

5. Start with the first page of the flip chart. Ask the strategic account manager to briefly summarize his or her experience and rate the account relationship on the one-to-five scale.

6. Ask the rest of the team for feedback about whether the strategic account manager has accurately assessed the quality of the relationship. If there is dissent, discover the reason and then decide how to rate the account. Write the current level at the left-hand top corner of the flip chart.

7. After you have rated all of the strategic accounts, start with the account that rated the highest. Flip to that page.

8. If the account is a four or a five, have the strategic account manager explain what he or she did to raise the account to that level. Summarize those actions as bullets on the flip chart. Remove that page and tape it to the wall.

9. If the account level is less than a four, open the floor to any ideas that might help the strategic account manager move the relationship to a higher level. Summarize those actions as bullets on the flip chart. Remove that page and tape it to the wall.

10. Repeat until you have cycled through all the strategic accounts or until the meeting time is consumed. Thank the team for its participation and close the meeting.

ADDITIONAL READING

With the ups and downs of the economy, businesses are looking for ways to maximize and economize at the same time; today, sales are an even bigger challenge than usual. One way to maximize sales while economizing on the expense of developing new accounts is to get more from the best of your customer base. If you do it right, you'll help your customers while you're helping yourself.

To learn how professional salespeople make the most of their best accounts, we talked to Michael Pisarski, who handles corporate sales for Bay to Bay Hardware and Pool Supplies in Tampa, FL, and Cecil Carder, regional sales manager for Havel, Giarusso and Associates Inc. in Olathe, KS. Pisarski says that making the most of his best customers means examining the 20 percent of his business that accounts for 80 percent of his sales.

"We're located in a very vibrant business community," Pisarski says. "But as the economy began to tighten, we realized that we needed to do more with less. That meant we needed to really listen to our customers."

Pisarski says that salespeople who have worked in one field for a long time tend to make sales assumptions that work against their giving the best service possible and getting the most out of their accounts.

"I've probably heard every possible plumbing problem that a client can encounter," he says. "Because of that, I'd gotten into the habit of mentally pricing the job out for my contractors as soon as they told me what type of job they were doing; in other words, I'd stopped listening. But in this economy, I've gone back to really listening to the job order and asking more follow-up questions. As a result, I'm picking up an additional 10 to 15

EXPERT ADVICE

UPSELLING STRATEGIES FOR MAJOR ACCOUNTS

☑ **DO YOUR HOMEWORK.** Monitor industry press and events with an eye toward finding ways your solutions can help customers navigate the market's changing tides, and then use your consultative selling skills to make further inroads.

☑ **DEVELOP RELATIONSHIPS.** Actively seek out other buying influencers within the major account. Create a blueprint for understanding who and what make things happen in the target department, and then find ways to use your product or service to make connections and solve problems.

☑ **ABO—ALWAYS BE QUALIFYING.** With good, long-term customers, salespeople risk falling into a rut and letting the relationship plateau. Instead, treat even solid customers like new prospects, and use your qualifying skills to ferret out new needs or concerns.

percent in parts orders from our core clients, not by forcing a sale, but by doing the job the way it should be done all the time. It makes me wonder why it took a slowdown to make me do things I knew I should be doing all along."

Carder says it takes a long time to develop an account to the point where you can get the most out of it. "Never lose sight of the fact that the client is always in control," he says. "But over time, if you can get to know a client and build a relationship with him away from the business, you develop a business relationship on a totally different level. That gives you some control over the account, as opposed to being in the store for an hour or two, where all you can do is make a presentation." Carder tries to spend time with clients on outings that range from a simple meal away from the business to a several-day hunting camp. These longer outings, he says, help create an atmosphere where most of the business for the year can sometimes be set up.

Since Carder sells outdoor products related to hunting, putting products into his clients' hands in the field has potential to increase his sales.

"Any hands-on experience with a product gives the customer a sense of ownership in that product line," he says. "When a retailer feels a sense of ownership in a specific line, he orders more of it. This helps create a sense of partnership between the retailer and us, so that now his inventory-control issues become our inventory-control issues as well. We have an obligation to keep his inventory of our products at a level that will give him the markup he expects."

> **"Any hands-on experience with a product gives the customer a sense of ownership in that product line."**

"Taking the time to build relationships also creates trust, which can lead to increased sales," Carder says. "Because the customer trusts us, over time we can increase the sale of items he hasn't previously carried," he says. "When you have that type of relationship with the guy across the table, where he knows you aren't going to just throw something at him that doesn't fit with his plan, you gain credibility."

"Sometimes I walk into a sales situation and put a product out on the desk and never say anything about it. At some time during the conversation the customer may ask about that product, and then the process begins. Is it right for the store at this time? Are the margins right? What about support? The retailer may also let me know that there's floor or shelf space for that product. That helps as well, because now I have a better idea of what kind of products to show him or not to show him."

"When you're working with your best accounts," Carder says, "never forget that the customer's needs always override your need to make additional sales. It's not worth putting a trusting relationship with a long-term sales partner at risk just to push an additional sale through. Trusting each other is essential to building a long-term relationship that will be profitable for everyone concerned."

Winning major account sales is a high-stakes game—it requires skill and patience. The salesperson who plays could win big . . . or waste lots of time. The player must be able to gather information that is not easily accessible and develop strategies for making the sale to everyone involved in the decision.

Rather than a one-stop call on a single decision maker, major account selling involves repeated sales calls over a period of time on a variety of customer contacts in different departments. To begin, rather than immediately leaping into your sales strategy, focus first on how the customer will make the decision.

To greatly increase your chances of success, use the five-step plan below.

STEP ONE: UNDERSTAND YOUR ACCOUNT'S PERSONALITY

Every organization has a unique personality, shaped by its history, the direction of its founders and top executives, industry forces, the organization's products, markets and competitors, and by financial, legal, and regulatory pressures.

Some sources that may help uncover and clarify an organization's personality include the company's annual report, 10-K reports filed with the Securities and Exchange Commission, articles from business and industry publications, investment company research reports, business school libraries, and online databases.

STEP TWO: ANALYZE THE COMPANY'S DECISION-MAKING PROCESS

Follow the customer's decision-making steps. We know the two ends of the process: identifying the need and implementing the solution. In between is probably a request for proposal (RFP) and vendor selection. Unfortunately, many salespeople spend most of their time at the RFP stage. The successful vendor, on the other hand, has probably spent time influencing the decision long before the company issues its RFP.

During their decision-making process, most major accounts follow these steps:

☑ Identify the need.

☑ Conduct a feasibility study.

☑ Assign a project team. This project team will likely consist of members with a vested interest in the solution, as well as members who are technically capable of seeking a solution.

☑ Identify potential solutions.

☑ Develop specifications. Affected departments will provide their input to the technical members of the team (i.e., purchasing and engineering), who will develop the specifications to which vendors will respond via the RFP process.

☑ Issue the RFP. The RFP is sent to potential vendors, requesting their proposals to meet the specifications stated in the RFP.

☑ Evaluate vendor proposals.

☑ Select the vendor.

☑ Conduct final negotiations. Before notifying all vendors, the company will approach selected vendors to negotiate any terms or conditions, quantities, delivery dates, or items not covered in the RFP specifications. In addition, the customer may ask the selected vendor to make concessions before signing the order.

☑ Implement the solution by ordering the equipment, training the users, installing and accepting the product, and paying the vendor.

To influence key people and stay in touch with those executives who participated in the development and approval of the business case, salespeople should get involved in the process as early as possible.

STEP THREE: DEVELOP THE SALES STRATEGY

If you have not yet contacted all the key players, especially those involved in the early stages of the decision process, know what to say when you do meet them. Also get to know all the technical, personal, political, and business issues involved in the project. Use this information to your advantage.

STEP FOUR: DEVELOP AN ACTION PLAN

The action plan is a sequence of tasks and activities required to get the order. It tells everyone involved in the project what to do and when to do it. Some examples are as follows:

☑ Give key prospects a tour of your design, engineering, or manufacturing facilities to demonstrate your company's commitment to customer support, quality, etc.

☑ Convince the customer of your technology and future direction with a technical briefing.

☑ Have your top management pay a visit to the customer's top management to assure them that your company stands behind the product or service you have proposed.

☑ Conduct a needs analysis or survey to show how the customer can benefit from your product.

STEP FIVE: ASSESS YOUR ACTION PLAN

After you have developed the action plan, step back and ask yourself, if I do all these things, how likely am I to get the order? If the answer is "somewhat likely" or "not very likely," take another shot at your strategies and your action plan until you are confident you will get the order.

THREE STRATEGIC SALES TOOLS

The three essential strategic sales tools for major account selling are: qualification, needs analysis, and testing your strategy.

Test if the sale is worth your time and effort by asking tough questions throughout the process. You will find out if you are on track and, if not, how to get back on track. If that is not possible, withdraw from the opportunity, pack up, and direct your efforts elsewhere.

1. Qualify the opportunity by asking the following questions:

☑ Are there identified needs?

☑ Is key management aware of the needs?

☑ Is there a compelling business reason to take action?

☑ Are key people willing to give us time and information?

☑ Is the decision maker available to us?

☑ Has funding been identified?

☑ Is there a pressing business reason to act?

☑ Is there a sense of urgency?

☑ Does this opportunity match up well against our strengths?

☑ Does our solution answer the customer's needs?

☑ Is our solution competitive?

☑ Have we established credibility and confidence with the customer?

☑ Are key people biased toward us?

2. Use the needs analysis to uncover needs, match them to your solution, and put a dollar value on soft benefits. Ask for your customer's full cooperation and involvement. Meet with all the decision makers, including top management.

3. Test your strategy and action plan with other members of your sales team. Everyone involved should understand the strategy, what is required of them, and how their efforts fit into the total plan. Not only will they be able to perform their role more effectively, but they may also suggest additional ideas and strategies that you have overlooked. The fact that they participated in the development of the plan will give them a sense of ownership which will in turn increase their level of commitment to the plan.

ADDITIONAL
READING

Major account sales involve many sales calls, spread over many months. They require a systematic selling process of one part strategy and one part tactics. Strategy includes identifying, surfacing, and addressing every element of a large account. In essence you must:

- ☑ Emphasize strategic planning as you uncover key information.
- ☑ Present solutions to key players on the buyer's team.
- ☑ Obtain gradual commitment that will ultimately lead to a win-win solution.
- ☑ Join in strategic planning with sales management and such internal resource departments as engineering, maintenance, and product specialists.

TACTICS

Use a well-thought-out questioning process and emphasize your company's unique strengths. A systematic sales process creates a common focus, a common language, and a common sales culture. It uncovers potential problems in the account and missing pieces of information; it tells you what has to be done next and lets you know where you are and how you are positioned throughout your sales cycle.

> **Use a well-thought-out questioning process and emphasize your company's unique strengths.**

INCREMENTAL CUSTOMER COMMITMENTS

Large account sales require incremental customer commitments at each step of the selling cycle. By definition, a large sale is a big investment on both sides. Both the salesperson and the buyer face significant investments of time, money, and resources as the buy-sell interaction moves toward a final decision.

A sales professional must obtain an incremental action commitment from the buyer equal to the increase in resources the salesperson's organization is making in its selling process. As investments in the sales process increase, so should investments in the buying process.

The salesperson has the ultimate responsibility to create this win-win solution with clear-cut incremental buying action commitments. A selling organization's limited resources must be protected and must be invested wisely if win-win selling is to become a reality.

THE BUILDING BLOCKS OF ACCOUNT KNOWLEDGE

Large account selling requires focus on building blocks of specific account information, market trends, business, and organizational issues. The salesperson must completely identify his or her prospect's internal decision-making process, including the number of players, their precise organizational roles, responsibilities, and individual focus.

The prospect's team usually has many players. However, often one person plays a powerful behind-the-scenes role in the final decision. Study and analyze internal politics, alliances and relationships, budgetary information, and the potential organizational and profitability impact of your sales proposal.

> **Study and analyze internal politics, alliances and relationships, budgetary information, and the potential organizational and profitability impact of your sales proposal.**

QUALIFY AND TEAM-SELL

Large account sales require concise identification of highly qualified prospects. A sales organization will pay a high price in wasted resources, selling time, and dollars spent in the pursuit of a large account prospect if it turns out the prospect did not want to buy in the first place.

Avoid this situation by systematically identifying highly qualified prospects. Establish a profile to describe your ideal customer, and then pursue only prospects who come close to that profile.

Large accounts require a cooperative team sell. Multiple players from the selling organization mean more eyes, varied experience and expertise, and a common focus with a common language. The more effective and systematic the use of team resources, the higher the probability of sales success.

Appointments

**A HANDS-ON GUIDE
FOR MANAGERS**

TRAINING GUIDE TIME REQUIRED: 55 MINUTES

GAIN ACCESS TO DECISION MAKERS

Who Are the Decision Makers?

Many sales reps think that somewhere inside their customer's headquarters building is a single decision maker, and if one could only reach that person, the deal could be quickly closed. Such decision makers are largely a myth. In today's business world, even CEOs try to reach consensus with their direct reports before making any important decision. In fact, the decision-making process for the purchase of any significant product and service is generally split among three individual roles:

1. **THE ACCESS OWNER.** This is the person in the organization who is prepared to talk to you, to give you inside information and access to the other decision makers. This person is absolutely critical to making things happen, because your initial credibility with the rest of the organization will be largely dependent upon his or her sponsorship.

2. **THE PROBLEM OWNER.** This is the person in the organization who owns the problem or challenge that your product or service is likely to address. The problem owner is unlikely to be an access owner or to normally be willing to spend time educating you about the organization, because people who own problems are generally too busy to give a sales rep much time.

3. **THE BUDGET OWNER.** This is the person in the organization who has control of the money the problem owner will need in order to purchase a solution to the problem. Typically, the budget owner isn't much interested in the specific problem or the specific solution, but whether the budget that he or she controls is going to be spent wisely. In other words, the proposed solution must have an easily articulated and measurable return on investment (ROI).

Most major sales decisions are made if, and only if, these three individuals agree that it makes sense to buy a particular product or service. This happens when the access owner says, "This company can be trusted to deliver," and the problem owner says, "This product will fix my problem," and the budget owner says, "This purchase makes sense financially."

Achieving this consensus is possible only through a selling effort that moves toward accessing each of the three decision makers and that addresses the concerns of each of the decision makers in a unique way. Here's how it's done.

Step 1. Get Access to the Access Owner

The first step is to get access to your initial contact, who functions as the gatekeeper to the rest of the organization. Unfortunately, in today's business world anybody who has time to see a sales rep probably isn't worth seeing. In order to get to an access owner who has enough clout within the target organization to act as an effective sponsor, the sales rep will have to demonstrate to that person that he or she can provide significant value.

Ideally, the access owner should view the sales call as an event for which the access owner's firm would normally pay a consultant. This presents a problem. Many sales reps know a lot about their company's products but don't know enough about a prospective customer to be able to add any positive value. (A product presentation, by itself, is generally perceived as a waste of time and therefore something that subtracts, rather than adds value.)

QUICK
TIP

CHECK LIST

Here's how to research a company on the Internet, quickly and effectively.

STEP 1:   **Gather Context.** Go to www.hoovers.com and search on the corporate name of the prospective customer. If there is a Hoovers listing, print it out. It will have a summary of the company, its finances and a list of its most important competitors. If there is no Hoovers listing, skip to step 2.

STEP 2:   **Gather Background.** Go the target company's Web site and print out the page that describes the company's mission and purpose. Check through the various pages on the company's Web site. Take particular note of case studies and press releases, because these often contain the names of individuals that might be potential access owners. Print out any relevant pages.

STEP 3:   **Gather Deep Background.** Go to www.sec.gov and click on "Search for Company Filings." Search on your prospect's corporate name. If the prospect is publicly held, you will receive a list of SEC reports. Examine the latest 10-K and 10-Q reports, which often contain detailed revenue information, the names of the corporate officers, the names of the top management team members, the organizational structure, the sales channels, the business models, and even the company's own analysis of the competitive threats that it faces. Print out any relevant pages.

STEP 4:   **Gather Competitive Data.** Repeat steps 1 and 2 for the prospect's major competitors. (Hoovers identifies these.) Print out the relevant pages.

STEP 5:   **Gather the Latest News.** Go to http://news.google.com and search on the name of the customer firm. Print out any news articles that seem relevant. Circle the names of potential contact points within the firm, as well as any analysts or experts who comment on that company.

STEP 6:   **Gather Personal News.** Go to www.google.com and do a search on the names of potential contacts (put them in quotes, e.g., "John Q. Scientist") along with the company name (in quotes, if it has more than one word, e.g., "General Electric.") Examine the first few pages of results. Click on any links that might be relevant and print out any that actually are. Repeat the process with each potential customer contact.

STEP 7:   **Gather Analyst Information.** Repeat step 5, only using the names of any industry analysts who study the firm or the firm's industry. The names of analysts are often included in news stories about the company in question.

STEP 8:   **Create a Notebook.** Put all of the above into a notebook with the following tabs: CORPORATE, COMPETITIVE, PERSONNEL, ANALYSIS, and NOTES. (The final segment is simply two blank pages.) Use this document to study and understand the company, its industry, and the market environment in which it works. Use the notes pages to record your thoughts and ideas about how to approach potential access owners.

In order to provide value to the access owner by supplying some of the function that a paid consultant would normally provide, the sales rep must learn about the target company and its industry. Fortunately, the Internet offers any sales rep the ability to learn an enormous amount. However, in order to use this information as a value-adding tool, the sales rep must apply analytical skills in order to generate some insight. And the sales rep will need to present that insight in a dramatic way, so that it opens the door to a meeting with the access owner. Here are examples of good openers:

- ☑ "I noticed that you presented a white paper on mega-widgets at the lastest MWUSA conference. Were you aware that your competitor in the mega-widget market is about to come out with a new product but lacks the money to expand its manufacturing capacity? I'd be happy to come over and share what I've learned and to see if there might be a way that your company could save some money in its own manufacturing processes."

- ☑ "I just read your book about electro-framistats and was wondering whether you had noticed that the market for electro-framistats seems to have leveled off after about three years of rapid growth. I think I know why that's happened and why there will be some additional growth next year. I'd love to come by and talk with you about that and to see if there's anything that my company can do help you get ready for the increased demand."

Step 2: Convert the Access Owner into a Sponsor

Access owners tend to be techies. As such, they are more interested in information and insight than in the specifics of your product or service. Because of this, it's generally a waste of time to do a traditional sales pitch to an access owner. Instead, your sales challenge is to exchange the information and insight that you've gathered in order to obtain access to the rest of the organization. In other words, this is not a social call! Many salespeople have customers they've been calling on for years and who love to see them, but who are never going to buy anything. The goal of meeting with the access owner is to trade your expertise for additional information about the prospective customer (e.g., who has the problem, who has the budget) and for access to the other decision makers (e.g., "Can you set up a meeting so that we can discuss the problem with the problem owner?").

In this effort, credibility is everything. When you ask an access owner to act as your sponsor, you're asking that person to put his or her own career and credibility on the line. Therefore, everything you communicate must be authoritative and reasonable. Extravagant claims and such marketing weasel-words as, "We turned XYZ Inc. around and doubled their profit," or, "We're well recognized as the best in the industry," are only going to damage your credibility. Worse, if the access owner is foolish enough to sponsor you, it's likely that the other decision makers will see through the bluster, making a sale unlikely. Your goal is to act and sound like a real-world consultant who adds value as part of the sales process. If you're seen as a talking brochure, you'll just be wasting your time, as well as the time of the decision makers.

> **When you ask an access owner to act as your sponsor, you're asking that person to put his or her own career and credibility on the line.**

Step 3: Sell a Solution to the Problem Owner

Problem owners tend to be managers responsible for a segment of the company's business. As such, they are interested in how a particular product or solution might solve their problem. Therefore, you have two goals here. First, you are trying to convince the problem owner that you have a workable solution to the problem. Second, you are also trying to convince the problem owner to give you access to the budget owner in order to complete the sale.

The best way to satisfy both goals is to add massive value to the problem owner by helping to clarify the problem and by proposing a workable solution, if appropriate. Ideally, this solution shouldn't be based upon what you have to sell, buy rather upon what the customer actually needs. You should strive to add so much value that the prospect will feel as if he or she should be paying for the sales call. In most cases, your product or service will be part of the proposed solution, because you have already learned enough about the target company and its industry to assure yourself that you have something valuable to sell.

Step 4: Sell the ROI to the Budget Owner

Budget owners tend to be financial types, such as CFOs and accountants. When the problem owner introduces you to the budget owner, forget about techie chit-chat or product/solution presentations. The budget owner will want to know how much your product is going to cost, whether the problem owner believes it will work, and how long it will take for your product to achieve an acceptable ROI. If you've gotten this far in the sales process, the problem owner and the access owner will probably be willing to help you build the ROI case in a way that will work politically inside the target company. However, you are going to have to continue to add value, in this case by understanding the potential ROI impact of your product and by having multiple, valid ways of calculating and expressing that impact.

Step 5: Close the Sale

If you have successfully worked through the previous steps, closing the sale is typically just a matter of gathering all three decision makers into a single room and confirming that the sale is to go forward. If you have conducted the entire sales process properly, the final closing is thus more of a formality than an ordeal.

QUICK TIP

QUICK TIPS FOR YOUR TRAINING SESSION

☑ The test of whether a sales call will prove effective is whether the information and insight that are conveyed are so valuable that the prospective customer would normally be willing to pay for them.

☑ According to research, prospective customers do not value information about products. They value information about the industry and the competition, providing it is current and up-to-date.

☑ Selling to the problem owner is more effective if the sales rep can clearly articulate the value of the product and the value of doing business with your firm.

☑ In order to sell, sales reps need convenient access to the Internet and sales management that considers sales research an integral part of the job.

☑ Companies that treat sales research as an afterthought or something that is best conducted off-hours will find it increasingly difficult to compete with companies that take sales research seriously.

NEIL RACKHAM was interviewed for this article. He has been the chairman of international consulting firms and is now a highly sought-after conference speaker. His books include the classic *Spin Selling* (McGraw-Hill) and a forthcoming release addressing the critical need for synergy—which is often absent—between corporate sales and marketing departments. He has worked closely with leading sales forces from such companies as IBM, Xerox, AT&T, Citicorp, and McKinsey & Company. He can be reached via www.neilrackham.com.

SALES MANAGER'S MEETING GUIDE

Below are 10 practical steps to help your sales team learn how to get access to decision makers. This sales meeting should take about 55 minutes.

1. Prior to the meeting, create a research notebook on a target customer, preferably one to which your company would like to sell, but where your salespeople have been having difficulty obtaining access. (See the checklist for the information-gathering process.) Make copies of the notebook for all participants.

2. At the beginning of the meeting, explain that the team is going to work on gaining access to decision makers and that this is one of the most important skills for any sales professional to develop.

3. Take five minutes and explain how decision making is typically split among three individuals and that getting access to the "access owner" is always the first step.

4. Hand out the research notebooks. Spend five minutes describing how you researched this material on the Web, so that team members can conduct their own research in the future.

5. Tell your team that the purpose of this exercise is to identify potential access owners and to come up with a creative and interesting approach that will open the door to those access owners.

6. Give your team 15 minutes to read over the notebook material. At the completion of this step, you should be 25 minutes into the training session.

7. Ask the team members to identify, based upon their reading, potential access owners. Put the names of those access owners on a whiteboard.

8. Have the team identify any significant information about each access owner that can be gleaned from the notebook. List that information (in brief) on the whiteboard, after the name of each potential access owner.

9. Have each team member attempt to craft a voice-mail message (or e-mail message if appropriate) that would intrigue and interest that access owner enough to open a dialogue. Each message should promise some sort of added value to the access owner.

10. Gather the messages and read them over quickly. Pick the best three. Read each of them aloud and conduct a discussion about whether the message would be effective in obtaining access and (just as important) whether the salesperson would be able to deliver the value promised in the message.

Without appointments, all the sales skills and all the knowledge in the world are just water down the drain. Here is an effective and detailed approach to getting appointments.

With this approach, you always achieve something positive even if you don't get an appointment the first time around.

You will get your name and details in the prospect's file, and make an impression that marks you as a professional and trustworthy individual. I call this approach Warm Calling because when you speak to the prospect, you are prepared and the prospect will be expecting your call.

STAGE ONE—TARGET YOUR MARKET

Begin by defining your ideal customers. Who is going to be most attracted by your particular package of features and benefits? Where do you stand out strongest against the competition and to which types of clients? Where have you been most successful in the past? Where is your competition most active? Start by analyzing and carefully targeting your market.

STAGE TWO—GATHER INFORMATION

The first call you make to the target account is only to get information. Simply highlight one or two key contacts and check addresses and other information. Curiously, five percent of the time you end up getting through to your prospect on this call, even though this is not your intention. Start by introducing yourself and company, explain that you have not dealt with the company before and would like to write a personal letter to the most appropriate person. Ask for help, then ask for:

- ☑ Name (with spelling) of the person responsible for . . .
- ☑ Address
- ☑ Best time of day to call back
- ☑ Any other piece of simple information that would be useful

STAGE THREE—WRITE TO INTRODUCE YOURSELF

A concise, interest-arousing, one-page letter with a brief overview of company, product, or proposition will do nicely.

STAGE FOUR—CALL TO GET THROUGH

Call within 14 days of mailing your letter. This allows time for the prospect to contact you by letter or phone (a few may), and does not seem unduly pushy. Your objective at this stage is only to get an appointment. Resist the temptation to give too much product or sales information—talk just enough to develop curiosity and give the prospect reasons to see you.

Take time to plan your call. Use an agenda or script—not word for word, but as a guide to your destination.

Use the alternative-choice close to arrive at a particular day and time. Once you have gained a measurable level of interest (judged mainly by voice tone), suggest that a brief initial meeting would be a good idea, and ask, "Do you have your diary handy?" This indirectly prompts the prospect to reach for his or her diary. "This week or next week? . . . Tuesday or Wednesday? . . . morning or afternoon? . . . 2:30 p.m. or 3:30 p.m.?" Suggesting a time slot on the half hour makes the prospect think that the meeting will only last 30 minutes, which is all it will last if he or she does not qualify as a serious prospect.

If the prospect is still reluctant, suggest that you are going to be in the area in a few weeks and would like to arrange a brief, introductory meeting. People are more likely to give you appointments further ahead. They are also likely to try to cancel these, which is where the next steps come in.

Repeat the appointment, say what you will be covering, who will be attending, your phone number in case of any changes, and that you will confirm in writing.

STAGE FIVE—CONFIRM IN WRITING

Either write confirming the appointment or allocate it as the next action in your file or on your prospect tracking system. The computer-based contact systems are ideal for this type of forward callback planning.

STAGE SIX—CALL 24 HOURS BEFORE

Phone the day before the appointment to check directions and to confirm.

STAGE SEVEN—FOLLOW-UPS

If you have done your target marketing properly, your prospect will probably need or be interested in your product—sometime. Ask when you might call back to check the situation then. Agree when you can call back and log this information in your tracking system. Most people are both flattered and impressed when you remember to call them back on the allotted date. Keep real "no-thank yous" on a mailing list and check back with them at least twice a year. By following this process, you'll have more appointments with more qualified prospects.

EXPERT ADVICE

A CALLING SCRIPT

Good morning, my name is _____.

Would you be able to help me gather some information about who is responsible for _____ in your company?

Would you know if Mr. Jones is at his desk today? Is he free to take my call?

Good morning, Mr. Jones. My name is _____.

Mr. Jones, I understand you are responsible for _____.

I represent _____. Perhaps you saw the letter I sent about a week ago?

I know your company has been looking for a solution to _____.

Our product has all the specs you seem to need.

We recently introduced a method of _____ that saves more than 16 percent on new parts and almost eliminates the need for service calls.

Tell me, Mr. Jones, if you would, just what level of efficiency are you looking for? Perhaps this Friday would be a good time to discuss it further. Would that suit your schedule?

Answer any questions or objections, then pin down the time and date for the meeting.

10 APPOINTMENT-SETTING TECHNIQUES THAT KEEP YOU IN FRONT OF CUSTOMERS

ADDITIONAL
READING

Not every call you make will end in a sale, but to even get a chance to close, you need an appointment with the decision maker. The stiffer the competition for your prospect's time, the more important it is to get your foot in the door before your competition does. To get your prospects to take you seriously, convince them that an appointment with you is time well spent.

These 10 tips will help you understand what to say and how to say it to get the appointments that help increase sales.

1. Start Tearing Down Buyer Barriers Immediately

To help you avoid being shut out by a wary gatekeeper, plan your greeting carefully. Politely identify yourself and your product or service. Use a friendly tone and impeccable phone manners to set you apart from the other salespeople who call on your prospect.

Be creative. An off-the-wall approach might throw a difficult gatekeeper temporarily off guard—just be careful not to say anything that might hurt your chances of getting an audience with your prospect.

2. Earn the Receptionist's Favor

In many cases the receptionist decides who will and won't get an appointment with your prospect. To make sure the receptionists you reach are on your side, treat them with respect. Ask for and use their names to show them that you view them as people and not just as petty annoyances standing between you and your prospects.

If you treat receptionists like the VIPs they are, they may be more likely to treat you like one. When you've collected the information you need, thank the receptionist warmly by name before you get transferred or hang up.

3. Tear Down Buyer Barriers with Your Prospects

Start building rapport from the moment you get through to your prospect. Ask open-ended questions that encourage buyers to talk and help you analyze their needs. Use words such as "may," "might" and "could," for example, and such phrases as "an opportunity you may find interesting" or "a plan that could cultivate new customers." If you establish yourself as a trustworthy, knowledgeable, and caring person before you start talking about your product, your prospect may listen more carefully—and buy more quickly.

75

4. Appeal to the Buyer's Best Interests

> **Instead of giving a long boring list of your product's bells and whistles, reassure your prospect that his or her needs come first by outlining how your product can meet those needs.**

To pinpoint your buyer's specific needs, do some homework before you make your first call. Make a brief but powerful benefits statement that grabs your prospect's attention and whets the appetite for more information. Instead of giving a long boring list of your product's bells and whistles, reassure your prospect that his or her needs come first by outlining how your product can meet those needs.

5. Answer the Buyer's Unasked Question

"What's in it for me?" Briefly outline how your product could meet your prospect's needs, then show how that affects your prospect personally. If your product could help reduce your buyer's workload or help impress top-level management, say so.

When you talk to your buyer, instead of using the phrases "your company's profits" or "your department's productivity," give your words more personal impact by saying "your profits" and "your productivity."

6. Appeal to the Buyer's Sense of Reason and Emotion

Some prospects base buying decisions on logic; others go with feelings and emotions. You might not be able to tell how your buyer makes decisions in the short time you have, so use a little of both to get the appointment. For the logical decision maker, use concise, rational arguments that emphasize the measurable positive results of using your product.

To win over the emotional decision maker, use image-building language and emphasize how product benefits will make the prospect feel (i.e., "Won't it feel great not to worry about production delays anymore?")

7. Establish the Offer's Credibility

If your prospect believes there's a sucker born every minute, you have to show that buying from you is safe and smart. Establish credibility by gathering facts and figures to back up your claims.

To make a positive impression on a wary prospect, for example, you might say, "XYZ Company used this product to decrease its product defects by 23 percent." This statement boosts your credibility by providing specific information on what your product can do and giving the name of a company prospects can call to verify it. Tell the buyer that you have a collection of testimonials from other satisfied customers.

8. Show Respect for the Buyer's Time

Tell prospects exactly how much time the appointment will take and emphasize that you know their time is valuable. Keep your conversation brief—save your product presentation for the appointment.

Use words that make it clear that you're trying to take up as little of their time as possible: "I'd like to very quickly tell you about this opportunity," or, "May I take a moment to discuss this with you briefly?" Your efforts to save the prospect's time help prove that you sincerely care about your customers.

9. Reassure Buyers That when You Meet with Them, You'll Provide All the Information They'll Need to Make a Decision

Your statement will help reassure them that you'll tell them everything they need to know, so they won't have to conduct any personal research to confirm your product's value or your credibility.

Emphasize that you want them to make an educated, informed decision and that the material you bring will allow them to do that. You might also shorten the buying cycle by suggesting that since they'll have all the information they need right in front of them, they'll be able to make a prompt and wise decision.

10. Confirm the Appointment

Send a brief, handwritten note with the date, time, and place of your appointment. Enclose your business card and an article that may interest the prospect, or maybe some product literature that addresses concerns raised when you arranged your meeting. On the day before your appointment, call again to make sure the decision maker is still able to meet you at the prearranged time.

Markets are so competitive and your buyers are often so busy that just getting an appointment—never mind a sale—takes an edge. By creating a strong first impression, you can give yourself the chance to tell your prospects about your product or service. A proven appointment-setting strategy can help give you greater access to prospects and sales.

FOLLOW CONSULTANT MICHAEL BRIZZ'S SIMPLE SUGGESTIONS FOR PHONING FOR APPOINTMENTS EVERY DAY

One precious hour a day can double your income. So claims consultant Michael Brizz, president of The Center for Professional Achievement. "Most salespeople squander their careers, and a fortune in commissions slips through their fingers each year," says Brizz, "because they fail to cash in on that single hour each day." That's one hour that should be spent phoning for appointments. It is easy to pull off if you follow the consultant's simple suggestions.

- ☑ **Devote one scheduled hour per day to phoning prospects for appointments.** Dedicate this time exclusively to setting appointments for selling. No service calls, attempts to close orders, or anything else. Just appointments.

- ☑ **Don't cannibalize phone time by visits to prospects.** Since you can set up five appointments an hour on the phone, seeing only one prospect during this time in place of setting up five appointments will put you in a hole.

- ☑ **Pinpoint the ideal time in your target market for contacting prospects.** Maximizing that time will put you at the peak of efficiency.

- ☑ **Keep track of your calls and results to upgrade your effectiveness.** Without an accurate record, you won't be able to tell if you are calling the right prospects at the right time and with the best selling message.

- ☑ **Set specific calling goals for yourself that tie into your sales-building goals.**

- ☑ **Put technology to use.** With low-cost tools such as headphones and speed-dialers, you can achieve a rate of 40 calls an hour. With a cold list, you can set at least two appointments per hour. With referrals, you can set five to seven appointments per hour. Go for it!

Rapport

**A HANDS-ON GUIDE
FOR MANAGERS**

TRAINING GUIDE TIME REQUIRED: 50 MINUTES

HOW TO BUILD RAPPORT

The rapport between the decision maker and the sales rep lies at the core of a positive customer relationship. When rapport is strong, each sale deepens the quality of the relationship, making successive sales easier. When rapport is weak, selling becomes difficult and awkward; when rapport is missing, selling becomes an exercise in futility. Therefore, learning how to build and maintain rapport should be at the top of every salesperson's list of critical skills to master.

The process of building rapport begins at the first customer contact and continues throughout the relationship. However, the process of building rapport changes over time to accommodate the changing requirements of the customer relationship. To understand this clearly, it helps to view the sales process as a five-step process:

1. Creating initial rapport

2. Gathering information

3. Proposing a solution

4. Appealing to the buying motive

5. Obtaining a commitment

Each step builds on the previous step. The first step is critical, because it sets the tone for the rest of the relationship and determines how easy (or difficult) it will be to maintain and build rapport during the lifetime of the relationship. If a sales rep creates a sense of rapport during the first customer meeting, the remaining steps are a natural development of the relationship. If the first meeting is bungled and a strong sense of rapport isn't established, chances are that the relationship will languish.

QUICK TIP

QUICK TIPS

☑ Nobody likes to be sold, but everybody likes to buy.

☑ Selling is a natural extension of rapport building.

☑ Find out what customers like, want, and need, and then show them how to get it.

☑ Gather information before proposing a solution, or you're shooting in the dark.

☑ Information gathering is supposed to be a conversation, not an inquisition.

☑ Rapport building thrives on mutual trust and credibility.

☑ Commitment isn't just a sale; it's a deepening of rapport.

☑ When it comes to rapport building, attitude is everything.

While many sales reps have a knack for building rapport, few understand the psychological dynamics that lie behind the rapport-building process. Rapport building takes place during any and all human interactions. For example, whenever people gather together in any social setting, there is always one person who becomes the primary center of attention. People want to be around that person and unconsciously seek his or her approval. This is because that individual is effective at building rapport. This skill may be (and often is) unconscious and even operates among people with limited social skills. At a technical conference, for example, the engineer who is best at creating rapport with fellow engineers will be the center of the discussion group.

While rapport building comes naturally to some, it is a mistake to believe that it's something that can't be consciously developed. Rapport building, like all human relationship skills, can be learned and taught. The key to doing this is to draw upon other experiences in your life where building rapport has come naturally.

When you meet any customer for the first time, visualize that customer as an honored guest in your home. If you're like most people, when you welcome guests into your home, you are typically glad to see them, and you want to make them feel welcome and at ease. While the specifics of what you might say to a customer are different from what you might say to a houseguest, the motivation and attitude behind the words should be the same. Just as you graciously do your best to make your guest comfortable, when you meet with a customer, try to find the place inside yourself that is truly grateful that you have this opportunity to meet this individual and to be of service.

Just as when you greet a guest, the first words out of your mouth set the tone of the visit and will determine whether the conversation will proceed to the point where a sale becomes possible. After an initial greeting, open the conversation with a remark that lets the customer know that you have put some thought into and done some research on the customer's firm. Then follow with a question about the business or the individual that will lead toward a conversation.

For example, you might begin a customer meeting with a technical expert by mentioning that you noticed that the expert had recently presented a paper at a conference and then ask a question that indicates your interest in the customer. "I was on the Web learning more about the widget industry, and I came across the text of a keynote speech that you gave at the last WidgetUSA conference. What kind of response did you get from that speech?" For a different decision maker, such as a CEO, you might remark that you noticed from the CEO's bio that his or her previous firm was in a different industry, and then ask what's different about being a leader in the current industry.

The specific content of the opening remark is far less important than what the remark shows about you as an individual and (by extension) your firm as a company with whom the customer might want to do business. The hidden message of the opening remark is that you really do care enough about this customer to take some extra effort.

Some salespeople mistakenly believe that it's best to open the initial conversation with a neutral compliment, such as something about the family photo, the autographed baseball on the desk, the view out the window, and so on. The problem with this approach is that it's incredibly trite. Dozens, perhaps hundreds, of sales reps who have come into that customer's office have already commented on these obvious conversation-starters. Furthermore, the fact that you've opened the conversation with an obvious compliment indicates that you haven't done any research and that you're winging it.

Another common error is believing that the opening question and conversation should be about a shared cultural experience, such as a recent sporting event or a world event. While such a conversation can indeed build rapport with the customer, that rapport is not easily redirected toward business and a sales opportunity. By contrast, opening with a business-related remark and question builds immediate momentum toward your goal of making a sale and (just as important) toward the customer's goal of having a problem solved or need fulfilled.

Just as important as the initial remarks is the overall tone of the meeting, because the tone is what the customer will remember long after the intellectual subject matter of the meeting is forgotten. As mentioned previously, a good way to set this all-important tone is to imagine the customer as a guest in your own home. Because you are in the customer's own environment, this idea seems a bit odd, but this is a case where a little imagination pays big dividends.

When a person comes into your home, you create a welcoming atmosphere so that he or she feels like a welcome guest. To create a similar atmosphere in the customer's office, think of yourself as "welcoming" the customer into your personal view of the world, where the product and services you sell are desirable and valuable. Just like a host who offers a thirsty guest a drink, you are about to offer a product or service that the customer truly needs.

When calling on a customer, it's useful to remember that five minutes ago some other sales rep was pitching somebody else's product. In order to differentiate yourself, you'll need to be personable, persuasive, and informed.

Contrast the following two examples:

Customer: I only have a couple of minutes.

Sales Rep: OK. I just thought I'd stop by with a brochure. Here's my business card. Please call us if you ever want some software for inventory control.

FREQUENTLY ASKED QUESTIONS

SALES REPS' FREQUENTLY ASKED QUESTIONS

Q: What is the most commonly made mistake when building rapport?

A: Trying to be too friendly too quickly. This makes it seem as if you're just a phony trying to make a sale. Instead, hold back on the friendliness and increase your level of curiosity. Be interested in the customer as a person and in the customer's motivations. Then let the friendliness evolve naturally during the conversation.

Q: How can I move gracefully from the initial rapport building to information gathering?

A: Don't push the process forward too quickly. Instead, let it evolve naturally out of the conversation. First ask permission to ask them further questions. For example: "Do you mind if I ask you a couple of questions so that I can understand your situation better and figure out if there's any way that I can help you?"

Q: How can I introduce a solution without seeming like I'm suddenly going into "sales mode"?

A: Don't try to be a hero who swoops in and solves the customer's problem. Instead, let the customer be the hero by positioning your solution from the customer's benefit and viewpoint. For example, don't ask, "What would it mean to you if we could solve that problem?" Instead, ask, "What would it mean to you if you could solve that problem?"

Here's a far more effective approach:

Customer: I only have a couple of minutes.

Sales Rep: In that case, I'm truly, truly grateful that you're willing to take the time to spend even two minutes with me. I'll bet one of the reasons that you're so busy is that you're getting ready for that big merger. I had an idea of how my company might be able to help you reduce inventory. When the new management looks at your department, how will they determine whether your inventory is running efficiently?

Regardless of how you handle the initial meeting, you want the customer to perceive you as the kind of person to whom people gravitate. This means exhibiting a genuine interest in the customer. When this is done correctly and casually, it doesn't seem pushy. And because your opening remark and question is about the customer, not about you and not about selling, it's very likely to lead to a conversation. The reason behind this is simple: most people enjoy talking about themselves and feel a natural rapport with anyone who is sincerely interested and willing to listen.

Rapport building does not end after the initial conversation, of course. Instead, it continues through the remaining steps of the sales process. While gathering information, for example, rather than antagonizing the customer by playing "20 Questions," guide the conversation onto subjects that will help you better assess how you can help the customer. Then, as you move from step to step, let your ideas and proposals emerge naturally from the conversation. Rather than just trying to sell something, you're doing your best to become the customer's ally in achieving the customer's goals. Because of your attitude and attention to rapport, the customer will be more inclined to make a commitment. Closing becomes more natural and less mechanical, because the commitment "feels" as if it's an extension of the relationship and a way to deepen the rapport.

QUICK TIPS FOR YOUR TRAINING SESSION

QUICK TIP

☑ The success of the training session will largely depend upon the time and effort that you put into devising an effective opening sequence.

☑ If your sales team works in a retail environment, the opening sequence will typically be a greeting followed by a canned set of questions.

☑ If your sales team works in a business-to-business environment, then the opening sequence will typically be a sample of a research-based question, which should be open-ended, so that it initiates a real conversation.

☑ The misdirection of the leadership role "A" and "B" in step 9 of the Sales Manager's Meeting Guide is intentional and important. Role-playing is more effective after normal group dynamics are disturbed. In most cases, the natural leader of the pairing will designate himself or herself as "A." Turning the tables tends to jolt both "A" and "B" out of their typical roles.

☑ As you monitor your team, pay special attention to the naturalness of the opening sequence. The purpose of the exercise isn't to learn a script, but to cultivate the attitude that will make the script seem natural. Note that varying the wording slightly can help keep the opening sequence fresh.

DR. EARL TAYLOR was interviewed for this article. He is a 30-year employee and master trainer at Dale Carnegie & Associates and is a global provider of locally delivered training in leadership, sales, and interpersonal and communications skills. The firm's clients include more than 400 of the Fortune 500 as well as thousands of smaller companies in more than 80 countries around the world. Dale Carnegie & Associates Inc. is located at 290 Motor Parkway, Hauppauge, NY 11788-5102. Telephone: 631-415-9300. Web: www.dale-carnegie.com.

SALES MANAGER'S MEETING GUIDE

SALES MANAGER'S MEETING GUIDE

Below are 12 practical steps to help your sales team build better rapport with its customers. This training session should take from 35 to 55 minutes.

1. Prior to the sales meeting, consider the nature of your customer base and come up with an opening sequence (remark and question) that, based on your experience, would lead toward building rapport with the typical customer.

2. Open the sales meeting by explaining that the team is going to work on rapport building during initial customer meetings. Explain that the team will be asked to do some role-playing and request that everyone participate to the fullest.

3. Review the five-step sales process with the team. Explain how each step builds on the previous step and that the first step is the foundation of the sales process.

4. Ask for a volunteer to act as a customer. Approach the customer with an opening that you know will be ineffective. For example, "May I help you?" "I suppose you're wondering why I'm here." Be sure to deliver this ineffective opening deadpan, so that the team can clearly see how ineffective it is.

> **Open the sales meeting by explaining that the team is going to work on rapport building during initial customer meetings. Explain that the team will be asked to do some role-playing and request that everyone participate to the fullest.**

5. Ask the team members whether they felt that this opening was effective. Discuss why it wasn't.

6. Repeat steps 4 and 5, but this time open with a totally irrelevant compliment. For example, "Nice tie." "What a lovely wedding ring."

7. Repeat steps 4 and 5, but this time use the effective opening sequence that you crafted prior to the meeting.

8. Tell the customer that you're now going to continue the conversation and ask the customer to play along. Open with the "effective" sequence and then lead the conversation into the information-gathering phase.

9. Separate the sales team into groups of two. Ask each pair to decide who is going to be "A" and who is going to be "B." Once they decide, tell them that "B" is the group leader. Have the group leader for each pair decide who is going to be the customer and who is going to be the sales rep.

10. Explain that the goal of this exercise is to create initial rapport and then move to the information-gathering step. Have the sales reps attempt an initial meeting with their customers. Move from group to group to check whether the conversations seem natural. Provide feedback when necessary.

11. Repeat step 10, but with reversed roles in each pair.

12. Break the pairs up and form new pairings. Repeat the same process until you feel that the team has learned this important skill.

BUILDING RAPPORT IN THE FIRST FIVE MINUTES

Establishing rapport is not about being a best friend to your customers.

"It's about respecting their time, understanding their needs, and offering your product or service to meet those needs," says Mary Parkhouse, a top Bausch and Lomb territory sales manager.

It's true that in order to be in sales you need to get along with all types of people, but as Parkhouse says, that doesn't mean you must be best friends to establish rapport. You just have to be prepared.

"Do your homework before you meet the customers, because in the first five minutes it's absolutely crucial that you gain agreement and establish a mutual relationship," she says. "You're there to convince them to do something, and the only way you can do that is to understand their needs and goals and how your product or service might help achieve those goals."

Parkhouse looks for such nonverbal clues as attitude, appearance, posture, and style. She also says you must be very respectful of your prospects' time. "Confirm how much time you've got and then move on quickly—introduce yourself, state your purpose, and then let them talk," says Parkhouse.

> "Do your homework before you meet the customers, because in the first five minutes it's absolutely crucial that you gain agreement and establish a mutual relationship."

MIRROR, MIRROR

So what if you're outgoing and your prospect is not? Does that mean there's no chance for a sale? No. The key is to mimic the other person's personality type.

"We are comfortable with people who are like us: that's human nature," says Bob Stiles, sales manager for Lassiter-Ware Insurance, a large Florida independent insurance agency. "Some people are very fast—they talk, move, and think fast. Some are very slow thinkers, talkers, and movers. Your job is to mirror each person, whether they're fast or slow."

Not only should you respond to prospects' speed but also to their personality temperature—warm or cold. How can you tell what type of personality they are?

Driver and analytical personality types are cold-natured. These people like to take control, and they want you to get to the point. Drivers talk fast and will seem irritated if you talk too much, explains Stiles. Analyticals tend to be a little slower paced; they have the need to be right and respected. Cold personalities tend not to like making eye contact and sometimes turn away or look down as they shake your hand.

"You can't be touchy-feely with these people," says Stiles. "Just get down to business."

On the other hand, warm personalities, the amiable and expressive types, look you in the eye. They like to talk and are naturally inviting and friendly. Amiables are slow-paced and family-oriented. They look for support and approval, while expressives are fast-paced and energetic.

Also, says Stiles, remember to respect someone's space. Don't lean forward across the desk if they have a cold personality. And, if they are warm, friendly people, don't put up barriers—by placing a briefcase on your lap, for instance.

Once you can relate to these people in their own personality style, you're on your way to establishing rapport.

OH NO! IT'S NOT WORKING

Even if you figure out personality types, sometimes things don't click. That's when you need to step back, take a deep breath, and quickly evaluate why it's not going well. Nine times out of ten, it's because you're doing most of the talking. When Parkhouse finds herself in this situation, she stops and asks a question that customers can expand on, so the focus is switched to their needs.

"Stop talking," she says. "Take it slow and pick up cues. Smile. If they don't smile back, the person's guard is really up and you need to get them talking."

Stiles agrees that people will relax if they are doing most of the talking. "When you enter a prospect's office, the scales are tipped against you, and the more you talk, the more they will tip. There's not a good balance," he says. "The only way you can change that is to get in and out of the conversation as soon as possible. Get the prospects talking. If you're telling, you're not selling."

The first five minutes are crucial to whether or not you will establish rapport. Like Mom always said, "The first impression is a lasting one, so make sure you make it a good one."

EXPERT ADVICE: AT EASE

EXPERT ADVICE

The following are four of the most important considerations when trying to develop rapport within the first five minutes, according to public speaker and sales trainer Mark Johns.

1. **APPEARANCE:** "When people first see us, they make judgments about whether they will like us, trust us, and do business with us. Determine if it's a formal or casual company ahead of time—know what they are expecting you to be like. If I were a financial analyst and I was calling on an auto repair shop, they would expect me to be in a suit and tie. If I was calling on that same shop as a parts seller, jeans would be appropriate—that's what they would expect me to wear."

2. **ATTITUDE:** "To create rapport with prospects, you must appear confident and service-oriented. You're there to help them, and you want them to be comfortable with you. Gain confidence by doing your homework and knowing what your customers' needs are before you meet them."

3. **COMMUNICATION:** "The best way to communicate is through mirroring. If they are very shy and withdrawn, I'm going to become a lot quieter. You can do this on the phone as well as face-to-face. Reflect the manner, volume, and rate of speech. Non-verbal communications can also make someone comfortable or uncomfortable; pay attention to posture, eye contact, body movement, gestures, and proximity—the space between you and the other person."

4. **MANNERS AND SOCIAL SKILLS:** "You can unknowingly make someone very uncomfortable if you have poor manners. Common courtesy is something we can't afford to forget".

"Finally, your goal in that first five minutes is to have them think, 'Gosh, I feel like I've known you all my life'."

MARK JOHNS, a public speaker and trainer on sales, customer service, and communication skills, is senior sales director for Sir Speedy Inc. in Mission Viejo, CA. For more information, call 949-348-5000.

HOW TO BUILD RAPPORT IN 60 SECONDS OR LESS

Times are tough—or at least, really tight. Everyone's feeling crunched. There's just no time for the niceties. So why not just ignore the getting-to-know-you games and get right down to the nitty-gritty of selling, closing, and moving on to the next account? Hey, wait a minute. That's exactly the wrong thing to do when everyone's feeling a bit desperate.

You may not have all the time in the world to develop a warm and fuzzy relationship with your prospect or customer, but you'll find that getting that first step off in the right direction can cement the account for the future.

Even though the time frame for building warmth and trust is no longer measured in 15-minute increments, you still have a few seconds to build rapport that can last for years. And remember, building rapport is not just a matter of shaking hands and coming out selling. It's the science of reading the buyer's verbal and nonverbal cues. How you respond can put a jingle in your pocket and a smile on your face—permanently.

> **...building rapport is not just a matter of shaking hands and coming out selling.**

That's a particular challenge for Charles Greene III. Greene is founder and president of Corporate Shuffle, a Washington, DC, company that provides magicians for meetings and exhibits. Most times he'll fulfill bookings himself—which means that he's the product he's selling. And that makes forging instant connections with clients all the more crucial. "What I do is based on personality," says the affable 42-year-old. "People hire me because they like me. They're not going to say, 'I don't like Charles, but I need his product.' Because I am the product."

Greene's ice-breaker isn't fancy or clever, but it's helped him build a thriving business with such blue chips as Johnson and Johnson, Monsanto, and Exxon. When Greene meets prospects at trade shows—either during performances for other clients or at shows where he has his own booth to promote himself—he'll gather such rudimentary information as budget, number of shows annually, and whether they've used magicians previously. Then, glancing at the city on their business card, he'll say, "So, you're from San Francisco. What do you do for fun?"

Seems like a simple enough question, but Greene finds that people are delighted to be asked. "I always try to find some area of connection other than the work itself," he says. "My asking them about their passions gets them to think about themselves a little." Prospects will open up about anything from travel to skiing to cooking—and give Greene an opportunity to find common ground. He'll note their interests so that the next time he

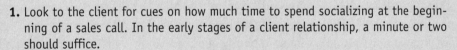

NONVERBAL SELLING TIPS

QUICK
TIP

1. Look to the client for cues on how much time to spend socializing at the beginning of a sales call. In the early stages of a client relationship, a minute or two
should suffice.

2. Come up with a few provocative questions that will help you understand your
clients as people.

3. Look around clients' offices for clues to their interests. Use them as conversational
openers and as insight into how they like to conduct business.

4. Try to connect with what the client is feeling. When you begin to feel a genuine
empathy with that person, your empathy will be transmitted through eye contact.

5. Segue to the meat of the meeting with an agenda-setting statement that recaps who
you are, what company you represent, and the purpose of the meeting.

calls, he's got a great conversational opener. Even better, it's an instant reminder of who
he is and of his warmth as a person and performer.

"When I go against other magicians, I know that some are stiff and not as personable," he says. "Hopefully, this gives me an edge."

Daphne Matalene, on the other hand, finds an edge by scrutinizing a client's environment. Matalene, the 29-year-old eastern account manager for *Budget Living Magazine*
which was recently named start-up of the year by *Adweek*, says that the props around a
prospect's office can throw off valuable clues about what makes him or her tick.

The following are two recent examples.

While waiting in the office of a vice president at a major Manhattan book publisher,
Matalene noticed several crumpled packets of aspirin on the woman's desk. "So I thought,
she's having a bad day." When the client did arrive, Matalene shifted her voice into low
gear and conducted the meeting in a calm, soothing tone. It worked. Matalene walked out
with enough information to put together a proposal for a volume deal that the client
subsequently bought.

Similarly, when Matalene called on a media supervisor at a major ad agency, she
looked around his windowed office and felt as if she'd parachuted into Jurassic Park. "It
was decorated with plastic models and pictures of sharks, alligators, dinosaurs, and all

sorts of fearsome, toothy beasts," she says. "I'm sure it was meant to strike fear in the hearts of people like me."

Matalene took the bait, though, and turned it to her advantage. When the supervisor swept into his office, she jokingly said, "I've noticed all these sharks. You're not going to eat me alive, are you?" By commenting on items in his office, "I was able to say, 'Okay, I know you, so now let's talk.' I also took my cue from all this shark stuff that I'd better move fast with this guy." Matalene dove right into the meeting—and 20 minutes later left with a sale.

Presentations

A HANDS-ON GUIDE FOR MANAGERS

TRAINING GUIDE TIME REQUIRED: 50 MINUTES

PERSUASIVE PRESENTATIONS

A sales presentation is not a "pitch"—a monologue that attempts to convince a customer to buy. A sales presentation is a rapport-building dialogue between the right salesperson and the right customer. This meeting of the minds leading to the transfer of value for money can be achieved consistently when only the salesperson has gone through a thorough preparation process. Ideally, your product and the customer's requirements should be like two gears engineered to mesh seamlessly.

Step 1: Identify Your Prospects

Many salespeople make the mistake of presenting to customers without knowing much about their market and potential customer base. These four steps will help you find the ideal customer to present to.

1. **SPECIALIZATION.** Determine your ideal customer, remembering that if customers experience positive feelings, they will feel that a sale is successful. Ask yourself the following questions: What specific benefit or improvement will your customers gain by using your product or service? How will using it make them happy? Who is most likely to experience, these positive feelings? What is their income, position, experience, and level of authority?

2. **POSITIONING.** Determine what's unique and wonderful about your company. Ask yourself the following questions: What is it you do that's better than any other company? Why should your ideal customer buy from you rather than the competition? If your competitors were asked (and they answered honestly), what would they say that your company does better than anyone else?

3. **SEGMENTATION.** Based upon the above, determine the specific type of customer that is the best match for your products or services. Don't make the mistake of

> **Don't make the mistake of thinking that success comes from a broad focus on many customers.**

thinking that success comes from a broad focus on many customers. You want to pick your shots. The key question to answer is, who are the customers who would value and appreciate what my company does better than our competitors?

4. CONCENTRATION. Focus on those few customers who can benefit the most from your company's products or services. Your ideal customer should want your product, need your product, be able to use your product, and be able to afford your product. Presenting elsewhere is a waste of time.

Step 2: Prepare for the Meeting

There are three steps to take before any sales presentation:

1. **DO YOUR HOMEWORK.** Learn everything you can about the customer. There is a wealth of information available on the Internet about virtually every company. You should never let yourself be in the position of asking the customer a question that's answered elsewhere.

2. **CREATE AN AGENDA.** An agenda positions you not as a salesperson asking for a sale, but as a consultant or advisor who is there to help. The agenda should be on your company's letterhead and should have the customer's full name spelled out, with the time and date. The agenda should consist of five to seven questions that focus the conversation on the customer's needs, going from the general to the specific. These questions should be spaced about an inch apart in order to leave space for you (and the customer) to take notes.

3. **PREPARE YOURSELF MENTALLY.** Remember that 80 percent of the buying decision will be based upon how the customer feels about you. The most important part of any sales presentation will be building trust and rapport, so visualize the percentages of time that you will spend at the meeting on different activities as an inverted pyramid, resting on the foundation of trust-building: building trust—40 percent; identifying needs—30 percent; presentation—20 percent; closing—10 percent.

Step 3: The Presentation

Once you've prepared, it's time to bring the process to fruition by actually meeting with the customer. There are four steps to doing this effectively:

SALES REPS' FREQUENTLY ASKED QUESTIONS

FREQUENTLY ASKED QUESTIONS

Q: What do I do when the customer won't stop talking long enough for me to continue my presentation?

A: Listening builds trust. In the early stages, this type of customer behavior is advantageous because it makes the customer more relaxed and allows you to learn valuable information. If the information stops becoming useful, compliment the customer and gently redirect the conversation. For example, say, "That's really a good point, Joe, and it reminds me of something I want to show you . . ."

Q: How do I handle a sales presentation where there are multiple decision makers in the room?

A: Do not make the mistake of addressing your presentation solely to the senior manager. While he or she may be the final decision maker, it's likely that you will have to convince others in the room to do business with you and your company. As you present, speak to each section of the audience, being sure to make eye contact with each person in the room. Make a point while looking at one person, then continue, making your next point while looking at another person.

Q: What do I do when they bring up the competition?

A: Never criticize competitors. Instead, praise them honestly for what they do well, but then show the customer why it would be a better business decision to work with your company. For example, say, "Well, ABC is an excellent company, and they've been in business a long time and have high standards. However, I believe, based upon what you've told me about your needs, that we can satisfy them better because. . ."

1. **MAKE A POSITIVE FIRST IMPRESSION.** Always begin by thanking customers for their time and acknowledging that you realize how busy they are. This is important, because even if customers have asked for the meeting, chances are that they'll be busy and stressed when the meeting time actually arrives. Then explain that you're not there to sell them anything, but only to ask a couple of questions and see if you can help them to achieve their goals. Then give each customer a copy of your agenda and explain that you've prepared an agenda to help use time most efficiently. When you say these things, customers will visibly relax, because you've taken away their fear that they'll be subjected to a sales pitch.

> **Think of the presentation as the torso of a skeleton, with the questions in the agenda as the spine and the resulting discussions as the ribs.**

2. QUESTION TO REVEAL REQUIREMENTS. Think of the presentation as the torso of a skeleton, with the questions in the agenda as the spine and the resulting discussions as the ribs. Keep coming back to the agenda in order to reinforce the fact that the meeting is moving forward and that you are respecting the customer's time, relieving any anxiety that the customer might have about the meeting going on for too long.

3. **SHOW HOW YOUR PRODUCTS AND SERVICES MEET THEIR REQUIREMENTS.** This should be easy because you've taken the time to understand the best features of your product or services and how they meet customer needs. In addition, you know in advance that this is a customer who actually needs that product. You've also carefully researched the customer, which makes it easier to tailor your presentation to that customer's needs.

4. **CLOSE THE BUSINESS OR CONFIRM THE NEXT STEP.** If you've followed the entire process described above and earned the customer's trust and if the customer understands the benefits of your solution, it will be very easy to close or move the sales process to the next step. If you do this correctly, the customer may even buy the product or service without asking the price.

Step 4: Honing Your Skills

There are four key thoughts to keep in mind as you refine your presentation skills:

1. **ALWAYS PACE THE CONVERSATION SO THAT THE CUSTOMER IS NEVER OVERWHELMED.** The average customer can listen to only three sentences before becoming overloaded. If you become an information fire hose, the customer will simply shut down and say, "I'll think it over." Instead, use questioning and requests for feedback to pace the conversation.

2. **LISTENING BUILDS TRUST AND RAPPORT.** When the customer talks, listen. Really listen; don't just sit there thinking about what you're going to say next. The golden rule of selling is to sell to your customers the way you'd like to be sold to yourself. Listening carefully also allows you to better sense the customer's true attitude and mood. Connecting with the customer in this fundamental way is the key element of turning a sales presentation into a sale.

3. **FIND OUT IF THE DECISION TO BUY WILL BE MADE WITHIN A REASONABLE AMOUNT OF TIME.** One of the biggest mistakes salespeople make is focusing on customers who aren't really going to buy. The best way to get this information is to ask. "If I show you exactly what you're looking for at a reasonable price, in what kind of time frame will you be making a decision?"

4. **SUBTLY PUSH POTENTIAL OBJECTIONS OFF THE TABLE.** If you're reasonably certain that a particular objection is likely to surface, you should preempt it by admitting it before the customer brings it up. For example, say, "Some people say that our product costs a little too much, but . . ." Admitting the cons of your product as well as the pros also enhances your credibility and positions you as an adviser rather than a salesperson.

QUICK TIPS FOR YOUR NEXT TRAINING SESSION

QUICK TIP

1. Explain that improving presentation skills is a lifelong process and that your primary goal is to coach your salespeople to do this better—not to criticize the way that they're doing it now.

2. When providing feedback during and after the training session, use the salesperson's natural desire for self-improvement to your advantage. Always let the salesperson self-evaluate his or her performance before giving your suggestions. In many cases, the salesperson will be more critical than you would be yourself.

3. Avoid the tendency to unload criticism every time one of your salespeople does a presentation. It's better to provide a suggestion prior to the next presentation rather than subject the salesperson to a criticism of the previous presentation.

QUICK TIPS FOR YOUR NEXT SALES MEETING

Here are key questions that your team should be asking itself:

1. Who is our ideal customer?

2. How do our products and services meet that customer's needs?

3. Can I articulate our value to the customer in 25 words or less?

4. What visual aids should I bring to the meeting?

5. What can I do to earn that customer's trust?

6. How can I make it simple for the customer to say yes?

BRIAN TRACY was interviewed for this article. He is chairman of Brian Tracy International, a human resource company based in San Diego, CA, with affiliates throughout America and in 31 countries worldwide. His customers include IBM, Hewlett-Packard, Arthur Andersen, McDonnell Douglas, and The Million Dollar Round Table. He's the author of numerous books and more than 300 audio and video learning programs. His company is headquartered at 462 Stevens Ave., Suite 202, Solana Beach, CA 92075. Telephone: 858-481-2977. Visit his Web site at www.briantracy.com.

SALES MANAGER'S MEETING GUIDE

SALES
MANAGER'S
MEETING
GUIDE

Below are 10 practical steps to improve your team's sales presentation skills. This sales meeting should take about 50 minutes.

1. One week prior to the meeting, gather marketing materials that describe your customer base and the products and services that your company offers. Select the material that is most relevant.

2. Three days prior to the meeting, distribute copies of this training module to your team members and inform them they'll be asked to give a five-minute sales presentation based upon the techniques described in the module.

3. Open the meeting by explaining that your team will be working on presentation skills, with the goal of closing more business. Ask team members to participate to the fullest, and make it clear that you consider this skill to be of the utmost importance.

4. Take five minutes so that everybody on the team can prepare an agenda. Some of your team may have already done so. If so, compliment them on their foresight.

5. Pair everyone up into groups of two. If somebody is left over, form a team of three. Have one person in each group give a five-minute presentation to the other, who acts as the customer. You may want to wander around the room during these presentations in order to assess each participant's performance.

6. When the presentation is complete, spend a few minutes letting each team discuss whether the presentation successfully hit the major points described in this training module.

7. Have the team members switch roles and repeat. When this is complete, you should be about 20 minutes into the meeting.

8. Have each person pair up with a new partner and repeat steps six and seven. Do this twice. By this point, each team member will have presented three times to three different people. When this is complete, you should be about 40 minutes into the meeting.

9. Open the floor for a discussion of presentation skills. Ask each participant to identify areas where he or she could use some improvement. If necessary, provide each participant with a constructive suggestion about how he or she might improve. Precede every suggestion with a meaningful compliment.

10. Summarize the preparation process and the presentation process described in the module and encourage participants to work on these skills on their own time.

In the future, when attending sales calls with individual salespeople, determine whether they've incorporated these skills; then provide additional suggestions for improvement.

HOW TO PREPARE FOR EVERY SALES CALL AS IF ANYTHING MIGHT HAPPEN

Preparation makes the difference between being unable to get your foot in the door at all and ultimately being invited to stay for a long and productive sojourn with a customer. "It's super important. You're an asset for the competition if you're doing cold calls without preparation. You're an asset for your company if you prepare," says Richard Trudel, senior account executive with Minolta Business Solutions in Miami, FL. With good precall preparation, you'll know very well the needs of a customer or prospect and be able to respond effectively to any objections or counterpoints.

Preparation is part research, part planning, and part critical thinking. The research aspect involves learning everything you can about the prospect company: In which markets does it operate? What relationships does it have with your competitors? What's its financial outlook? What are its strategic objectives? "You have to do your homework beforehand and evaluate the customer, their products and services; which of your competitors they're using; and whether their whole business plan is a good fit for you and the markets you cover," says Mark Eggert, sales manager of the Midwest division of United Window and Door Manufacturing.

The key is to have enough information so that you can effectively demonstrate why the prospect should either meet with or purchase from you. "It changes the momentum of the meeting. It gets people from being put out that you're just there to get a contract to thinking creatively about their needs and what you can do for them," says Trudel. Sufficient precall research also can shorten the sales cycle. "If you know ahead of time the problems a customer is having, you can be prepared to offer solutions at the time you're meeting," advises Eggert.

Trudel's research often includes identifying existing customers who operate in the same industry or even the same office complex. "I use that as much as possible. It helps with the response to 'Why should I see you?'" he says.

Planning and critical thinking prior to either telephone or face-to-face encounters help identify goals and plot strategies for achieving them. When Eggert travels with a salesperson, the two prepare an analysis sheet that outlines what they expect to accomplish from each meeting. "We establish objectives, discuss the competition, agree on strategies, and discuss the possible objections of the customer," he says.

Another aspect of preparation is establishing the roles of both salesperson and sales manager. "We decide beforehand which role I'll play—if I will hit hard or go soft. Depending on the personality of the salesperson, I'll adjust my approach accordingly," says Eggert.

Precall role-playing is another must for identifying and preparing for customer objections. "We use that a lot, especially for large accounts. We work as a team and come up

PRECALL PLANNING CHECKLIST

QUICK
TIP

There's nothing you can do to guarantee that your next appointment will go well, but by preparing well, you can at least tip the scales in your favor. Before any sales call, be sure to go over the following five-point checklist.

1. **WHAT'S MY SELF-TALK?** Instead of mulling over all possible catastrophes, remind yourself that you're there only because the customer has already seen enough merit in you and your company to meet with you. Remember that you're doing the customer a favor by sharing your expertise and thoughts.

2. **AM I REALISTIC?** Recognize that you are not omniscient and can't be expected to know everything. If the customer asks a question you don't have a ready answer for, it's OK to say so and promise to get back with an answer promptly.

3. **AM I FLEXIBLE?** Don't be rigid about sticking to a script, or you may risk missing unanticipated opportunities. Determine to let the conversation flow while keeping an open mind.

4. **DO I KNOW MY BEST QUESTIONS?** Every sales rep should be armed with five terrific open-ended questions that nearly always set the customer to thinking and envisioning the challenges ahead—and the possible solutions.

5. **WHAT'S MY END GAME?** One area where you don't want to be too flexible is with the close. Resolve to ask for the order, and be sure to do so with the confidence that your solution will solve key customer issues.

with objections that the customer might throw at us for why they shouldn't buy from us or shouldn't buy at that price," says Trudel.

There's not too much you can do to prepare for or prevent the occasional incendiary. "A purchaser sometimes likes to throw a curve at you. Sometimes it's just to play, or it may be a way to let you know he's not interested without saying it directly," Eggert explains. The best response to off-the-wall remarks and outrageous questions or requests is to say you don't know the answer and will have to get back to the prospect. "Never say anything you can't commit to," advises Eggert.

Preparation also doesn't help much with people who are annoyed at taking your call and make it clear they don't want to talk. However, Trudel finds benefit from adjusting his own attitude. "Before I pick up the phone, I smile just sitting at my desk. I believe people can feel your smile through the phone."

EXPERT ADVICE

EXPERT ADVICE: DO YOUR RESEARCH

As important as preparation is, it's where many salespeople miss the mark, according to The Professional Sales Coach, Anita Sirianni. "The number one mistake is failing to identify what you hope to accomplish and to detail what information you expect to collect. People don't do due diligence to collect the appropriate data they need to earn a sale. They think they can just show up and wow a customer with everything they know about a product or service," she says.

Good preparation combining research and critical thinking enables you to form questions that open the doors of opportunity. Contrast the clunker unprepared question, "Do you operate in other markets?" with "How effective has your expansion into three new markets been?" The latter gets the prospect thinking about opportunities to improve and puts you in the position of partnering with him or her in that process. "You need to identify several areas about the competition or the client's current condition and formulate questions—not statements—that get the prospect to discover the need for at least a conversation or discussion," says Sirianni. "It's that prethinking that gives you the edge going in."

Stay ahead of customer objections by writing down all the objections or questions raised in phone calls and face-to-face meetings and reviewing them regularly. "Slow down long enough to come up with reasonable, informed answers," advises Sirianni.

The research part of the preparation equation should include identifying a sales advocate within the prospect organization if possible. "That's not necessarily a decision maker. It's someone who finds an interest in you or in helping you get your product or service to their organization," says Sirianni. Use the person to locate sales opportunities and useful information and to help you steer clear of organizational land mines.

For more information, call 1-800-471-2619 or visit anitasirianni.com.

OK, so you're not performing at Radio City or Las Vegas. So you're not going to win an Emmy if you make the world's best presentation. Still, you want it to go smoothly. You want your audience—even if it's an audience of one vital prospect or customer—to stay tuned in to your message.

ADDITIONAL READING

You want, in essence, to present your message in such a way that you and your client enjoy the experience and want to close a deal. But that doesn't mean you have to put on a Broadway production. Everywhere you look, it seems, people are talking about getting more bang for their presentation buck. "Should I incorporate more slides?" they ask. "Should I add music?" "Do I need to beef up the visuals?"

But it's not about overhead projectors and cool graphics. A solid presentation is not made through upgrading your PowerPoint program or wowing the crowd with eye-popping photos. It's both more difficult and simpler than that. A great presentation—one from which the presenter and the client both leave excited about doing business together—is about people. It's about understanding what a company needs and offering to meet those needs in the best possible way.

The good news is, there are a few techniques that will help you communicate with your client and make your presentation more meaningful. Although there is no secret formula, there are a few universal truths about giving winning presentations.

First off, nobody is a natural. Nobody, but nobody, nails the presentation the first time through. At least that is what we heard over and over from sales reps and consultants. Second, everybody can learn. Really. So relax, sit back, and get ready for some hard-earned wisdom from two seasoned professionals.

1. DON'T PRETEND YOU'RE SOMETHING YOU'RE NOT

John McGrath, a consultant at Runzhiemer International who makes four to five presentations a week, has been giving presentations in one form or another for 15 years. "Those early presentations can be tough," says McGrath. "It's not quite fair, because you're not as much of an expert as you're supposed to be." McGrath suggests that the best policy if you're new to your firm or to the presentation game is honesty. "Just say, 'Look, I've only been here six months, I'm learning right along with you. But anything you need to know, if I don't know it, I will find out for you.'"

Cathy Lanski, an executive sales rep at Worldcom in Buffalo, NY, agrees. "People aren't looking for you to fail. If you tell them you're new, they're going to be on your side." And if you don't know the answer to a question, don't lie. Just say, "I don't know." But make sure that next time you know.

2. GET TO KNOW EVERYONE

> **Make sure that you've read up on the company you are presenting to, and customize your presentation to fit the needs of this particular client.**

"Personalize it," says Lanski. Make sure that you've read up on the company you are presenting to, and customize your presentation to fit the needs of this particular client. "Find the hot buttons at that company," says Lanski. "Every company has them. Use them."

McGrath believes the key to a good presentation lies not in getting all the facts about your company across to the client, but rather in getting to know the client. He believes that people get off track by thinking that a presentation has to be a monologue. "It's a dialogue," says McGrath. "Ask questions. Get to know them."

McGrath has found that people may start on the defensive. "You have to bring them around." Go in with a humble attitude. "I don't walk in thinking, 'I've got something to teach these people.' I go in thinking, 'I'm here to learn. I'm here to assist.'"

QUICK TIP

TELLTALE SIGNS THAT YOU NEED TO KEEP PROBING

Customers are not going to come right out and tell you to keep asking them questions, but they will offer signals that you need to keep probing. Just a few of such signals include:

☑ **BODY LANGUAGE.** Prospects who cross their arms, turn away, lean back, or avoid eye contact are communicating that you have yet to find the right approach. Change your tactics and ask a different set of probing questions.

☑ **SHORT ANSWERS.** When customers offer only curt responses to your questions, try asking different questions, ones that key on thoughts or feelings, such as "What was your thinking behind making the strategic decision to focus on that new market?"

☑ **VAGUE ANSWERS.** If a customer offers up a vague nonanswer to one of your questions, follow up with a "What does . . . mean to you?" inquiry. So when the customer says, "I want a system with good security," say, "What does good security mean to you?"

☑ **OBJECTIONS.** When customers say, "Your price is too high," "I'm happy with my current supplier," "We don't have the budget," or any of the dozens of other objections you probably know all too well, what they're really saying is, "You haven't figured out enough about my needs to offer me a compelling reason to act." Keep probing to get to those hidden needs.

3. KEEP NO SECRETS

"Nothing's taboo during my presentations," says McGrath. "No subjects are off-limits."

McGrath believes that when you enter the presentation room, you have to be willing to talk about anything. So don't shy away from the tough questions. "I want to know their fears, their hesitations," says McGrath. "I want to know their doubts. If there's something they're afraid to ask, then there's something they're holding back, and that could be the key to the sale."

4. MAKE IT INTERACTIVE

During a presentation, you want people to interrupt you; you want them to ask questions. It means they are engaged.

"One guy even brought a bag of Hershey's Kisses," says Lanski about a presentation she recently attended. "Every time you asked a question, he tossed you a kiss." It sounds hokey, but it worked. "I wanted some chocolate, so I asked a question. And you know what? It did get me involved."

You don't have to have a gimmick. You just have to be open to questions. And if you don't have some cool trick to break the ice, "just say it," suggests McGrath. "Say, 'Please comment. Please ask questions. Ask anything you want!'"

5. KEEP IT SIMPLE

Over and over we've heard, "Keep your slides clean." "Don't have too many handouts." "Don't overload them with stuff."

The trouble with those high-tech, super-cool presentations is that you can get bogged down in your own technology. You don't want to get so involved in all your gimmicks that, when someone raises a hand to ask a question, you find yourself thinking, "Great, now I'll never get to that really amazing slide."

6. PRACTICE, PRACTICE, PRACTICE!

The more you do it, the better you get. It's as simple as that. The key to a good presentation is being comfortable with your material—and yourself. So find ways to practice your public speaking.

Lanski suggests that sales reps look for opportunities to speak outside of work. "Join Toastmasters or the PTA. Any opportunity to talk, take it," says Lanski. "It will get easier. I promise."

PROVEN PRESENTATION TECHNIQUES AND HOW TO USE THEM

All salespeople have their own unique approaches for presenting and closing a sale. While the objectives, goals, and selling steps in the typical selling presentation are basically the same, everyone has a different style. Let your style move the sale forward.

There's a story of a shatterproof-glass salesperson who was the top producer in his company. When asked how he sold so much shatterproof glass, he responded by saying he would visit a prospect, explain the benefits of the glass, take out a square of it and, in front of the prospect, smack it with a hammer. Of course, it didn't break, and he closed a lot of sales.

The next year the salesperson once again won the top spot, but with many more sales than the year before. When asked how he did it, he said that instead of hitting the glass with the hammer, he handed the hammer over and asked the prospect to hit it. He involved the prospect, and that made all the difference.

Is there a single best presentation technique? Is it using PowerPoint? Is it engaging the prospects and getting them involved in the process? Is it your attitude and enthusiasm when you present? Or is it a combination of all of them? The following are key strategies from Kelly Rossman, president of Rossman and Martin Associates, a public relations firm in Lansing, MI, and Michele Duval, advertising account executive for the *Nashville Tennessean* newspaper.

Rossman's firm specializes in "issue management," a segment of public relations where the goal is to maximize public support or minimize public opposition to issues. She believes that the best presentation technique is not bringing in "bells, whistles, and trinkets," but basically talking to and communicating with prospects.

"We found that our ability to talk directly to prospective clients—I mean really talk to them, tell them what we think, how we view where they are, and what it is that we can bring to the table for them—ultimately wins over the majority of clients," says Rossman. "The over-reliance on trinkets, bells, whistles, and packaging eventually ends up as a disadvantage to the competing firm's reps,

> . . . the best presentation technique is not bringing in "bells, whistles and trinkets," but basically talking to and communicating with prospects.

because they don't spend a lot of time strategically thinking about the prospects' needs."

While Rossman doesn't make PowerPoint presentations or supply the customer with imprinted T-shirts, hats and coffee cups, her firm has come up with some creative ways to present itself to prospects, including handouts and audiovisual presentations.

"We often feel that we are the black-and-white TV up against the color TV," says Rossman. "One of the things we do to counter the bells and whistles is to open our presentations with a quick, in-house-produced, person-on-the-street video that basically gives the prospects the lay of the land based on what our limited research efforts show.

"For example, we did a video to pitch a hospital where we simply asked people the names of the hospitals in town," says Rossman. "It was a snapshot, and we felt it was ground zero, and that's where we were starting from."

"It did a wonderful job of setting the stage with the client and allowed us to address, 'Here's where you are, and here's what we can do to help you fix this,'" notes Rossman. "That's the only type of audiovisual thing we do at presentations."

Why not PowerPoint? Rossman feels that, in many cases, companies rely on the technology as a crutch and don't pay attention to the personal interaction.

"By the time you're at the oral presentation stage, it's almost like a dating ritual," says Rossman. "It's a matter of how we are going to work with the prospects: Do we think alike, do the groups click together, and are the personalities right? PowerPoint minimizes the personal interaction and diminishes the opportunity for eye contact and interactive discussion.

> "... it's almost like a dating ritual. It's a matter of how we are going to work with the prospects: Do we think alike, do the groups click together, and are the personalities right?"

"I know of a company that had a client literally in the palm of its hand based on a written presentation and was one of three firms brought in for an oral presentation," says Rossman. "The team went in, spent 10 minutes dinking around with their equipment, turned out the lights, and did their PowerPoint presentation. They never really talked with the client, and when they left the room, one of the clients said, 'I don't know how to put it better: They turned out the lights on us, literally and figuratively.'"

Rossman freely admits that she is PowerPoint biased and believes that presenters should be able to sell themselves, think on their feet, and articulately respond to client inquiries, concerns, and interests. She also believes that salespeople need to practice.

> "Organize your presentation and do dry runs so that you know exactly how that presentation is going to go."

"Organize your presentation and do dry runs so that you know exactly how that presentation is going to go," says Rossman. "In our firm we present to each other, because we think we are our own worst critics."

SALES MANAGER'S MEETING GUIDE

MANAGER'S MEETING GUIDE: PRESENTATIONS

Much as they might want to, sales managers can't deliver presentations for their salespeople. The best the manager can do is to prepare salespeople in a way that gives them the best opportunity for success in closing the sale. Following are a few key topics to discuss during your next sales meeting to help your team members deliver tight, composed, and effective closing presentations.

1. **KNOW THE ROOM.** Get the lay of the land in the room where you'll be presenting. Plan out where you want the decision maker to sit and how you can use the full space to your advantage. Check out the lighting and whether the air-conditioning system is loud and distracting, and make sure all the equipment you'll need is available and fully operational. If possible, rehearse your presentation here as well.

2. **KNOW YOUR INTRO.** If you're nervous, the first 90 seconds of your presentation is where it will show. For this reason you should hone your opening until it's razor sharp and then practice it until you know it cold. In a good intro you should thank all in attendance for their time, make sure everyone is ready, and then dive in with enthusiasm.

3. **KNOW YOUR MATERIALS.** Fumbling with an overhead projector or mislabeling pages in your PowerPoint presentation is not going to win you any points. Practice using all your materials until you can weave them into your presentation seamlessly.

4. **KNOW YOUR ANSWERS.** The buyer will likely have questions for you, and how well you address those questions will largely determine your success. What questions are you likely to face from this particular customer? How can you prepare your responses to answer the concerns and move the presentation forward?

5. **KNOW THE CLOSE.** Practice your phrasing ahead of time so you can close in a way comfortable for you. Conclude your presentation by asking for the order. Don't falter! Close on the sale!

Duval of the *Nashville Tennessean* believes that successful presentations are based on putting yourself in the customers' shoes, communicating exactly what you can do for them, and being a consultative salesperson. "Make sure you understand what customers want and how they want to be treated, help them understand the program you're offering, and be consultative with the relationship and their business," says Duval.

Unlike Rossman, Duval has used PowerPoint as a sales tool, depending on the prospect, and emphasizes that salespeople have to know their products inside and out and, above all, be honest, sincere, and enthusiastic.

"Some people want PowerPoint, and some people just want you to talk to them on a one-to-one level: 'Just shoot it to me straight and help me understand,'" says Duval. "If you don't have professionalism and knowledge of what you're selling, the customer will smell the fear and know that you're not for real.

"During any presentation it's imperative that you make eye contact and establish trust," adds Duval. "Honesty, in terms of what you're telling the person, is of prime importance. People don't buy from people they don't trust.

"You have to be enthusiastic about whatever it is you do, and that is apparent to your clients. If you enjoy your job, they will know. If you hate your job, you aren't going to be successful. If you're not excited about helping them, they're not going to be excited about trusting you and allowing some of their advertising budget to come to you."

Proposals

**A HANDS-ON GUIDE
FOR MANAGERS**

TRAINING GUIDE TIME REQUIRED: 55 MINUTES

THE MYSTERY OF EFFECTIVE PROPOSALS

A proposal is a sales tool, not an information packet. The purpose of a proposal is to make a persuasive case that leads to a sale. In order to write a winning proposal, the salesperson must understand how customers make decisions. With proposals, there are four stages to this decision making.

Stage One: Do I Know You? The customer looks at the cover pages of the proposals and separates them into two groups: (1) those that come from vendors with whom they're familiar and (2) those that come from vendors with whom they're unfamiliar. Proposals from unfamiliar vendors are thrown into the trash without being read.

Stage Two: Is It Compliant? The customer reads the executive summary of the surviving proposals and separates them into two groups: (1) those whose proposed solution clearly matches the criteria that the customer has set and (2) those whose proposed solution seems off base or doesn't address what the customer wants. Proposals that are noncompliant are thrown in the trash without being read in full.

Stage Three: Does It Make Sense? The customer reads the surviving proposals and separates them into two groups: (1) those whose contents provide credibility to the proposed solution and the vendor who will deliver that solution and (2) those whose contents indicate, for whatever reason, that the vendor lacks sufficient credibility and understanding to generate a viable solution. Proposals that don't make sense are thrown into the trash.

Stage Four: Does It Provide Value? Based upon preproposal positioning, the executive summary, and the contents of the proposal, the customer assesses the persuasive case that each of the few surviving vendors has built. The customer then makes a final decision based upon the customer's belief about which vendor will provide the greatest value. The vendor who did the most effective groundwork and wrote the best proposal wins the business. The almost-rans end up in the trash.

Winning proposals (and preproposal activities) leverage this decision-making process, leading the customer naturally through these four stages. There are four key steps to writing a proposal that accomplishes this.

Step One: Lay Your Groundwork

Your proposal will not be read unless, before you write and submit it, you've done marketing and sales activities that establish recognition in the mind of the decision maker. In a global sense, this is accomplished through advertising, public relations, sponsoring conferences, sending speakers to conferences, publishing newsletters, and other marketing activities. In individual sales situations, a salesperson can establish recognition through sales calls and customer meetings.

Step Two: Do Your Research

Your proposal will eventually be rejected if you fail to uncover the customer's true decision criteria and decision makers. In order to be compliant, the proposal must address the customer's real concerns, which may lie deeper than the customer's stated problems. In order to make sense, the proposal must state the solution in terms that the customer understands and accepts. In order to provide value, the proposal must address the specific value system and concerns of each set of decision makers. Engineers, for example, have a different set of value criteria from accountants, and therefore a proposal targeted at a mixed group of decision makers from both engineering and accounting will need to provide a value proposition for both disciplines.

Step Three: Write the Executive Summary

Many salespeople wrongly believe that an executive summary should be a summary of the contents of the proposal. As a result, they write the executive summary last, after all the information has been gathered into the body of the proposal. In fact, the executive summary does not summarize the proposal; it summarizes the reasons why the customer should buy from you. It is your key sales tool and should be written first, in order to set the tone and direction of the body of the proposal. As we shall see, the primary function of the body of the proposal is to create credibility for the executive summary.

In order to help the customer through the decision-making process, leading to a successful sale, the executive summary should have the following structure:

- ☑ **THE PROBLEM/NEED/GOAL.** Clarify why the customer wants to buy. The definition of the problem/need/goal is more than a paraphrase of the customer's original requirements. Instead, it should reflect the results of your research into the customer's situation.

- ☑ **THE EXPECTED OUTCOME.** Create a mental picture of the potential impact on the organization if the problem is solved, need is fulfilled, or goal is achieved. This is not a

discussion of features, but a statement of how the customer will benefit from your solution. For example, "When problem A is solved, you will have 50 percent less downtime . . ." "Achieving goal B will allow you to open your products to new markets . . ."

- ☑ **SOLUTION OVERVIEW.** Provide, for the nonspecialist, an overview of the solutions being proposed. Each element of the solution overview should tie back to the expected outcome. For example, "We are proposing 'A' because it solves the problem of . . ." "We are proposing 'B' because it provides the following value to your firm . . ."

- ☑ **THE CALL TO ACTION.** Ask for the business. This needn't be complicated and can even be something as simple as, "We're eager to work with you."

The executive summary does not contain information about your firm or attempt to create recognition. This is because if you don't already have recognition, the executive summary will not even be read. The executive summary is a customer-focused document. As a rule of thumb, the name of the customer should appear three times as frequently as the name of the vendor. Similarly, if the executive summary (or indeed the body of the proposal) contains jargon, it should be the customer's jargon, not your company's idiosyncratic jargon. You don't want the reader of the proposal to be wondering what you're talking about because you introduce unfamiliar terminology.

The executive summary should include the price only if the customer has specifically requested that the price be included in the summary. While most salespeople believe that customers are focused primarily on price, they are usually focused on value, of which price is only one element—and often not the most important. Emphasizing price in the executive summary implies that what's being sold is a replaceable commodity. By contrast, emphasizing what you can do for the customer and what's unique about your solution creates a perception of value that can raise your proposal above the rest, even if other solutions might cost less.

Step Four: Write the Body of the Proposal

The body of the proposal provides background and credibility for the claims and promises made in the executive summary. It also provides evidence that you can supply the proposed solution on time and on budget.

Every part of the proposal body should be crafted to enhance your credibility. In order to do this, the proposal must contain the right level of detail. Many proposals are chockablock with irrelevant technical details, because salespeople usually overestimate the technical expertise of the decision makers. On the other hand, many proposals miss opportunities to create additional credibility with brief answers that communicate a fact but don't add to the value proposition.

For example, suppose the customer's request for proposal (RFP) contains the question, "Do you have 24/7 support?" As a proposal writer, you have three possible responses:

A. Answer, "Yes" and move on to the next question.

B. Include pages of technical detail about the mechanics of your support infrastructure.

C. Describe how your 24/7 support is better than the competition's and will reduce the customer's overall costs.

Approach A has too little information, while approach B has too much. By contrast, approach C turns answering a simple question into an opportunity to create the perception of value that will lead to a successful sale.

Because the proposal is a product of your firm, you must make certain that it represents the quality that your firm is offering the customer. Needless to say, there can't be any glaring inconsistencies in the description of the products or services that are to be provided. But appearance can be as important as content. There should be no obvious

QUICK TIPS FOR YOUR NEXT SALES MEETING

Ten reasons why proposals get thrown out:

QUICK TIP

1. Customer doesn't know who you are.

2. Proposal doesn't follow the specified format.

3. Executive summary doesn't address customer needs.

4. Proposal is swimming in your company's jargon.

5. Boilerplate material contains another customer's name.

6. Writing is flat and technical, without passion.

7. Proposal doesn't convince customer you can deliver.

8. Proposal contains glaring grammatical errors.

9. Proposal doesn't address key decision criteria.

10. Proposal doesn't build a persuasive value proposition.

grammatical errors and an absolute minimum of typographical errors. If boilerplate (standardized material from other proposals) is included, it must be carefully customized to match the customer's own situation. Be extremely careful to edit any passages that might contain the names of other companies for which the boilerplate was used in the past. Many proposals have been thrown out simply because the proposal writer left the name of one of the customer's competitors in a paragraph lifted from an old proposal.

FREQUENTLY ASKED QUESTIONS

SALES REP'S FREQUENTLY ASKED QUESTIONS

Q: How long should the executive summary be?

A: Shorter is better. A single page should be sufficient for any proposal that's less than 50 pages, while a proposal from 50 to 75 pages long might need up to two pages. For every additional 25 pages, you should add about half a page. Needless to say, if the customer provides guidelines for the page length of the executive summary, follow them.

Q: How can I write proposals faster?

A: Write more proposals. Like anything else, proposal writing gets easier and faster when the skill is practiced regularly. Beyond this, it helps to break a proposal into parts and have different people work on each part. Make use of boilerplate, but always be certain that it's customized to match the customer. Don't waste time on elaborate graphics and fancy words. Customers are interested in content, not whether you might have a second career as a graphic designer. There is also software available to help salespeople write effective proposals. Contact the Sant Corporation for further information.

Q: Do I have to follow the customer's outline for the proposal?

A: Only if you want the business. Failure to follow a format precisely will tell customers that you can't be trusted to adhere to their specifications. However, while the presence of predetermined structure makes it more difficult to walk the customer through the decision–making process, the proposal (and especially the executive summary) must still be written in a way that fulfills its primary function as a sales tool.

TOM SANT was interviewed for this article. He is the author of *Persuasive Business Proposals* (Amacom). He is also the founder of the Sant Corporation, a provider of proposal-generation tools used by many Fortune 100 companies. A much-in-demand public speaker and consultant, Sant can be reached through the Sant Corporation, 10260 Alliance Road, Suite 210, Cincinnati, OH 45242. Telephone: 513-631-1155. Web: www.santcorp.com.

SALES MANAGER'S MEETING GUIDE

SALES
MANAGER'S
MEETING
GUIDE

Below are 10 practical steps for improving your team's ability to create effective proposals. This sales meeting should take about 55 minutes.

1. A week before the meeting, locate a customer RFP that is approximately two to three pages in length. If you do not have an RFP of this size, then create a fake RFP based upon a customer with whom you are familiar. (In either case, use a fictional name to avoid any confusion in the future.)

2. Prior to the meeting, create a brief slide presentation summarizing this article, with an emphasis on the correct structure for an executive summary. Make copies of the fake RFP.

3. Open the meeting. Explain that the team will be working on proposal writing, specifically the executive summary, which is the key to any proposal's overall effectiveness.

4. Present the overview slides. Confirm, through questioning, that the team understands the critical role that the executive summary plays in the customer's decision-making process.

5. Distribute the fake RFP. Have the team briefly review it, asking team members to keep in mind what they've just learned about proposals and executive summaries. When they've completed this process, you should be 20 minutes into the meeting.

6. Set a time limit of five minutes. Have each member of the team write a short paragraph (one to three sentences) describing, in the customer's language, what the customer wants to accomplish.

7. After five minutes, have the paragraphs handed to the front of the room. Select three paragraphs at random and read them to the entire team. Take five additional minutes to discuss with the team which paragraphs worked, based upon the intended purpose of the executive summary.

8. Repeat the same process with the expected-outcome segment of the executive summary and the proposed-solution segment of the executive summary. When you have completed this, you should be 50 minutes into the meeting.

9. Ask the team members to clear their minds and pretend that they're the customer. Based upon the conclusions that the team reached during the writing process, read aloud the best statement of need, followed by the best expected outcome, followed by the best proposed solution. Confirm with the team that these three paragraphs would help result in a proposal that could function as an effective sales document.

10. Thank the team members for their participation and close the meeting.

ADDITIONAL READING

In many cases, winning the sale comes down to the written word. In short, your written proposal can move your sale to the contract stage. But first you must be able to make all your points in a brief, convincing, written document. And, for many salespeople, that's a tall order. If you don't know how to write a proposal that gets the business, now's the time to learn.

In many ways a written proposal mimics your personal presentation. And the first rule is simple: Don't waste your time writing a proposal unless you have qualified the prospect thoroughly.

> ... the first rule is simple: Don't waste your time writing a proposal unless you have qualified the prospect thoroughly.

Some salespeople who write proposals often and know what clients are looking for have a standard format. "I target Fortune 500 companies, and most of the time they put out requests for proposals (RFPs)," says Ted Massouras, client/business manager at AT&T in Chicago, IL. "Proposal writing probably takes up about 25 percent of my time."

Before actually writing, however, do your homework. Massouras advises salespeople to make sure that a request for proposal is really a valid one—not merely an excuse to obtain useful information. "You have to make sure your customer is qualified," he says. "Sometimes customers put out an RFP just to make sure that what they have today is what they should have. You need to determine whether the RFP is just a price exercise or the customer is really interested in making a purchase. At AT&T we follow a 'bid, no bid' process."

Keep it simple, Massouras adds. Present only what the prospect is interested in and don't clutter the proposal with unneeded or unwanted services. "Capture background information on the prospect, not only in direct conversation but also by using the Net," he says. "Make sure you're on target. The applications that you present in your proposal should be exactly what the customer is looking for. Don't try to offer a laundry list of services. If your customer is interested in a virtual market, don't try to sell 800 services."

David Kaylor, director of sales for shared services at Host Pro, an Internet services provider in Bellevue, WA, also stresses prewriting research to make sure salespeople know what the customer wants and needs. "Then," he says, "use gathered information to create a customer benefit-oriented proposal. Get to know your client very well and make sure you know exactly what that client needs and wants to accomplish so you can tailor and customize your proposal. Be clear and specific. Don't try to wow them with everything your company can do, and don't include additional fluff."

"Make sure that in the very first paragraph you summarize the content and description of the proposal so the client immediately understands its nature. The first paragraph should be an appropriate, concise recap regarding the customer's needs."

Massouras believes a customer should first see an introductory letter in a proposal. He also emphasizes that proposals should look "sharp"—without grammatical or spelling mistakes. "Start out with an executive overview letter," he explains. "It should state what you are proposing, describe product services and benefits, and close with a summary. It has to be personalized to the customer and be short and sweet."

"We put a lot of emphasis on making sure everything is perfect before a proposal goes out, even if I have to ask for an extension. If proposals don't look professional and have misspelled words and grammar errors, you're sending a message to your customers that you're not willing to take the time to care about their business."

Presentation is also important. "We include graphics, charts, graphs, and even color to clarify important points and make the proposal more interesting." Massouras adds. "If it's gray and dull and just all verbiage, the prospect may just put it aside and go on to the next one."

Host Pro's Kaylor feels that customizing a proposal to the individual client is more important than embellishing it. In the Internet industry, he finds elaborate proposals are not always the way to go. Sometimes speed of delivery takes top billing. "There's a big difference in how you package a proposal to a Fortune 500 company, a midsize business, or a mom and pop customer," he points out. "For the smaller business you probably don't need to include a lot of graphs and images."

"In our industry, when it comes to format, a proposal should be noiseless, simple, and delivered fast. It's better for us to put together a short and concise proposal because most of our customers prefer to have something back to them quickly instead of waiting for a more comprehensive proposal. They're looking for the bare statistics they need to make a major technical decision within a relatively short time frame," Kaylor advises.

Sometimes the little things can make a difference. "Don't assume that everyone knows what your acronyms stand for, and use plain English," advises Massouras. "And there is no rule of thumb regarding length. The specifics of the executive overview should be short and to the point, and the details that follow should take as much space as needed to make your case."

Massouras adds, "Make sure you attach an appendix with white papers, trade magazine articles, and testimonials."

Both Massouras and Kaylor agree that your company history should appear toward the end of a proposal. "A proposal should focus on the customer's needs first. The company history and description of range of services should appear later on in the document," says Kaylor.

Here's one last point. If you're iffy on proposal writing, look for software that can crank out proposals that you only have to tailor to individual customers. After all, there's no sense in reinventing a wheel that already works.

EXPERT ADVICE

EXPERT ADVICE: WRITE YOUR WAY TO BUSINESS

"Your client may love your approach, love your products, and even love you; but in order to get the business, you need to put it in writing," says proposal writing consultant Tom Sant. "And because many companies involve multiple decision makers, your proposal has to walk the client's corridors speaking on your behalf."

Sant feels that all proposals are evaluated based on three criteria. "Initially, clients want to get the right solutions to their needs and problems," he says. "Secondly, they want to be assured that the company can do what it says it can do. Finally, they have to believe that what you're offering is a fair value and it's worth their time to work with you."

According to Sant, a competitive proposal must always offer the following four elements.

1. Statements—including the title of the proposal—showing that you clearly understand the client's needs, problems, and issues. "If you are working with a boilerplate format, where you start out telling the client how big you are, what you can do, and your company vision, you're destroying all the rapport that you built up in person," notes Sant. "You're telling the clients that you're more important than they are."

   "It's really important to make the proposal as customer specific as possible and focus on your client's business needs and objectives first. This shows that you have listened and considered their interests."

   Sant adds, "Never title your proposal 'Proposal.' If you wrote a book, you wouldn't title it 'Book.' Instead, write a title that states a benefit to the client."

2. Specific recommendations about how you can solve the client's problem. "Tell the client exactly how you're going to solve the problem, step by step, item by item," Sant advises, "and how your approach delivers the right results and contributes to the client's return on investment."

3. Information that differentiates you from other vendors and prioritizes your uniqueness or competitive advantages. "Reassure the decision makers so they know that you can do the job and not waste money or time," says Sant. "If you're doing something different, tell your customers how they benefit from it."

4. Reasons why the client should choose you over any others. "In other words, ask for the business," says Sant. "Ask for it in the cover letter, ask for it in the executive summary, and ask for it when you deliver or present the proposal. Being passive doesn't work. You have to ask."

TOM SANT is president of the Sant Corporation, specializing in communications, training, and consulting. He is the author of *Persuasive Business Proposals: Writing to Win Customers, Clients and Contracts* (AMACOM, 1992) and creator of the ProposalMaster software. For information call 1-888-448-7268 or visit www.santcorp.com.

HOW TO DECIDE IF CREATING A PROPOSAL IS WORTH YOUR TIME AND EFFORT

You've been courting this prospect for what seems like forever. He's working with someone else and says that he's satisfied. Still, he takes your calls, and you're confident that you're now the second vendor of choice. All you have to do is wait in the wings until the numero-uno vendor goofs up on an order or can't deliver what he said he could.

Then you can gleefully charge in, save the day, write a ton of business and live happily ever after.

Then one day it happens. The prospect calls you up and asks you to submit a proposal for a project and is sending you the specs. Hallelujah!

This scenario isn't limited just to a prospect that you've been working on. A request for a proposal or quote could simply appear on your desk from out of the clear blue, and you might not have a clue who the prospects are or what their needs are.

Is it for real, or are the prospects just tapping you to provide a blueprint they can use to shop around? Or are they just staying legitimate by having additional proposals submitted, even though they already know who they're going to award the project to? And what should you do?

"It's easy for a prospect to call you up and ask for a proposal, but proposals require a lot of time and effort," says Ann Baldwin, partner of Baldwin/Alverio Media Marketing in Hartford, CT. "You really have to pick and choose which ones are worth your time, which ones you have a shot at, and which ones you're going to pass on."

Baldwin, whose firm specializes in public relations, marketing, and crisis communications, believes that the major priorities are to research the prospect and understand the parameters of the request.

"That means formulating such questions as, What's the budget? What's within the budget? What does the prospect want to accomplish?" says Baldwin. "The goal is to determine what their intent is in requesting the proposal. Is it a legitimate request, or are they just looking for a blueprint to negotiate with or award to a competitor?"

Speaking of competition, Baldwin thinks it a must to establish the playing field, as in who the other players are. She doesn't think it hurts to just simply ask. "Schedule a needs-analysis meeting where you can ask your benchmark questions and make sure to find out who you're up against," says Baldwin. "Then gauge the competition, and based on the responses to your questions, make a strategic decision as to whether you actually should submit a proposal.

"If someone looks you straight in the eye and says they really want you involved in the process, then you need to be involved," says Baldwin. "It's a good indicator that they appreciate your expertise and lets you know that you have a pretty good shot at getting in on the project.

"In a lot of situations you just have to go with your gut," says Baldwin. "If it doesn't seem right, just walk away."

The bottom line is, in most cases, even if you suspect they're just asking you to get something to share with another contender, you still have to do it. It's part of the business.

When John Cheney, senior account executive for StillSecure, a provider of computer network security and infrastructure products and services, receives a request for proposal (RFP), he immediately jumps into the qualification and due-diligence mode.

"Pursuing business that is unqualified is a total waste of time," says Cheney. "Responding to an RFP requires numerous work hours and is resource intensive. Initially, I ask one of our engineers or consultants to read over the RFP to help pinpoint the direction of the prospect's vision."

Cheney then contacts the prospect and "demands" a meeting with the buying decision maker and the IT decision maker.

"The meeting is a prerequisite for me responding to the bid, because I need to determine who actually wrote the RFP," says Cheney. "In some cases, it's an internal RFP. Usually, in 9 out of 10 cases, the competition has aided in writing the RFP, and it's geared toward their product or service. Basically, it's a slam dunk for them.

"If the prospect refuses your meeting, it's most likely because a competitor wrote the RFP, and that clarifies your position in the decision-making process," says Cheney. "If they won't take the meeting, you won't meet the bid, and you're going to lose."

If the prospect does agree to a meeting, Cheney develops a set of clarifying questions used as much to gain information about the RFP as to learn about his competition and how to position himself, regardless of whether he decides to actually submit a bid or not.

"Use the questions to discover why they're leaning toward a particular vendor and provide a benchmark to move into your value-added services," says Cheney. "The meeting defines the fact that you have the expertise to provide what they need, determine hot buttons, throw a few darts, and open for business down the road.

"At the end of the meeting, you may decide that you don't want to take the time to be a second or third vendor and just walk away from submitting the

> "At the end of the meeting, you may decide that you don't want to take the time to be a second or third vendor and just walk away from submitting the proposal."

proposal," says Cheney. "Still, you've established the fact that there may be components of the proposal that you can do better than anyone else."

In many instances, Cheney will write a proposal even though he recognizes that the competition may have had a hand in writing the RFP or the prospect is looking to "farm it out." But the saving grace is that by being part of the proposal process, he positions his company to capture business it may not have had a shot at.

"In one instance, we had a meeting, walked away from a bid, and about three months later, received an RFP for managed services, submitted a postaward bid, and got the business," says Cheney. "The company that won the proposal got the product in, but couldn't manage it . . . and they thought of us."

EXPERT ADVICE: HOW TO EVALUATE THE RFP

EXPERT
ADVICE

The very first step a salesperson needs to take is to validate the authenticity of a request for a proposal or a bid, says Tim Breithaupt, author of *Ten Steps to Sales Success* (AMACOM, 2004) and president of Spectrum Training Solutions Inc.

"Ask yourself if it's a legitimate request or if the customer is just pursuing a price-shopping exercise or if they want you to do all the work just to hand it off to someone else," says Breithaupt. "It's a tough call, and before you can make a decision, you need to do due diligence."

That due diligence includes finding out more about the prospects. Have they ever done any business with your company? How long have they been with their current vendor? How often do they change vendors? Have they requested proposals from you before? If it's a customer you've been working with, you should already know most of this.

"If you find out that they've been doing business with the same vendor for 15 years, it lets you know that it might be tough to win them over just by filling out a quote," says Breithaupt.

Once you've done your homework, the next step is to request a meeting to evaluate the prospect's needs and expectations regarding the proposal. If you're granted a meeting, it's a good sign that the prospect is serious. But if you can't get a meeting, it's a red flag.

"If you're not granted an audience to discuss a tender, determine prospect needs, and present your service, that means there is no actual value mesh," says Breithaupt. "Then, just return it."

According to Breithaupt, while scheduling a meeting is critical, another signal about the validity of a request for a proposal is whom you meet with.

"You need to find out who's who in the zoo," says Breithaupt. "You want to meet with the decision maker, 'the bag of money,' or at least an ally," says Breithaupt. "But we often get stuck talking to 'the bag of wind,' and that's not a good sign."

If you are granted an interview with "the bag of money," there are three questions that absolutely need to be asked to clarify a proposal or bid, and they all revolve around money.

1. What if we're a little bit higher . . . would we still get your business?

2. Do we have to be the same price to get your business?

3. Do we have to offer a lower price to get your business?

"If you ask these questions straight off, it reveals the mind-set of the 'bag of money,' demonstrates how serious that person is, and gives you an opportunity to present value-added solutions."

Creating proposals and completing quotes take time, and salespeople need to balance out the time involved with the return on time investment and potential benefit, especially if they have a suspicion that they're just being used.

"It really is a tough call and has a lot to do with, after due diligence, how much integrity the salesperson thinks the customer has and what the potential is," says Breithaupt. "If the return doesn't equal the time and effort invested and the salesperson feels it's not for real, don't do it.

"Salespeople have only 1,760 selling hours available a year, and they need to be doing major things during major time," says Breithaupt. "If you're doing a proposal or quote during your valuable selling hours, you'd better be sure it's validated and is a legitimate request."

For more information, visit www.spectrain.com.

Consultative Selling

 **A HANDS-ON GUIDE FOR MANAGERS**

TRAINING GUIDE TIME REQUIRED: 55 MINUTES

CONSULTATIVE SELLING STRATEGIES

The basic concept of consultative selling is to view the selling process as helping a customer to solve a problem or achieve a goal through the use of the seller's offering. However, while most salespeople are familiar with the concept, they have no idea how to go about implementing it. This is because most salespeople have been trained to believe that the best way to sell a product is to educate the user on the product.

Such product-oriented selling is inefficient and ineffective. It inevitably leads salespeople to swamp customers with exhaustive menus of product features and detailed product demonstrations that have little or nothing to do with the problems and goals of the customer's organization. This alienates customers, especially managers and executives who have little interest in technical details.

As a result, salespeople trained in product-oriented selling often take the path of least resistance and focus their sales efforts on low-level technical employees who are willing to discuss products at the feature/function level. However, technical employees are usually not the final decision makers, which means (at worst) that the salesperson is wasting time or (at best) that the salesperson will be unprepared to describe the benefits of the product to the actual decision makers, even if the salesperson eventually obtains access to them.

Product-oriented selling can easily lapse into product evangelism, with the salesperson attempting to convince the customer of the superiority of the salesperson's product. This is ineffective. Pushing a product too hard drives a customer to raise an objection, because that's the only way the customer can reclaim the conversation. The basic error is spending too much time talking about the product and not enough time listening to the customer.

Unfortunately, many companies encourage product-oriented selling by providing internal sales training that's focused on product features. Ironically, product training is generally the responsibility of product managers who are familiar with the product but who have never had an actual conversation with a customer. Sales managers and sales teams must therefore take responsibility for translating product features into customer usage, so customers can understand the benefits of using the seller's product offering and the salespeople can act as consultants rather than just as ineffective product pushers.

There are three steps to accomplishing this.

Step 1: Rethink the Sales Process

Moving beyond product-oriented selling and into consultative selling requires a change in your attitudes and beliefs about sales. There are four aspects to that change.

1. You must change what you're selling from a noun into a verb. Products are always nouns and solutions are always verbs. This is a subtle but powerful distinction that's best illustrated by example. If you are a salesperson who works for a firm that makes industrial glue and you think that your job is to sell "glue" (a noun), you will tend to talk to the customer about product features, such as bonding ability, pressure requirements, adhesion characteristics, and so forth. By contrast, if you think your job is to sell "gluing" (a verb), you will want to discover your customer's gluing needs and then show how your glue will fulfill those needs.

2. You must begin thinking about selling as a process of helping the customer, rather than a process of making a sale. Unfortunately, most salespeople habitually think about selling in terms of convincing, persuading, and overcoming—activities that assume the salesperson is in contention with the customer. Instead, you should redefine selling as the process of helping customers visualize how (if they had your product) they could solve their problems and achieve their goals.

3. You must consider a sales call successful when you disqualify a prospect because the buyer does not actually need your product. Most salespeople get so caught up in quotas that they try to foist unwanted products on customers, who naturally resent such behavior. Rather than adopting a dogged determination to make a sale, you should make it clear to customers that you're willing to leave if your product can't actually help them.

4. You must learn to communicate with customers primarily through questions rather than through statements. Don't confuse telling with selling. Rather than talking to customers about the product, you must use questions to lead them to the natural conclusion that they need your product because it will help them solve a problem or achieve a goal. Most people would rather buy than be sold. The best way to

move a prospect toward becoming a customer is to ask intelligent questions that the prospect is capable of answering.

Step 2: Create Sales Prompters

The questions you ask customers must be planned out ahead of the sales call. The best way to do this is to create a series of "sales prompters," which are lists of relevant questions prepared especially for each type of decision maker within the customer organization. Each sales prompter has two types of questions:

1. **DIAGNOSTIC QUESTIONS.** These help customers articulate needs and goals by identifying potential problems and potential opportunities that are biased to the seller's capabilities.

2. **USAGE SCENARIO QUESTIONS.** These help customers visualize how their problems can be solved and their goals achieved through the use of your product.

The salesperson asks the diagnostic questions first and then, based upon the responses, asks the appropriate usage scenario questions. For example, a salesperson selling an inventory control system to a manufacturing firm might use the following diagnostic questions:

1. How often are products late because component parts aren't in the supply chain?

2. How do you deal with customers whose products aren't shipped on time?

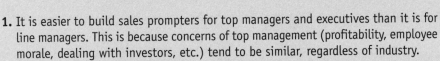

QUICK TIPS FOR YOUR NEXT TRAINING SESSION

QUICK TIP

1. It is easier to build sales prompters for top managers and executives than it is for line managers. This is because concerns of top management (profitability, employee morale, dealing with investors, etc.) tend to be similar, regardless of industry.

2. When you're playing the role of the customer during the initial sales presentation, avoid being combative or belligerent, even if your customers sometimes act that way. The focus needs to be on why the product-oriented selling process fails and why consultative selling is more effective.

3. Building effective sales prompters is a time-consuming process, but well worth the effort. You may want to hire experts to help you identify questioning sequences that would be most likely to reveal problems and opportunities and be best able to help customers visualize solutions.

FREQUENTLY ASKED QUESTIONS

SALES REPS' FREQUENTLY ASKED QUESTIONS

Q: What do I do when a prospect identifies an unexpected need?

A: First ask, "What are you hoping to accomplish?" in order to determine whether the apparently unfamiliar need is actually a familiar need in disguise. If it is, then move to the appropriate usage scenario questions. If not, then say, "I'm not sure I can help you with that. We're really good at [whatever your firm is good at]. I'll go back to my office and ask."

Q: What do I do when my diagnostic questions don't identify a need?

A: Thank the customer for his or her time and end the meeting. A big part of consultative selling is being able to walk away from situations where your products or services won't help the customer.

Q: How can I keep the questioning process from sounding rote?

A: Memorize the questions and use them verbatim during practice sessions. Then, when you meet with a prospect, rephrase the questions in your own words as part of a conversation with the prospect.

Q: Can I be a consultative salesperson to an executive, even though I'm just a novice salesperson?

A: Probably not. Consultative selling is possible only when the seller can add substantial value to the conversation. Consultative selling is not possible without a deep understanding of the buyer's environment or how he or she would use the product to achieve a goal or solve a problem. Under these circumstances, the only way to become a consultative seller would be to study the customer's industry until you can add substantial value to the discussion.

3. Have you ever lost orders, or even customers, because products weren't shipped on time?

Assuming the first set of questions exposed a customer need, the salesperson moves to a related set of usage scenario questions, such as:

1. Would it have a positive financial impact on your company if there were one-tenth as many inventory failures as you currently experience?

2. When you have a delay in shipments, would it be useful to be able to automatically inform all your customers that their shipment will be late?

3. When dates for delivery of components slip, would it be helpful for the system to identify all orders that will be affected, so you can proactively notify customers and minimize the impact to your business?

Sales prompters must be customized to fit the requirements of each decision maker inside the organization. Fortunately, in every sales situation there is generally a predictable list of key decision makers, so sales prompters, once created, are often reusable. For example, the sale of a CRM system to a large corporation might involve sales presentations to the CFO, the VP of sales, the VP of marketing, and the CIO. Because each decision maker has a different set of concerns, each person must be approached with a different set of questions. In this case, the salesperson would ask the CFO about cost savings, ask the sales VP about the importance of increasing sales revenue, ask the marketing VP about ad campaigns, and ask the CIO about system compatibility.

Step 3: Use the Product as Proof of the Solution

In product-oriented selling, the salesperson uses the product to educate and generate customer interest, often through use of a demonstration. However, because the salesperson is unaware of customer needs and goals in the early stages of the sale, its likely that the demonstration will not be effective, especially if the salesperson runs through a plethora of the features, hoping to strike a chord with the customer. This technique is known as "spray and pray" or, worse, "death by demo."

In consultative selling, the salesperson uses the product to demonstrate the proposed solution that emerged from asking the usage scenario questions. For example, a salesperson for a company that makes inventory control systems might say, "You told me that, if at the end of each month you could view a report of inventory sorted by date of last use, then you could reduce overall costs. Now let me show you how easy it is to get that report."

QUICK TIP

QUICK TIPS FOR YOUR NEXT SALES MEETING

Have your sales team assess its ability to do consultative selling by asking the following questions:

1. If you were in your prospect's shoes, knowing what you know about our product, what kind of help would you want to receive from a consultative salesperson from our firm?

2. What are three ways that our offerings can actually help customers solve problems or achieve goals?

3. Under what conditions would customers be unable to do without our offerings? What would be the best way to get them to visualize and understand that they have that need?

4. What are some problems that we should walk away from because we don't have a strong solution for them?

MICHAEL BOSWORTH AND JOHN HOLLAND were interviewed for this article. They are the cofounders of CustomerCentric Systems and the coauthors of *CustomerCentric Selling* (McGraw-Hill). Bosworth has been a lecturer at the Stanford Graduate School of Business, and Holland has 20 years' experience in sales and sales management for technology companies. Their customers include Rockwell, Hewlett-Packard, and Microsoft. CustomerCentric Systems is located at 2055 Seaside Ave., Del Mar, CA 92014. Telephone: 858/350-5570. Web: www.customercentricsystems.com.

SALES MANAGER'S MEETING GUIDE

SALES
MANAGER'S
MEETING
GUIDE

Below are 12 practical steps to help your team begin selling in a more consultative manner. This sales meeting should take about 55 minutes.

1. Before the meeting, create a sales prompter intended for a key player at one of your firm's target customers. Be sure to include diagnostic questions and usage scenario questions.

2. When you begin the meeting, make certain that your sales team members know that you consider this training to be important and you'd like them to participate enthusiastically.

3. Ask for a volunteer from the team. Tell the volunteer that he or she will be making a sales call on you, while you will be role-playing the customer for whom you made a sales prompter.

4. After the preliminaries (introduction, some rapport building, etc.), ask, "So, how does your product work?" This will probably result in a product description or a list of features and functions. While the presenter talks, keep track of how many times he or she asks questions.

5. Let the presentation continue for a while, then end the role-playing, thank the volunteer, and explain basic concepts of consultative selling and the importance of asking questions, based upon this training module.

6. Ask for another volunteer. Tell the volunteer that he or she will now be the customer while you will be the salesperson.

7. After the preliminaries, begin asking the diagnostic questions. Let the "customer" do the majority of the talking. (This may require some prompting on your part.)

8. If your diagnostic questions reveal a need for your product, jump to step 10.

9. If your diagnostic questions do not reveal a need for your product, thank the customer for his or her time, and end the sales call. Point out to your sales team that this was a "win" even though you didn't make a sale, because you are acting as a consultant rather than a product pusher. Then go back to step 6 and begin again.

10. Move to your usage scenario questions, helping the "customer" to visualize how your product would help with the problems or opportunities revealed in step 7.

11. Use the product (or a description of the product) as a proof point that the solution that you've proposed will actually work.

12. Obtain specific commitments from the sales team to draft sales prompters for the different types of decision makers inside your customer's organization.

At your next meeting, review the prompters as a group and then break into groups to practice consultative selling. Continue to monitor and track progress, reporting to your team any successes that team members have achieved using this sales method.

ADDITIONAL READING

When customers view your product as a commodity, price becomes the major factor in their purchasing decision. When that happens, your company faces reduced margins, and your sales commissions may suffer. No matter how you look at it, that's not a good scenario.

To differentiate your product from other, off-the-shelf solutions, you might have to change the way you sell by trying a consultative approach.

There are two basic underpinnings of consultative selling. First, you want to maintain your price and profit margin. Second, to accomplish this, you must demonstrate how your product or service can result in higher profits for your customers.

Lisa Ciampi, account executive for Design Display Inc. in Birmingham, AL, feels consultative selling is all about being a marketing adviser and problem solver. "To me, consultative selling is an attitude or mind-set toward the whole selling process," she says. "It's understanding the products you sell, your competition and the market, and making recommendations that are in the client's best interest, not necessarily in your own."

"You have to become almost 'all knowing' in the industry and have an answer for everything your customers are trying to do. I want my customers to feel that if they have a problem or need an answer, they can just call me up."

Ciampi points out that the consultative selling process necessitates getting deeply involved in all areas of the customers' business—marketing, competition, and company objectives. She also advises salespeople to remember that although customers may think they know what they want, it may not be what they need. It's up to salespeople to recommend something that's in their customers' best interest.

"From our end, we want to become totally involved in the overall marketing process and understand what their goals are and even who their competition is," explains Ciampi. "That allows us to better design a total exhibitor package."

"Asking questions is key. Our goal is to incorporate and reinforce the points customers make in their printed material in the display, and keep everything constant, especially from a graphic perspective."

"Sometimes customers come to us thinking that they know what they want, and it's important for us to offer options that make more sense for them. For example, they may think they want a brushed aluminum laminate, and we point out that, over time, that material will scratch considerably. If they're going to do a lot of exhibiting, we'll recommend something that won't need to be replaced as often, which boils down to a cost savings."

Just selling an exhibit isn't enough. "You have to show customers direct benefits of using your product or service," says Ciampi. "In our case, an exhibit may bring customers

EXPERT ADVICE: THREE STRATEGIES TO HELP CREATE VALUE

Consultative salespeople are not vendors out to sell a product. They must become consultants focused on helping their clients' businesses grow, says Mack Hanan, international business consultant and author of *Consultative Selling: The Formula for High Margin Sales at High Levels* (AMACOM, 1999).

According to Hanan, consultative selling has three strategies. First, position salespeople as value adders in dollar terms. In other words, have them sell profits rather than products and services. Second, train them how to present profit improvement proposals that quantify dollars. Third, make salespeople problem solvers, comanaging with their customers as partners.

"Consultative selling is true customer-driven sales strategy, instead of a product-driven process," says Hanan.

To base a price, Hanan suggests looking at comparative performance—the features and benefits of a product. "If your product is a commodity, prices will be low because of equalization by competition," he says. Also, look at the value created in a customer's business by using your product. "When you create that value, you cease being a commodity."

So, how does a salesperson establish value? "Salespeople need to be trained in their customers' businesses," Hanan explains. "They need to understand where the key areas and the cost centers are. Value comes not from the product, but from the ability to apply it to your customers' businesses so that costs are reduced or revenues are increased. Either way, profits are improved."

MACK HANAN is an international consultant on accelerated business growth and inventor of the Profit Improvement Proposal.

100 more leads than a booth that wasn't fully thought through. Or, our booth may have fewer connectors, which reduces set-up time and labor costs." That's a direct saving.

"In consultative selling, you have to care about your client, add value, and not worry so much about the numbers," Ciampi sums up.

"A consultative salesperson really has to understand the customer's business and what motivates the customer. That means asking the proper questions to discover the hot buttons and niches," says Allen Carmack, regional sales manager with RPS in Memphis, TN. "In our business we believe that people really don't want to be sold—they want us to lead them to the best possible buying decision."

SKILL SET

1. **BE A VALUE ADDER.** Sell customers profits rather than goods and services.

2. **FOLLOW-UP.** Contact current customers and find out where the products you sold them went, learn how they're being used, and quantify the results in dollars.

3. **BECOME A MARKETING CONSULTANT.** Learn from prospects exactly what they want to accomplish and then tailor a program that reduces costs or increases revenues—without lowering your price.

4. **BE A PROBLEM SOLVER.** Actively comanage your program's application with customers, to achieve the desired results. They make higher profits, and you take the credit.

5. **LOOK LONG TERM.** Forge a lasting relationship by providing consistent, solid support and continuously reinforcing the buying decision.

"It's very important for our salespeople to sell to as many different levels within an organization as they can, from the president down to the hourly worker on the back dock. We want understanding at all levels, from customer service to the accounting department, so we can design a program that has benefit for everybody."

"Consultative selling means finding ways to directly reduce customer costs or increase revenues," Carmack points out. "We always look to find ways to drive costs out of our customer's system without lowering our price," he says. "For example, suppose there is a company that ships to Canada. Instead of shipping individual packages, they might reduce costs by having us move them across the border in one drop ship. Or we might be able to cut their receivables cycle by getting their inventory delivered a day quicker."

Carmack adds, "It's turning features into benefits. You might have a lot of nice features, but if they're not benefits, they have no value to the customer. We constantly emphasize our goal is to create partnerships. We want our customers to think about changes they can make to their warehouse operations or other areas and how these changes affect how we do business together. It's important that we position ourselves deep in the process."

"If we can provide a two-hour-later pickup that allows a company to move more merchandise more efficiently, we take credit for that because the value we're providing directly equates to greater savings. We've now established a profitable relationship and, in essence, become a part of their company."

Carmack believes it is important to consider the sale as just beginning once a company signs on the dotted line. "We're not a sell-and-run company, and, in our opinion, the sale really just starts when we get our commitment from the customer," he explains. "We just don't sell and then never see the customer again. We put great emphasis on support after the sale."

"People want to do business with people they like. It gets down to building a relationship and providing a service that positively affects their bottom line. If you bring customers value, they're going to keep doing business with you."

ADDITIONAL READING

Consultative salespeople (CSs) do more than simply seek the exchange of money for services or products. They create an integrated relationship between the supplier and the purchasing company. They create a relationship, an information transfer, a support for client goals, and enthusiasm for their success. The CS realizes the need to look beyond one sale.

While the principles of consultative selling apply in every type of sale, they are particularly effective in business services and finance and with highly technical products—all areas in which the customer needs the salesperson to provide expertise as well as a product.

Mike Hill, business development director with PricewaterhouseCoopers based in Dallas, TX, says, "We need to get away from a selling mentality and let the customers tell us their needs. Consultative selling requires the mind-set of helping clients to solve problems, not a focus on purchasing." Hill directs a team approach to CS. In the process of selling analytical business services, he views the first meeting not as a sales call, but as a first analysis of the clients' business needs.

"Our view is that we are building a relationship, based on trust in our expertise, that can help them solve problems," Hill says. "We have a vast number of experts in our company. They talk to our clients. We do a lot of research on the prospects, on issues important to them, and on their competitors. When we make a call to a prospect, we have to be experienced and knowledgeable."

"As a sales manager my work is to get my staff to ask questions and gather information to begin the relationship process." Hill notes that a CS needs a different sort of goal setting from traditional sales. "We have revenue goals rather than sales goals. The key is a mind-set that is oriented to putting the client first. We put a good quality product in front of the clients within the time frame they specify. We talk about our approach and sometimes don't even need to ask for the business. The client often asks us."

Jack Napton, sales consultant with Scientific Visions Systems, a medical video equipment sales company in Carlsbad, CA, is often a part of a team effort meeting with the client. "We bring our technical person with us," Napton says. "Actually, I am often the support person to a sales staff for a machine where our product will be added to provide visuals. We are also selling advice on the video portion of a CT scanner or ultrasound device."

"I am called in, and the client often does not even realize that I am with another company. It doesn't matter. I study their needs and determine how that integrates with the overall product being sold—how our piece of equipment fits into the puzzle to make it all go well. This requires listening. We can't afford to have any preconceived notions. Research is very important. To make the seamless connection, I have to know and understand the end-user's requirements well. I have to know my product inside out and be able to provide solutions to the client's problem. If I don't provide a solution, the sale is dead," says Napton.

"You don't sell blue sky and promises—just what can really work. I must act in a consultative way both toward the end user and toward the sales staff of the primary medical machine, for example, the CT scanner."

In a sale where technical expertise or complex product meshing carries most of the weight, the salesperson must be willing to let his or her own personality take a backseat to the importance of the sale. Cooperation between client and sales staff to find the right solution to the client's problems is a hallmark of the consultative sales approach.

THE ESSENCE OF CONSULTATIVE SELLING

EXPERT ADVICE

Jeffrey Gitomer has been writing about selling skills since 1992. Contrasting traditional selling and the CS approach, Gitomer says both types of salespeople make calls, but their attitude, approach, and commitment differ. The CS is willing to forgo short-term gains to achieve greater long-term benefit. A CS builds relationships on a foundation of trust, credibility, respect, and performance.

"To be a consultant rather than a salesperson, you have to be resourceful, a value provider, and a friend to clients. If you're not, clients will shop for price or, these days, just go to the Internet," says Gitomer.

"Consultative selling is not a system—all systems are manipulative. You have to be real—put the costumers' interests first," he notes. "In most sales you are trying to convince the clients that they need your product. The consultative approach builds trust in your expertise so that customers know they need you and are willing to pay for your expertise."

According to Gitomer, salespeople need to raise their level of selling skills to a point where the prospect wants to learn more. How do you know if you have achieved that new level of skill? One measure is returned calls. Clients return the calls of those they like and trust. Another measure is referrals. People refer salespeople they trust.

"Selling is a committed process. Unless you are willing to commit to excellence, consultation is never going to occur," advises Gitomer.

He notes that customers are always more interested in achieving their objectives than yours. A CS works hard helping customers succeed—not just helping customers purchase. The CS combines great ideas to help the customer's business grow with a solid understanding of what it takes to earn the order.

These are the five components of Consultative Selling:

1. Find and understand the customers' needs.

2. Partner with the customers.

3. Show customers how they can achieve their objectives with your product.

4. Believe that your business, product, and service are the best.

5. Believe in yourself. A positive attitude makes it all work.

Gitomer adds, "Consultants believe that the knowledge they offer is valid and valuable. Salespeople are trying to earn a commission. It's all a matter of focus and vision. The consultative salesperson thinks past the sale to the relationship. Belief in yourself is part of that process, and it has to be real—you can't fake it."

Objections

A HANDS-ON GUIDE FOR MANAGERS

TRAINING GUIDE TIME REQUIRED: 60 MINUTES

HOW TO HANDLE OBJECTIONS

Most salespeople hate objections. They think an objection means that they might not make the sale. That's exactly wrong: until you hear an objection, you're not even close to making a sale. When a customer hears a little voice saying, "I want it," the next normal emotional response is to come up with an objection. That's when your job as a salesperson really starts.

Until you hear an objection, you're strictly a visitor and an information giver. Customers who don't come up with objections either aren't qualified to make a decision or don't have the money or credit to make a purchase. If customers don't challenge you in one way or another, or fight the purchase with at least one objection, then they aren't serious about buying. So, if you hear an objection, get excited! You now have a chance to make the sale.

Step 1: Shelve the Objection Until After the Presentation

When you hear the first three words of an objection during a presentation, the natural tendency is to jump in and attempt to handle the objection. Chances are that you'll end up answering the wrong objection and, worse, give the customer a brand-new objection to worry about. Instead, when the customer comes up with objections during your presentation, don't interrupt; listen to the objection, acknowledge it, but then shelve it until the end of the presentation.

Salesperson: . . . and here's the second benefit . . .

Customer (interrupting): This is going to really cost me, right?

Salesperson (acknowledging the objection): Are you worried about the cost?

Customer: Yes.

Salesperson: I can understand that. I'll get to the price in a minute, and I think you'll be pleasantly surprised, especially since our product has this second benefit . . .

Shelving the objection is important, because if you attempt to answer the objection immediately, the customer will continue to focus on the objection. As you continue with the presentation, you can craft your words to emphasize the benefits that will provide the future ammunition you'll need to overcome the objection. Shelving the objection has another side effect. By the time you're done with the presentation, the customer may no longer consider the objection valid or, even better, may even have forgotten all about it.

Step 2: Feed the Objection Back to the Customer

Objections aren't real unless the customer brings them up more than once. If an objection reappears at the end of the presentation, then you know that it's something you need to handle. When this happens, hear the customer out and make sure the customer knows that you understand the objection. Then ask for more information or a clarification of the objection. This request encourages the customer to provide you with valuable information that you'll need in order to answer the objection. For example:

Customer: That copier is too expensive.

Salesperson: Yes, things today are expensive. How much were you looking to spend?

Customer: We've been paying around $500 for our copiers.

Salesperson: Are you looking for something that's of equal or higher quality than what you currently have?

Customer: Well, probably something better than what we have. We have to produce some brochures this year.

Salesperson: I have several copiers that might be appropriate for brochures.

Step 3: Pinpoint the Real Objection

Almost every time a customer says no (regardless of how that "no" is expressed), the customer is actually surfacing an objection, which you as the salesperson can overcome. However, an objection can bring the sales process to a screeching halt when it turns out that the customer either has no money to make the purchase or can't get the credit to obtain the money for the purpose. These are the only two solid objections, and it's up to you as the salesperson to find out through questioning whether the transaction opportunity is dead on arrival. If not, then it's your job to handle the objection and to make the sale.

SALES REPS' FREQUENTLY ASKED QUESTIONS

Q: How do I handle "I can get it cheaper elsewhere"?

A: "In today's world we can almost always get something cheaper. I've found that when smart people invest their money, they look for three things: the finest quality, the best service, and the lowest price. However, I've also noticed that no company can consistently offer all three. Which two of the three—the finest quality, the best service, and the lowest price—do you think will be most important for your long-term enjoyment of this product?"

Q: How do I handle, "I have a friend in the business"?

A: "That's great. You know, there's an old saying—I don't know how true it is—that sometimes friendship and business don't mix. If you bought from a friend, you might not say anything if you weren't happy with the purchase, but with me, you can just get on my case until you get what you want."

Q: How do I handle, "I did business with people from your company in the past and they were unprofessional"?

A: "I can really appreciate that. I really hate it when that kind of thing happens to me. Suppose the shoe were on the other foot and it was your company that had acted unprofessionally. You'd probably fire the person responsible. That's probably what we had to do, and now it's my job to make certain that you're treated right."

FREQUENTLY ASKED QUESTIONS

Many objections are initially vague, often varieties of "I want to think it over." The average salesperson, when confronted with such a remark, hands over a business card and then never hears back from the customer. As a professional, you must delve into the customer's thinking to discover the real objection, so that you can come up with an appropriate response. For example:

Customer: I want to think it over.

Salesperson: That's fine . . . obviously you wouldn't take the time to do that if you weren't serious, right?

Customer: I guess not.

Salesperson: Just to clarify my thinking, what is it that you need to think about? Is it the quality of service?

Customer: Not really.

Salesperson: Tell me, could it be the money?

Customer: Yes.

Step 4: Question the Importance of the Objection

Most objections can be overcome by comparing them to the benefits that you describe during your presentation.

Customer: The taxes are too high on that house.

Salesperson: Yes, the taxes are a little higher than the surrounding neighborhoods, and that is probably why the public schools are so much better. Which is of greater concern to you, the taxes or the quality of education your children will receive?

But be careful that you don't tread on any toes or make the customers look foolish.

Customer: I heard this isn't a good area for property appreciation.

Salesperson: Whoever told you that doesn't know much about real estate.

Customer: My father told me that.

Ouch. Here's a better approach to this situation:

Customer: I heard this is not a good area for property appreciation.

Salesperson: We can check the appreciation rates when we get back to my office. Would that be critical to your decision about making a purchase in this area?

> **Reminder: Customers who don't come up with objections either aren't qualified to make a decision or don't have the money or credit to make a purchase.**

You can often reduce the importance of objections by changing the metrics by which the customer is measuring them and then comparing the objection to something trivial. While this technique involves some quick math, it's generally worth the extra effort.

Customer: That car is $5,000 more than I want to pay.

Salesperson: I can appreciate that. You know, $5,000 comes down to about $2.50 a day for the length of time you will have it. What might you be able to change in your daily life to be able to afford to invest an extra $2.50 a day for this vehicle, which you really seem to want?

Step 5: Confirm That You've Answered the Objection and Then Change Gears

After you've answered an objection, be sure to get the customer to agree that you've answered it. This prevents the objection from resurfacing later, because people feel inconsistent and foolish if they bring up issues that they've already agreed are no longer important.

Customer: We don't have the money in this year's budget.

Salesperson: That's OK. We can finance the investment so part of it falls into next year's budget. Does that work for you?

Customer: I guess so.

Salesperson: So that settles that, doesn't it?

Customer: Right.

Once you've gotten the customer to agree, change the subject by asking a question on an unrelated matter. (A good choice might be the benefits of the product or service that you're selling.) Here's an example:

Salesperson: . . . so that's taken care of, right?

Customer: Right.

Salesperson: Great! By the way, did you notice that our reference accounts include some of the largest companies in the world . . .

TOM HOPKINS was interviewed for this article. He is the author of 12 books on sales training, including *How to Master the Art of Selling*, which has sold more than 1.6 million copies. Since 1976, Hopkins has presonally trained more than 3 million students on five continents, including sales presonnel from ADT Security, 24 Hour Fitness, and Card Services International. His company, Tom Hopkins International, is located at 7531 E. Second St., Scottsdale, AZ 85251. Telephone: 480-949-0786. To find out when Tom Hopkins will be delivering training workshops in your area, go to www.tomhopkins.com/seminar_schedule.asp.

SALES MANAGER'S MEETING GUIDE

SALES MANAGER'S MEETING GUIDE

Below are 12 practical steps that can help you and your team create more effective responses to the most common and difficult customer objections.

1. Three days prior to the meeting, send out a message to all participants asking them to write down the five most frequently heard and most difficult customer objections. Tell your salespeople that your objective is to brainstorm better and more effective ways of responding to customer objections. This task should take no more than 10 minutes to complete.

2. The night before the meeting, set up your conference room so that you have a flip chart in the front of the room and a chalkboard or a whiteboard. Divide your writing space with one vertical line. Write customer objections on the top left and best responses on the top right.

3. Get a set of 3 × 5 cards. Write six common customer objections on each card, such as, "Your price is too high," or, "I have to think this over," or, "I have to speak to my boss about this." Have one card ready for every three salespeople in your group. You will use these cards for the role-playing session during the meeting.

4. Open the meeting by explaining the rules. The first objective is to explore better strategies for handling customer objections. The second is to help your team increase its skills and comfort levels with handling customer objections. Don't let the meeting slip into a griping session.

5. Ask one salesperson at a time to share a customer objection with you. After you hear each objection, thank the salesperson for contributing and write the objection word for word on the flip chart or whiteboard. Pause after you've collected five objections.

6. Tell your salespeople, "These are all very valid objections. Let's ask ourselves, are those the real objections? Or could there be other reasons hiding behind these objections?" Invariably, your salespeople will agree that further probing questions are needed to pinpoint the real objection.

7. Ask your salespeople to think of questions to ask to pinpoint the real objection. Write down the best answers. Reinforce the lesson that it is not a good idea to respond to any objection unless we've followed up with questions and isolated the real reason for resisting the purchase.

8. Ask your group about the emotional challenges involved in responding to customer objections. Explore two major subject areas: the customer's emotional turmoil and the salesperson's corresponding apprehension. Then ask your group for effective ways to defuse the emotionally charged atmosphere. Agree that the best way to reduce the tension is to accept and acknowledge the customer's feelings with such "empathy statements" as, "I'd like to thank you for sharing this with me," "I understand how you feel," or, "This must be a difficult decision for you." Underline the customer's need for reassurance.

9. Ask the group to share the next set of five objections and brainstorm effective responses for each objection.

10. Conduct a brief role-play. Divide your salespeople into groups of three, each group member assuming the role of a buyer, a salesperson, or an observer. The salesperson should make a two-minute presentation to the buyer. The buyer listens and voices one or two objections during the presentation. The observer takes notes and discusses afterward what was done well and explains why. Next, go over what could be improved and how. Ask the players to switch roles. The person who plays the first buyer selects two objections for the role-play from your 3 × 5 card with your six customer objections. After the first role-play is completed, the card should be handed to the next buyer, who will in turn select two different objections.

11. Conduct a quick debriefing session. Ask each group to report new ideas for handling objections. Write them down and thank each salesperson for contributing.

12. Conclude the meeting by asking for feedback. Solicit ideas for your next meeting and end with your promise to e-mail each participant a summary of the objections discussed and the best responses to each.

In his 25 years of superstar real estate sales, Floyd Wickman developed a system to counter any price objection in every selling situation. Sales consultant Wickman shares five steps for countering price objections.

However, before you can implement his five-step plan, you must learn Wickman's three sales fundamentals for every call you make:

1. **BE THE FIRST PERSON SOLD ON THE PRODUCT.** If you do not approach a customer confident of the value of your product, your insincerity will show, and the prospect will never believe that your product is worth the price.

2. **NEVER DISCUSS PRICE UNTIL THE CUSTOMER IS SOLD ON THE PRODUCT OR SERVICE.** Many salespeople are too quick to broach the price issue. Understand that buyers are motivated more by the heart than the wallet. If price were the most important factor, everybody would be driving a Yugo. When you open your discussion with price, it becomes the central concern. The real issue should be whether you and your product are right for that customer.

3. **ANTICIPATE THE CUSTOMERS' CONCERNS.** If you do your homework in preparation for selling your product or service, you will be better able to counter any objections customers may have to your price. As we shall see, letters of testimony from previous buyers, a list of your product's ingredients, and simple charts comparing your product with the competition's can be extremely handy in closing the sale.

FIVE STEPS TO COUNTER PRICE OBJECTIONS

When price is the only barrier keeping you from closing the sale, Wickman suggests that you use this simple, five-step response to counter any price objection. In order, the steps are: Cushion it; Question it; Isolate it; Handle it; and Close it.

For example, you have explained to customers the quality and value of your product, and they agree that it serves their needs, but say, "It just seems like a lot of money to spend." First you must cushion the objection by agreeing with them. Say something such as, "I can understand what you're saying. After all, it does seem like a lot of money to spend." By agreeing with them, you further portray yourself as their friend, and they will be more willing to open up to you about what specifically they object to about the price. This helps in the next stage, when you question them.

Next, ask them a probing question about the objection. "Out of curiosity, what concerns you? Is it that you feel you can get a better price elsewhere? Is it that you think the price may come down?" Once you have narrowed down their concern, you can isolate it. "Is that the only thing preventing you from buying today?" This is an essential step. If they say yes, you can move on to handle that objection knowing that the customer won't catch you by surprise with another objection. If, however, they mention another concern, you must begin again and cushion that objection as well.

There are many potential price objections and just as many ways of handling those objections, if not more. Let's assume that you are selling a $20,000 automobile and have discovered that the customer feels the price is too high. First, Wickman counsels, determine by how much the price is too high. If the customer says that he feels it is $2,000 too much, you have made the sale much easier on yourself.

> **There are many potential price objections and just as many ways of handling those objections, if not more.**

You are now dealing with the $2,000 difference, which is much easier than dealing with the sum total. Always discuss the difference and reduce it to the ridiculous. If they plan on financing the purchase over three years, explain that for two dollars a day they are getting all the advantages you enumerated before. Now sell them again on your product, but based on the ridiculous two-dollar-a-day amount. "For two dollars a day, you get the CD player, the power disk brakes, the sun roof . . . You wouldn't want to give those up for a mere two dollars, would you?"

If, on the other hand, the customer feels that she can save money buying from a competitor, you can be prepared for that as well. If you have done your homework, you can show the customer on a graph or flowchart exactly what services, features, and benefits she will be giving up by choosing the lower-priced competitor. Say, "These extras are something that at some point are going to be important to you."

Or, say to the customer, "If I could prove to you that this automobile is worth every penny of that $20,000, would you buy it?" Having done your homework, you can then go to your records for a blue book or lists and receipts of comparable sales. As Wickman puts it, no one likes to be a pioneer buyer and often just showing customers that others have made comparable purchases is enough to convince them that they are making the right decision. This is a very powerful way of putting a price objection to rest.

Sometimes, Wickman admits, none of these methods will be sufficient to close a particularly intransigent customer. Wickman advises putting the ball back in the customer's court. Recapitulate your methods and say, "I've tried to demonstrate why I think my product is right for you. What is the one thing I would have to show you right now that would convince you this is the right time and product to buy?" Perhaps they won't be able to think of anything either, and you will walk away with a particularly satisfying sale.

EXPERT ADVICE

FIRST, SAY NO

What do you do when a customer says, "Will you lower your price/commission/ etc. . . . ?" Do you hem and haw and apologize for your price? Wickman says, "Don't!" If you wriggle under pressure, you are implying to the customer that a price break is possible. Here's the Floyd Wickman response:

Look the customer in the eye and, with an air of humor, merely say, "No." Thirty percent of the time the prospect will say to himself, "Hey, it didn't hurt to ask." Admittedly, 70 percent of the time it won't work, but often the prospect will feel the obligation to ask, and a simple no can put the issue to rest.

If the prospect persists, however, and says, "If you lower it, I'll buy," you can respond with "If I say yes to that lower price, that means that I was lying to you about the previous price. Now Mr. Prospect, I don't ever lie. I think that would be a terrible way to create a business relationship, don't you?" Often an appeal to a prospect's sense of honesty—and need to test yours—can be just the leverage you need to get a signature on the dotted line.

GO INTO PRICE NEGOTIATIONS WITH AN EDGE THAT CUTS THE DEAL

Although we all go into negotiations determined to come out on top, we often give away more than necessary to close the sale.

ADDITIONAL
READING

It may be easy to jump into the negotiating arena, but winning at the game is another matter. Your effectiveness will increase dramatically if you become aware of the most common negotiating mistakes and then learn how to avoid them.

MISTAKE #1—UNDERESTIMATING YOUR POWER

When you want someone to buy your product, it is natural to feel anxious. Before you realize it, you may become preoccupied with how important the sale is to you, both for your ego and for your income. While there is nothing wrong with looking at the situation from your own point of view, you may lose perspective.

In negotiating, your strength and power lie in focusing on what you can do for your customer, not on what your customer can do for you. Keep in mind that your product is going to solve some very serious problems for your customer. To negotiate from a position of power, you must sincerely believe that doing business with you is a plus for the customer.

MISTAKE #2—NEGOTIATING WITHOUT THE FINAL DECISION MAKER

Even seasoned professionals sometimes fail to make sure they are negotiating with the final fund releaser. This is not to say that you foolishly forgot to ask, "Can you make the final purchasing decision?" Very often the answer to this question is "Yes." When the crunch comes, however, a mysterious committee that has to give final approval suddenly surfaces. The trap is that you are pushed to give your best and final price, only to find out that the committee has to approve. The committee, not surprisingly, wants you to offer a better deal again. Now it's back to the concessions board.

To get around this setup, pin down all decision makers: "Is there anyone, aside from you, who will be involved in making the final decision?" Also establish the rules for negotiating. Ask, "If we worked out an agreement that is comfortable for you, would you be prepared to complete the paperwork today?" These questions will force out the true situation. If you find that a committee must approve, push to attend the committee meeting yourself. If this is not acceptable, you have two choices—either put in your price/term package and leave yourself

159

room to negotiate, or give them your best package and make it clear that you will not make any changes. If you take the second course, stick to what you have said.

MISTAKE #3—THINKING ABOUT YOUR PRICE IN A VACUUM

Because it's the fastest, most effective way to get you to lower your price, customers will usually tell you that your price is too high. Since it works, they reason, why not continue to use it?

Price is always too high if the purchaser is not getting anything for the money spent. If I said, "I am asking $5,000 for a stone I am selling," you would probably say that I was crazy.

> **Price is always too high if the purchaser is not getting anything for the money spent.**

But if the stone was a one-carat unblemished diamond, you might grab at the opportunity to turn a profit. The mistake is in thinking about price in a vacuum.

Always talk about price in relation to the value purchased by the money being spent. Will the purchase increase productivity, improve ease of daily operations, increase sales, reduce expenses, or increase the bottom line in some other way? Then when your customer talks about the price being too high, you can talk about how the expenditure will be recovered or what benefits that purchase will bring to your customer's company.

MISTAKE #4—FORGETTING TO JUSTIFY YOUR PRICE

If we were not slaves to our emotions, it would appear quite logical to explain the rationale for our prices again rather than quickly reducing the price. After all, when your customers say that your price is too high, they mean that they do not appreciate the value of your product. At this point, before you even consider reducing your price, you must review the benefits that your product will provide and the price tag attached to the opportunity to enjoy these benefits.

MISTAKE #5—LOWERING YOUR PRICE TOO QUICKLY

To negotiate without dropping your price, you can extend your service contract a couple of months, offer some consultation time to solve a particular problem, provide a free maintenance check, or do a small piece of additional work at no extra charge. Or throw in a couple of additional concessions on your company's part: add 30 days to the terms of payment, improve speed of delivery, or provide product storage. If you can tie it into a problem that your customer needs to solve, whatever you offer will be extremely effective.

MISTAKE #6—NEGOTIATING YOUR PRICE TOO SOON

Your customer says, "Your price is too high." You respond with, "Well, how would a 2 percent discount sound to you?" You drop your price immediately. In doing so, you probably don't realize how you have weakened your selling position. Your action says, "This product really isn't worth very much in itself. It is only worth what you will pay for it. So why don't we agree on what you want to pay for it, and as long as you are reasonable, we can make a deal." In the end your customers may lose trust in you for attempting to rip them off with your (initially) high price.

When your customer first requests a price reduction, ask, "What makes you feel that the price is too high?" Let your customer put forth his or her argument for why you should accept the price reduction request. Insist upon a reason.

MISTAKE #7—REDUCING YOUR PRICE WITHOUT ASKING FOR A RETURN CONCESSION

When you do make a price concession, be sure to ask for a concession from your customer in return. "If you give in to a price negotiation once, why shouldn't you give in again?" your customer reasons. On the other hand, if you ask for a concession from your customer, he or she will think twice about continuing the negotiation game. It is not as rewarding if he or she has to give up something, too.

> "If you give in to a price negotiation once, why shouldn't you give in again?" your customer reasons.

In exchange for a price reduction, you might ask your customer to purchase additional quantities of the same product, or some related add-on product. You can ask your customer to extend the service contract with you for three to six additional months, request shorter terms of payment, offer fewer features, vary the delivery schedule, or reduce the product quality.

MISTAKE #8—FORGETTING THAT YOU ARE GIVING AWAY YOUR COMPANY'S PROFITS

Negotiations can become so all-consuming that you can lose sight of the big picture. Every dollar that you negotiate away comes off your company's profits and your own sales commission.

To stay on top of profits, watch the zeros. Don't negotiate in round numbers. Never offer a 1 or a 2 percent discount. Always connect your price concessions to actual reductions made on parts of the deal. For example, if your total package is $62,535 to include product and service, cut it down slowly by saying, "Well, maybe we can cut down on the second service call and charge you $____ for our engineer's time." By looking at specific aspects of the deal, it will be easy to slow down the negotiations and keep your counteroffers low. Again, don't forget when you make your concession to ask your customer to give you one in return.

Negotiating successfully is a game of strategy and tactics. Although it takes years of concentrated effort to become a master negotiator, you can certainly increase your effectiveness immediately if you realize one thing: you are valuable to your customers. They want what you are selling, and no matter how much they play the indifferent buyer role, they would not be negotiating with you if they weren't interested in your product or service. Use this knowledge to your advantage and stand your ground. You will be amazed at your results.

Negotiation

A HANDS-ON GUIDE FOR MANAGERS

TRAINING GUIDE TIME REQUIRED: 30 MINUTES

THE ART OF SALES NEGOTIATION
What Is Influence?

Most people confuse influence with persuasion. There is a difference. Persuasion is the process of altering somebody else's attitudes or beliefs. Influence is the process of changing somebody else's behavior. While persuasion can be a tool to create influence, for a sales rep, influence is far more important—higher sales can only result from a positive change in the customer's behavior.

It is a common misconception that the ability to influence is a character attribute some people possess and others lack. It's true there appear to be individuals for whom influence comes naturally. Fortunately for everyone else, scientific research conducted over the past 30 years indicates that virtually anybody can apply the principles of influence to change the outcome of personal interactions, including the sales process. This research is based upon extensive observation of top-performing salespeople inside a wide variety of industries, including insurance, automobile, photography, charity, advertising, public relations, and so forth. Through decades of trial and error, organizations have learned what works in sales situations.

Through comparing the sales successes across these fields, scientists have identified patterns of behavior and speech that increase the likelihood another person will say "yes" to a request. While sales reps (and others) have good reason to believe that getting to "yes" is a matter of offering a product or service that is of value to the customer, research indicates the individual or organization that presents its offering in an influential manner will capture the lion's share of the sales.

What Are the Principles of Influence?

According to the research, you can greatly increase the likelihood of closing a sale if you use one or more of six basic principles of influence. The six principles are as follows.

THE PRINCIPLE OF RECIPROCATION

Customers feel obligated to say yes to those they owe. For example, when charities include small gifts in direct mailings, they double the response from recipients. To implement this principle, always enter a sales situation with the thought of helping rather than of being helped. When this is sincerely felt and expressed, it creates an obligation that the customer will find extremely difficult to ignore. Similarly, one of the best ways to get a referral from a customer is to give that customer a referral. Create a sense of obligation, and you'll make more sales.

THE PRINCIPLE OF SCARCITY

Customers are more likely to say yes if they believe the product or service being sold is rare or dwindling in availability. For example, when GM announced the end of the Oldsmobile product line, the Oldsmobiles that had been on the lot for months suddenly sold in a matter of days. One way to use this principle is to reveal to the customer any circumstance that would make your product or service difficult to get in the future. Another is to focus the discussion on what the customer will lose without your product or service, rather than on what the customer will gain from having it.

THE PRINCIPLE OF AUTHORITY

Customers are more likely to say yes if they view the sales rep as having special knowledge or unique credibility. For example, high-tech firms often bring their CEOs into the sales process in order to close a big sale. To implement this principle, always reveal anything about your background or experience that would tend to increase the customer's perception of you as an authority. Another way to use this principle is to emphasize your firm's reputation in the industry and its history of success.

THE PRINCIPLE OF COMMITMENT

Customers are more likely to say yes if saying yes is consistent with a prior commitment they have already made in your presence. For example, market research firms double the number of people who agree to be surveyed by simply asking the prospective survey-taker the following question: "Are you a helpful person?" To use this principle, obtain commitments from the customer about goals and preferences, and then match your product or service to those goals and preferences. Even better, get the customer to make a public commitment that defines the customer's identity. Then, when you tie purchasing your product or service to that identity, the customer will want to say yes because saying no would be inconsistent with the customer's self-image. For example, if the customer says, "I feel personally responsible for the security of this organization," you say, "Then you'll be really interested in how our product will make your facility more secure."

THE PRINCIPLE OF CONSENSUS

Customers are more likely to say yes if they are presented with evidence that people just like them are also saying yes. For example, television infomercials get a much larger response when they interview people who have bought the product and are willing to talk about how wonderful it is. One way to use this principle is to provide the customer with examples and references that as closely as possible match the profile of that customer. Another way is to invite the customer to a user's group meeting where the customer will be exposed to dozens of your (presumably happy) customers.

THE PRINCIPLE OF LIKABILITY

Customers are more likely to say yes if they know and like the sales rep. For example, television commercials often use celebrities as spokespeople because consumers feel that they like and know celebrities. Likability is difficult for most sales reps, because it seems to be a matter of personality and chance rather than of behavior and intention. However, likability is no big mystery. To use this principle, find similarities between yourself and the customer and raise them to the surface. Are you in the same business? Is there anything similar about your backgrounds? The principle of likability is also complementary to the principle of reciprocation. If you can find something about the customer that you truly like and respect, then the customer will naturally like and respect you. While this may seem manipulative, it's not, because if you truly like the customer, you will be certain that the customer is treated well.

Remember that these principles must be applied before you ask for the business. Research indicates that this prepositioning of the sale is the major differentiator between opportunities that result in sales and opportunities that fester and die. This is not to say a product's features, contract issues, and other elements of the sales process are not important. Creating a receptive psychological environment for a sales request, however, is the single most important element of closing a sale.

How to Apply These Principles

The key to applying these principles is preparation. Prior to every sales call, you should find out what you can about the customer, the customer's interests, and the customer's role inside his or her organization. The reason for this is simple: The better you understand the customer, the more likely you'll be able to apply one or more of the principles while you preposition for the close.

Prior to the sales call, go through the six principles, one after the other, and decide whether that principle is available to use in this sales situation. During the sales call, preposition the close by bringing the principles to bear—gradually and naturally as part of the conversation. Needless to say, you should adjust your approach to match any additional information that you gather during the sales call. For example, if you discover that a customer has frequently bought products from your firm in the past, surface that prior commitment by asking the customer to provide more details about when and how those purchases took place.

ROBERT B. CIALDINI, Ph.D. was interviewed for this article. He is an expert in the fields of persuasion, compliance, and negotiation. His books, including *Influence: Science and Practice* (Allyn & Bacon, 2000), have sold almost 1 million copies and are available in 20 languages. In addition to serving as Regent's Professor at Arizona State University, Cialdini is also president of the training and consulting firm, Influence At Work. For additional workshops, training, consulting, or keynotes, contact 480-967-6070 or www.influenceatwork.com.

SALES REPS' FREQUENTLY ASKED QUESTIONS

FREQUENTLY ASKED QUESTIONS

Q: We're a global company. Will these techniques work to influence people who are from a different business culture?

A: Yes, but the specific elements of the techniques will vary according to the peculiarities of the culture. For example, in Asian cultures, businesspeople are more likely to be influenced by appeals to authority than in Mediterranean cultures, where businesspeople tend to react more positively to appeals to friendship. Both biases differ from that in the United States where the main points of influence are obligation and reciprocation.

Q: What is the difference between influence and manipulation?

A: Ethics. It's influence when you honestly believe that by selling your product or service you are truly helping the customer to achieve a goal or overcome a problem. It's manipulation if you're trying to fool a customer into buying something that's neither wanted nor needed.

Q: Our product is better than the competition's. Why do we need to use influence to sell it?

A: In most cases, a higher-quality product will sell better than a lower-quality one. However, all things being more or less equal, sales reps who use influence effectively will outsell sales reps who fail to do so. If you use influence, you'll not only outsell the competition but also your own firm's sales reps who aren't using the principles of influence. One of the elements of a quality product is a well-trained sales force that can help a customer make a good decision, so your ability to influence is actually an element in whether a product is truly best in class. Because of this, a company with a weak product but a strong sales force can sometimes provide more value than a company with a strong product but a weak sales force.

SALES
MANAGER'S
MEETING
GUIDE

SALES MANAGER'S MEETING GUIDE

Below are 12 practical steps to help your sales team utilize
the principles of influence to preposition a sales opportunity
for closing. This training session should take approximately 30 minutes.

1. Prior to the meeting, copy and trim the wallet-sized "Quick Tips for Your Next Sales Meeting" reference card from the next page.

2. Prior to the meeting, create a one-paragraph profile of a fictional customer who is close to the average customer on which your sales team calls. Make copies of that paragraph for distribution during the meeting.

3. Open the sales meeting by explaining that the team is going to learn how to influence customers to say yes more quickly and more frequently. Explain that you will be asking team members to do some role-playing, and request that everyone participate to the fullest.

4. Break the meeting into groups of two. Have each pair designate who will be A and who will be B. Distribute the paragraph describing the fictional customer. Tell the A's they are the customer, and the B's are to act as the sales rep.

5. Explain that the B's have obtained three minutes with customer A, and this is an excellent opportunity to move a sale toward closure. Have the B's conduct a sales call, during which the A's take brief notes on what the B's say.

6. After three minutes, stop the role-playing and thank everyone for participating. Ask everyone to take out writing materials and take notes on what you're about to tell them.

7. Describe the six principles of influence to the best of your ability, giving examples from your own experience when you have used these principles to close business. Spend about 10 minutes doing this. You should now be 15 minutes into the meeting.

8. Repeat the role-playing exercise, but with A's selling to the B's this time. Have A attempt to use one or more of the principles of influence during the call. Be sure to point out that small, subtle changes in approach are likely to be the most effective.

9. After five minutes, end the role-playing. Have the A's and B's brainstorm on how A could have made the sales call more productive through the application of the principles. Spend about five minutes on this.

10. Repeat the role-play with B once again conducting a sales call with A as the customer. Have B attempt to subtly use the principles to move the call toward closing the sale.

11. Open the floor to discussion. Ask the teams to share what they did or heard that seemed effective. Provide additional coaching as necessary to ensure the teams get as much as possible out of the exercise.

12. Hand out the wallet cards, and suggest they refer to them before calling on customers.

QUICK TIPS FOR YOUR NEXT SALES MEETING

QUICK TIP

☑ How can I help this customer? If you help the customer, he or she will feel obligated to say yes. (Principle of Reciprocation.)

☑ What will it cost the customer not to buy? A customer is more likely to say yes if there's loss connected with saying no. (Principle of Scarcity.)

☑ What are the sources of my authority? A customer is more likely to say yes if he or she believes you are knowledgeable and credible. (Principle of Authority.)

☑ What similar commitments have already been made? A customer is more likely to say yes if he or she has already made public commitments consistent with purchasing your product or service. (Principle of Commitment.)

☑ Who among the customer's peers is also our customer? Customers believe that saying yes entails much less risk if the customer knows of similar people who have already said yes. (Principle of Consensus.)

☑ What is it about this customer that I can truly like and respect? A customer is more likely to say yes to somebody who is likable, and likability is a reflection of your own attitude toward the customer. (Principle of Likability.)

A STEP-BY-STEP PROCESS

A professional salesperson negotiates everything from appointment times to the selling price to the service contract.

For those who understand negotiation, the process can be as enjoyable as the end result. Even though sellers and buyers work from separate agendas, negotiation usually results in more equitable settlements. It's the way to conduct business. These six ideas will help you hone your sales negotiation skills.

First, be prepared. Knowledge is power. The more knowledgeable and prepared you are, the better the solution you'll create. Review what you already know about the customers. What will they ask for, and what concessions will they make? List your demands in advance. Know what you must have versus what you would like to have. In what ways are you flexible? What are your limits of authority? How much bargaining is permitted? There is a direct relationship between your preparation and the results you achieve. The more front-end time you invest, the greater the return.

> **Be direct with your probes. Focus on customer problem areas where you feel you offer unique solutions. Concentrate on buyer pressure points—areas which induce buyers to make nonprice decisions.**

Second, proactively probe. Ask questions early in the negotiating process. Determine the buyer's wants and needs as soon as possible. Are there buyer absolutes? Be direct with your probes. Focus on customer problem areas where you feel you offer unique solutions. Concentrate on buyer pressure points—areas which induce buyers to make nonprice decisions. Examples include timing, limited inventory, high demand, and bad experience with your compensation in the past.

Once you've asked questions, listen. Use your eyes as well as your ears. What is the buyer saying or not saying? Is anything obvious because of its exclusion? Observe the buyer's nonverbal signals. Is he or she relaxed, open, or defensive? Be perceptive to all signals coming from the buyer.

Third, remember that everything is negotiable. Whatever demands the buyer makes are the results of internal negotiations within the company. You deal with the end results of this internal bargaining. A corollary to this is that anything can be renegotiated. For example, the customer's budget for your product may be renegotiated internally if the customer feels convinced of your product value. No product is overpriced unless it's undesirable.

Never assume that the "final" offer is the last offer. How many times have customers said: "This is my final offer—take it or leave it," and 10 minutes later revised the offer?

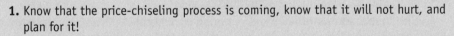

SKILL SET

QUICK TIP

1. Know that the price-chiseling process is coming, know that it will not hurt, and plan for it!

2. Get to know the people you will be dealing with before you meet with them. Find out what their decision-making capabilities are. Then build a relationship.

3. Find out the prospects' or customers' real needs before you go in or while you are on a call by asking open-ended questions. Once you find out their needs, strive to show them how your company will satisfy their needs.

4. Build your greatest benefit to that customer in your proposal. Go in with options.

5. Let customers know up front what is off-limits for you, such as price slashing or buy-one-get-one-free gimmicks.

6. Do a mini search for change before you leave your customer. Then build that change into your next call.

Fourth, use funny money for concessions. When you must concede on your end, look for funny money, or soft dollars. This includes free training, extra services, extended warranty, free delivery, longer payment terms, and so on. You are making concessions, but they're indirectly related to costs. It's easier to get management to concede on these non-price issues, and it allows the customer to save face while experiencing a real gain. Carry a list of funny money options. Know what you may offer. It could be just enough to cinch the deal.

Fifth, use time patiently. Most salespeople have the word "hungry" embossed on their foreheads. And buyers read this signal. Buyers also know that prudent foot-dragging on their end generally opens up the concession box. I drag my feet a little, and you give a little. I drag my feet a lot, and you give a lot. As a salesperson with a quota to meet, you want to close the deal as soon as possible. You've learned to close early. Close often. Close always. Ironically, it's this same frantic pace that signals the buyer to hold out for a better deal. Buyers need the solution just as quickly as you need to help them. Drag your feet sensibly to embrace the quality of your offer.

Sixth, focus on win-win results. In sales there are only two possibilities: win-win and lose-lose. The win-lose scenario is a deception. When you win and the customer loses, it's a double loss. You may win the order, but you've lost the bond with your customer. That's a lose-lose result. When it's lose-win, it's still a double loss. The customer may get the best of you on this deal, and you will resent the business and provide mediocre service. You may even avoid this customer's business in the future. Again, it's a double-loss situation. Focus on win-win. It builds the relationship and feeds customer loyalty. You feel better, and the customer is satisfied.

As a salesperson, sooner or later you're bound to negotiate. It's not an *if* question; it's a *when* question. Be prepared. Ask questions. Remember, everything is negotiable. Look for nonprice concessions and wait for the best solution for all parties.

HOW TO NEGOTIATE WITH PURCHASING MANAGERS TO STRIKE A WIN-WIN DEAL

Why can't sales be simpler? Why do purchasing managers always have to hammer you on price? You know you've got what they need; why is cost always number one on their list? Because that's their job.

And yours is to lead them in a more fruitful direction.

It's your job to find out what that customer is looking for, says Myers. He advises asking open-ended questions to get at the customer's true needs or problems. "A simple question I will ask is, 'How's the quality of your product?' If they answer, 'Good,' I ask, 'Can you define good for me?' This lets me find out exactly what they are looking for. Then, I can key in on what they really want, build up the value of my services, and minimize the price issue," he says.

> "A simple question I will ask is 'How's the quality of your product?' If they answer, 'Good,' I ask, 'Can you define good for me?' This lets me find out exactly what they are looking for."

If, for example, prospects are trying to get Myers to lower his price but Myers knows that color selection is important to them, he focuses on the fact that his company offers more color selection than his competitors do. "Having 21 colors to offer will throw the price issue right out the door," says Myers, "especially if the competitor only offers six color choices."

Myers admits that there are times when a person is what he calls a "bottom liner—a price buyer."

"These are instances in which you have to take a look at what you're going to get in return," he says. "If I'm giving away price, I need to get something in return. Maybe I'll get two or three referrals that will make it worthwhile. Ask yourself, 'What's the risk?'"

Price-chiseling situations arise all the time in Gil Strader's business. "In today's selling environment, you should expect it," says Strader, a district manager for Syngenta, a worldwide leader in the manufacturing and marketing of crop protection products. "Most often, customers think they are doing their job by chiseling down the price or asking for add-ons from salespeople. I advise my team to plan for it. A salesperson will find few clients to call on who do not try to chisel you down or ask for add-ons beyond limits. Don't feel threatened or take it personally. Even my best customers, who know me very well, will try to chisel me or force 'wraparounds' on a sales call. They are just doing their job and keeping me on my toes. My objective is for this to happen occasionally, not occur as a standard practice in meeting with our customers."

**EXPERT
ADVICE**

EXPERT ADVICE: NEGOTIATE WITH PURCHASING MANAGERS

"If you are being chiseled down, you are in a negotiation," says Marilyn Nyman, president of Nyman Associates, a communications firm that provides coaching, consulting, and customized training. "Unfortunately, people are accustomed to viewing a negotiation as a win-or-lose situation. The better thing to do is to look at negotiation as building a relationship. At our company, we use a three-pronged approach to doing that."

First, Nyman suggests that you choose a strategy before meeting with the purchasing manager. She recommends an interest-based strategy. "Go in with the idea that you are looking for common ground," she says. "What are their needs? What are their concerns? You also need to know what the purchasing manager's role is in that particular company. What kind of power does the purchasing manager have? Is the person just there to body-block and say no, which is sometimes the case, or can this person make his or her own decisions? Know your audience: Where do they fit in the organization? What pushes their buttons? Oftentimes they have more flexibility than they let on."

Nyman stresses that the relationship-building phase should not be overlooked. "People like to do business with people that they like," she says. "Use the art of the question. Ask a few open-ended questions to find out their needs. Let the other people talk so they can help you understand what they want. Remember, money is only one part of decision making," Nyman adds. "No purchasing decision is made just on dollars. See this as a process. Go in and build a relationship and then come back to negotiate."

The second part of the approach is dealing with emotion. "Most negotiations are driven by emotions," she says. "Manage your emotions and manage their emotions. How? Manage their emotions by reading their body language, listening to their tone of voice, and seeing everything they say as a concern that you have to address. If you go in with an idea of building a relationship instead of being uptight, you can focus on clients and read their emotions better."

The third and most important part of the approach is to help your client (in this case the purchasing manager) see your negotiation in terms of options and consequences. "If the purchasing manager says, 'We can only do it for this price', don't say yes or no, say, 'Well, that's an option; the consequence may be that you won't get the kind of service that you want,'" Nyman advises. "Go in with three kinds of options; maybe one option is that if they pay less, they get less. Another option is that they can go with a competitor, but then they may find that the competitor doesn't have your track record. Option three is that you agree to the pricing and go ahead with the sale."

> "The primary thing to remember is that you need to build a trusting relationship," says Nyman. "Sometimes that may mean that you don't get this particular sale, but remember, you will win in the long run."
>
> An executive speech coach and certified speech pathologist, **MARILYN S. NYMAN** is president and founder of The Nyman Group, a communications firm that provides coaching, consulting, and customized training. See www.nymangroup.com.

Strader, whose sales team covers New Jersey, Maryland, Delaware, Virginia, and West Virginia, adds, "Sometimes it's a shock—this art of negotiation. When your customer's an expert negotiator, it can throw you into a tailspin, leading to unsuccessful results. You have to realize that this tactic is part of the purchasers' responsibility to their companies. Thinking of it this way always helps take the emotion out of it."

Strader also advises his sales reps to list what they anticipate the customer will ask for and be creative when they think about it. "I tell them to think of every legal and ethical thing that the customer would ask for and have an answer for each," he says. "Figure out how much, (if any) flexibility in pricing, discounts, and add-ons you will have in your proposal. Also, write down where and why you can't go further. If you have a logical business explanation of why you can't go lower, it will be accepted and understood."

"Build your reputation on value to the customer," adds Strader. "This is not done by playing some give-and-take negotiation game. You can accomplish this by knowing what you can do and need to do based on what your customer needs. When you build it in up front, you reinforce to your customers that you know them and their business, and you have already taken care of them to the highest level. When you can get across to the customers that they don't have to 'play the role of a customer,' then you have won a big battle. Make it known that you will always plan and present the greatest value to them during your calls and that their time is too valuable to waste with chiseling-down tactics. You need to let your customers know that they have won—or at least make them feel that way."

Strader also lets customers know up front what decisions his sales reps can and can't make. "Our salespeople do not have the authority to change price, terms, and discounts associated with our brands," he says. "However, they can help develop and execute sales plans and strategies to capitalize on market opportunities. Promotional activities, training meetings, and minor equipment assistance are all examples of what we can build into our customers' plans."

"Finally," says Strader, "I have been working with some customers for more than 12 years. They are the same people with the same name on the business, in the same location, but customers constantly change. Their market environment changes, their bottom line changes, the people that they work around and report to change, and their customers change. So, before we leave every customer, we do a 'mini search' for change. If we find a change, it is something that we will need to build into our next call or proposal. This is a must."

"You want to build a solid, long-term relationship with your customers," Strader concludes. "What better way to do this than to build the greatest value into your proposal up front. Don't wait for the customer to ask or beat it out of you. Go in with options."

Rejection

A HANDS-ON GUIDE FOR MANAGERS

TRAINING GUIDE TIME REQUIRED: 50 MINUTES

THE ROLE OF REJECTION IN SALES SUCCESS

Successful people understand the value of rejection in the process of developing clients. The more they enjoy rejection, the more they enjoy contacting prospective clients. Rather than taking rejection personally, they realize their attitude and reactions to rejection are critical in developing new business. They enjoy the challenge of converting resistance into receptivity so they can develop relationships that ensure results. First, let's review the three objectives of the client-development process, which is similar to the process of building a pyramid.

> **Rather than taking rejection personally, they realize their attitude and reactions to rejection are critical in developing new business. They enjoy the challenge of converting resistance into receptivity.**

Objective No. 1

In sales we begin by building our client base, which is the base of the pyramid. This requires contacting people five times, on average. Within each of these five contacts, we have a goal to achieve, including gaining their awareness of who we are and what we have to offer, developing an interest in what we can do for them, having them evaluate our product or service, trying our product and analyzing the benefits they will gain from it versus what they are presently using, and adopting our recommendations.

Objective No. 2

The second part of the pyramid is developing a stronger relationship with our existing clients to achieve such objectives as earning the right to ask for referrals, gaining repeat or additional business, and exploring other applications.

Objective No. 3

The peak of the pyramid is to take our success to the top by contacting the highest-level decision makers—the most affluent prospects—and seeking the largest opportunities.

Each of us in sales understands the importance of achieving these objectives—making the calls, getting more involved with existing clients, and calling on more important people. We have to wonder why—if we are all motivated to contact people, build stronger relationships with our clients, and explore greater opportunities—so many salespeople avoid these challenges. As we are motivated by the need to achieve and gain recognition, we can also be unmotivated by the opposite need to avoid failure and rejection.

Fear of failure and rejection can cause salespeople to lose their enthusiasm, their confidence, and their initiative. There are, however, two kinds of rejection—one that can amuse us and one that can be damaging to our ego. One word separates the two, and that is the word *personal*. If we do not take the rejection personally, we might react with humor, but if we take the negativity or unkindness personally, we might become disappointed, depressed, and defensive.

QUICK TIP

QUICK TIPS FOR YOUR TRAINING SESSION

Following are examples of beliefs regarding the value of failure that can ensure our success.

1. The more I fail, the more I succeed. Failure is part of the process of succeeding.

2. There are only two ways of failing. One is by not trying, and the other is by quitting.

3. Failure gives me insight into where change might occur.

4. Failure is an experience in which I must know what I have gained.

5. I never see failure as failure but only as an opportunity to try new ideas.

6. I learn more from my failures than my successes.

7. I am paid for the number of times that I fail.

Ask your people why rejection and negative feedback might have more value than positive feedback and acceptance. Following are examples of beliefs regarding the value of rejection as part of gaining acceptance.

1. Negative feedback is the information I need to make changes in my direction.

2. If the rejection is invalid, then I cannot take it personally.

3. Rejection, rather than being humiliating, renews my humility.

4. My self-esteem is not based on the reactions of others but on my own sense of value.

5. Rejection reminds me not to take myself too seriously.

6. People who are saying no to me are speeding me on to someone who needs me.

7. If people are going to reject me, let it be from someone important.

8. I view rejection as raindrops off a duck's feathers.

9. I raise my self-image and fly above the storm.

Our beliefs determine our attitudes toward failure and rejection—though beliefs and attitudes are separate subjects. While we might take rejection personally, because we believe we need the acceptance of others to accept ourselves, we can still develop an attitude that overrides any self-defeating assumptions and beliefs.

Our beliefs affect our attitude; our attitude influences the way we perform; and our performance determines our results. Attitude is critical, but attitude is not everything: performance is everything. If we think negatively, we can still perform positively.

Before we discuss how successful people react to rejection, consider the two negative reactions to rejection: (1) avoiding the situation, backing off, and retreating and (2) counterattacking, becoming more aggressive, and overreacting. If we understand which of these two reactions we are most likely to use, we might then realize our own solution to dealing with people who are resistant to us.

Charisma is the trait of balancing opposite qualities into a personality with which most anyone can identify. In creating this ideal balance, answer two questions: What do you believe to be Charlie's best quality? What do you feel is Lucy's primary strength? If your answers are sensitivity and aggressiveness, then the ideal reaction to rejection is to be aggressively sensitive or relentlessly compassionate or perseveringly pleasant.

There are three reasons we might take rejection personally. Each of the following relates directly to the three sales objectives in building the client-development pyramid.

1. **FREQUENCY.** Everyone can deal with some rejection. The question is, how much failure and rejection can you experience before you start taking the negative feedback too much to heart? This is why salespeople have difficulty contacting people and developing their client base. Before they have made enough calls to find a prospect, they become discouraged and stop trying. How many prospecting calls can you make before you become discouraged? How many times can you contact a qualified prospect, who is always negative toward you, before you begin taking it personally?

2. **EMOTIONAL INVOLVEMENT.** How emotionally involved can we become with someone before we believe the person knows us so well that whatever he or she says might be true, causing us to feel vulnerable and defensive in our behavior? This is the reason some people can send out promotional material, but have difficulty making cold calls. Or, when they do make calls, they are reluctant to get an appointment to meet people personally. Or, they may enjoy meeting people and

FREQUENTLY ASKED QUESTIONS

SALES REPS' FREQUENTLY ASKED QUESTIONS

Q: Can you really change beliefs that are based on experience?

A: Most people are convinced their beliefs are completely valid because they can remember times when those beliefs proved true. However, because beliefs influence the way people see the world, they were probably ignoring evidence that ran contrary to the belief, while noticing evidence that confirmed it.

Q: How do I know when a belief is not a law of nature?

A: Any law that, at its base, contains the phrase "and because of that, I feel bad" (or something of the sort) is a belief that can be changed. Such beliefs combine an interpretation of reality—an attempt to put meaning into a situation and then use that meaning to produce an emotional state. While there are situations (such as a death in the family) where sadness is appropriate, being rejected in a sales situation is simply not all that important.

Q: What's the key to dealing positively with rejection?

A: Five words sum it up: do not take it personally. Things happen. Customers have bad days. The economy goes up and down. You have the choice to make those events an excuse for failure, or you can work on the four things that you have under your control: your beliefs, your attitude, your emotions, and your performance. Take care of those four, and the fifth—good results—will take care of itself.

> **If we believe someone is more important than we are, then our respect for that person will cause us to feel that whatever he or she says might be true.**

easily develop a friendship and perform the necessary follow-up, but they avoid asking for a decision for fear they might confront buyer's remorse.

3. PERCEIVED IMPORTANCE. If we believe someone is more important than we are, then our respect for that person will cause us to feel that whatever he or she says might be true. The idea that he or she might reject us can cause us to avoid contacting people of this level. This is the reason salespeople call on people who fall within their own self-image, and they have difficulty taking their success to a higher level.

Checklist

Recognize that there are two kinds of rejection—valid and invalid. If we identify which of the two we are confronting, we will know how to react appropriately.

QUICK TIPS FOR YOUR NEXT SALES SESSION

Following are examples of beliefs or thoughts for enjoying failure and being amused by rejection.

QUICK TIP

1. I love rejection.

2. Rejection turns me on.

3. Negative feedback ignites energy.

4. Hostile people amuse me.

5. I attack my fears.

6. Failure sharpens my objectivity.

7. Adversity makes me resilient.

8. Failure is a maturing process.

9. I do better under pressure.

10. Stress stimulates my creativity.

If the rejection is valid, then you want to know what you did to irritate your prospect. Critical comments are the information you need to make the necessary adjustments in your strategy and selling skills.

If the rejection is invalid and the prospect is just using you to release frustration, then you have to be concerned about what is causing the anger, rather than taking the unkindness personally.

If we believe we need to achieve and be accepted by others to feel good about ourselves, then we will be vulnerable to failure and rejection. Successful people thrive on failure and rejection because their self-esteem is based on their own sense of value. They believe they can gain more from failure than success and that negative feedback can be of greater value than positive feedback. This is why—whether they fail or succeed—they always feel good about themselves.

ART MORTELL was interviewed for this article. He is the author of *The Courage to Fail* (McGraw-Hill) and *World Class Selling* (Dearborn Trade Pub). A top motivational speaker, Mortell has given more than 4,000 programs at leading corporations including IBM, Merrill Lynch, PricewaterhouseCoopers, and Lockheed Martin. Address: PO Box 721, Malibu, CA 90265. Telephone: 310-457-2551. Web: www.artmortell.com.

SALES MANAGER'S MEETING GUIDE

SALES MANAGER'S MEETING GUIDE

Below are nine practical steps to improve your team's ability to turn rejection into a sales advantage.

1. Prior to the meeting, develop a presentation that reviews the key points of the module, as well as a handout for each of your people.

2. Open the meeting by asking your people to decide on which of the three sales objectives they will focus.
   a) Prospecting to develop clients.
   b) Getting more involved with existing clients in order to gain referrals and additional business.
   c) Taking their success to a higher level by seeking greater opportunities, such as contacting higher-level decision makers, more affluent people, or larger orders.

3. Ask your people to think of why they might have difficulty achieving these objectives.

4. Discuss how the fear of failure and rejection can cause us to become defensive and avoid our objectives. Now get more specific with your people.

5. Focus on those sales activities that cause the greatest difficulty, such as cold calling on the phone, gaining the administrative assistant's cooperation in speaking with the decision maker, confronting objections, or closing.

6. Have each person share a success story, about what he or she did to convert rejection into acceptance. Prepare a brief presentation on how thoughts determine emotions.

   Create the following visual:

   Thinking that:
   I will succeed
   Causes me to feel:
   Excited and enthusiastic
   Creating performance that:
   Perseveres and stays on target

   Thinking that:
   I do not want to be rejected
   Causes me to feel:
   Apprehensive and defensive
   Creating performance that:
   Seeks to take on less-threatening responsibility

7. Ask your people to write down what they believe successful people think about failure and rejection. What causes them to do better when confronting such experiences?

8. Develop, with your people, sales techniques that can disengage their fear of rejection.

9. Have your people decide how many cold-call conversations are required to find a prospect, how many prospects are needed to gain a new account; and, therefore, how many calls in total are needed to get one new client.

ADDITIONAL READING

A salesperson who never hears a "no" is no salesperson, only an order taker. Rejection is as much a part of sales as getting dressed in the morning, and salespeople who can't handle rejection had better find another career.

Having said that, even the heartiest of selling souls sometimes caves in after a steady diet of rejection.

If you look at sales as strictly a numbers game, noes are actually quite valuable. If you know your closing ratio and your average unit of sale, you can calculate how many noes you need to hear before you hear a yes. If your average unit of sales is $5,000 and you have a 20 percent closing ratio, every rejection you encounter is worth $1,000. It's like saying your glass is half full, not half empty.

How can you stay positive and let rejection roll off your back? The experts agree that the main point to keep in mind is that customers don't reject you, they just reject what you happen to be selling at the time you're selling it.

"The very first thing to remember when handling rejection is that you just can't take it personally," says Gavin McIntyre, senior consulting engineer and account executive for Bryan Research and Engineering of Bryan, TX. "In any business, you can't sell prospects every time you call on them. Chalk it up to experience."

"I put major emphasis on building a relationship, whether they are buying customers or not," says McIntyre. "Once you get that relationship built, more often than not those noes become yeses."

QUICK TIP

SKILL SET

1. Don't take sales rejection personally. A customer is not saying no to you, only to what you're selling at the moment.

2. Every "no" is not final. If your qualified prospect and your product are a good fit, your prospect may ultimately have a need.

3. Don't give up. Your next call may result in the sale of a lifetime, but if you don't make that call, you'll never know.

4. Learn from rejection. Find out the real reasons why a customer chooses not to buy.

5. Continuously analyze your skills to identify areas in which you can improve. Then go do it.

McIntyre, who sells high-end process simulation software for the oil and gas industry, says, "The complexity of the product affects the sales time curve and increases the
amount of rejection for the salesperson."

"In our case, it's a long-term process, and it takes me three to six calls before I've
spent enough time with customers to show them the benefits," says McIntyre. "It's a lot
of rejection, but I keep believing that I'm there for a reason and my product can benefit
them. They just haven't realized it yet."

As sales and district manager for Air Components & Systems Ltd. of
Charlotte, NC, Scott Avey believes it's critical for salespeople not to take rejection
personally and for demoralized salespeople to regain an objective viewpoint.

"A 'no' is not a personal rejection, and professionals realize they do have value to
customers. When customers say no, it's really a loss for them," says Avey.

"I sit down with salespeople and let them tell me what they're currently doing, review
their current style of opening and presentation, and basically let them use me as a dummy,"
says Avey. "I have them do a pretty good dry run of what they say and how they do it.
I take notes and then try to refresh their understandings of customers' needs, wants,
and likes."

"In many instances, it's a case of salespeople simply not communicating correctly
with customers," says Avey. "We repackage what they say and how they say it and develop
a new presentation."

"It really helps to take demoralized salespeople and get them to just stop and
rethink what's happening from a strategic aspect—to put themselves in their
customers' place and ask themselves, 'Why should I, as a busy customer, invest my
valuable time in talking to you? What are you going to do to make my business more
successful?'"

Once salespeople understand where they're falling short and have modified their presentations, Avery spends time emphasizing the company itself, going over its good points
and what resources are available, and reinforcing the salesperson's role. Finally, he tells
them to practice, practice, and practice their presentation.

"The next step is to go out and practice, rehearse, and fine-tune it with your
colleagues, spouse, or friends," says Avey. "The continuous activity of refining the presentation increases the salesperson's knowledge base and results in more confidence and
a better selling attitude. Then I tell them to 'go out and redeploy.'"

McIntyre feels that hearing noes can actually be a positive thing in that it allows salespeople to think about their sales strategies and how their products fit into a solution. He
also believes that since needs and personnel change; every time you're rejected, it puts
you one step closer to a yes.

"A 'no' can be a good thing and provide great information, especially if it's for a specific reason," McIntyre explains. "It gives us the chance to think about our strategies or learn about something that's flawed that we don't see and then fix it."

"Every 'no' you hear is a potential 'yes' the next time you call," adds McIntyre. "Turn it around. It's another day and companies' needs and personnel change. If you give up and don't call back, you've just lost the business."

"Since salespeople are in the forefront of the selling process, many feel as if they're lone wolves and beat themselves up when they get rejected," states Avey. "They tend to forget that the whole company is supporting them."

"Salespeople work in highly negative environments and have pressure to 'bring home the bacon'. They get downtrodden when they receive too much rejection," Avey says. "They need to remember that they're still valuable people doing a service for their company."

EXPERT ADVICE

HOW SALES MANAGERS CAN HELP

According to sales consultant Andrea Moses, the salesperson who hears an inordinate number of noes is doing something wrong. The first thing a manager has to do is get salespeople to recognize and admit there is a problem.

"Get salespeople to admit and acknowledge that there is a problem and encourage them to freely talk about it," says Moses. "They may not want to talk about the reality of it."

Once it is established that there is a problem, the sales manager has to identify what the problem is, put a price tag on the lost sales, and find a solution.

"You need to approach [the matter] from a practical standpoint. Conduct an audit to find out what the problem is, why it's happening, what it's costing the company, and what can be done about it." Moses advises.

"It could be that the salespeople are stuck handling price objections, falling short on rapport building skills, need to beef up on product knowledge, or one of any number of things," she adds. "Many times the solution is simply to go back to the basics and take it step by step."

"Salespeople need to address emotion and not obsess about rejection or take it so personally," says Moses. "When they get rejected, it's easy to fall into the 'poor me' syndrome and experience hurt, anger, and fear. But the super salespeople get over it, stay focused and aggressive, and continue on."

"When salespeople are feeling 'down in their cups,'" Moses advises, "help them to rethink the way they're evaluating their sales performance."

> "Instead of evaluating themselves on the number of closed sales, tell them to look at the progress they're making in each component of the overall sales process," explains Moses. "They may be getting more appointments, making more presentations, or meeting more decision makers."
>
> "Remind them that selling is more sophisticated today than ever before, and successful salespeople don't get caught up in their own emotions."
>
> **ANDREA MOSES** is the author of *Street Smart Selling: The Guide to Ultimate Masterful Powerbase Consultants* (Powerbase, 1990).

"We try to deemphasize that single individuals are responsible for the sale. While the salesperson has a key role, everyone plays a part in our success."

"We bring together sales, engineering, purchasing, and management, and strategize on specific accounts; and we stress that it's more of a team effort than an individual effort. It helps salespeople psychologically to know that if we lose a sale, the monkey's off their individual backs. We're all in the soup together."

Bryan Research's McIntyre advises salespeople who are feeling rejected "to place greater emphasis on preparation and, above all, not to succumb to fear if they're not reaching their goals."

"First and foremost, you have to know as much about your product and prospect as you possibly can," he advises. "If we take the time to invest in ourselves, learn and grow, and make our best effort, we'll get the business down the road."

"Obviously, salespeople have to sell if they want to stay on the job, and goals are important, but not the primary focus. Salespeople need to feel secure and confident in their company, product knowledge, and selling skills and give it their best effort."

ADDITIONAL READING

What do you do when a bad day stretches into a bad week, which somehow ends up being a bad month? You know how it is—every prospect you call on says no or puts you off. Even customers who gave you verbal agreements are changing their minds. Pessimism and dejection take over. Are you losing your skill? Should you seriously consider changing careers?

Larry Doubt, account manager for Allen Foods in St. Louis, MO, and Jeff Engler, director of new business for Agri-Dairy Products in Ada, MI, have both experienced this type of discouragement. Nevertheless, they have found the means to come back—and still stay in sales. What's their secret? They recommend three strategies: Put things in perspective, get advice and support, and motivate yourself to get going again with a positive attitude.

Engler uses the law of thirds as a guideline. "Remember that one-third of your prospects will buy from you, no matter what," he explains. "Another third will never buy from you, even if you are the best salesperson in the world. The final third may or may not buy from you, and it is only this last group that your selling skills have any potential for influencing."

For example, if you contact 30 prospects in a week and all of them are in the group that will never buy from you, it's easy to become discouraged. However, next week you may encounter 15 prospects who will say "maybe" or "yes" to you—even though you have done nothing differently. Simply remember the three groups and realize that rejections are inevitable.

Engler's reps classify each customer into one of his three groups, based on the initial telephone conversation. "If prospects are willing to see us and hear our quoted price, they may be in the middle group," he says. "But if they always buy from their brother's company, we'll never win their business."

Not all customers, or industries, are created equal. Doubt suggests finding out the average number of calls required to close a prospect in a particular field. "In my industry, five calls are usually required," he notes. "If it takes five calls to close most customers and I've only made three, why worry? I still have two more calls to make before I even need to get concerned."

Also, the marketplace has changed in recent years. Doubt says that it is harder to close prospects today than it was 25 years ago when he started out. "Most businesses use just three vendors. I am the only supplier for many of my customers," he explains. "There's no way you can win every prospect's business. So stop beating yourself up for something you can't control."

The hardest type of rejection for Engler is when customers who have given a verbal commitment change their minds. His reps try diplomatically to find out the reasons for the change. Usually it's because of price. Then they try either to compete on the basis of better value for the customer's money or lower their price. However, the key is not to take these challenges personally.

Furthermore, to help keep things in perspective, don't let your work be the only focus of your life. Engler recommends striving for a balanced life away from work. Spending time with friends, taking part in support and interest groups, and staying in shape keep him from becoming overly depressed during challenging times in his sales career. "Some people I know take time out to go to an afternoon movie to recharge their batteries," he says. "I call a friend or significant other to chat, remind myself of what is good in my life, and realize I don't need to define myself by temporary setbacks in my sales career."

Remind yourself of what you are doing right at work. Doubt asks a manager or other reps whom he respects to come with him on some of his sales calls and suggest ways he can improve. He also carries letters of reference from several current clients, reads them to remind himself of what he is doing right, and uses them as references to show potential customers.

HOW TO CHART YOUR MOOD SWINGS

QUICK TIP

☑ **HOW'S YOUR FUNNEL?** Salespeople riding high frequently tend to ignore the critical front-end grunt work that produces sales down the road. Have you been prospecting, asking for referrals, and networking as diligently as you should?

☑ **HOW'S YOUR DELIVERY?** Bad habits can sneak up on you unexpectedly. Try taping yourself on the phone or doing a little role-play with a colleague. Now, painful as it may be, go over the tape and listen for ways you can improve your delivery, energy level, body language (if you videotaped), and attention to the little things that close sales.

☑ **HOW'S YOUR CYCLE?** What does your selling cycle look like? Draw up a detailed chart of a typical sale. Have you been neglecting or racing through important steps? In what stages of the sale are you the weakest? Focus on improving those areas, and your overall effort will improve dramatically.

☑ **HOW'S YOUR MANAGER?** Go to your manager and ask for help, or have your manager come along on sales calls, particularly the tough calls. Then ask where you can improve. Let your manager know that you want honest criticism, and then swallow your pride and express thanks for any help you receive.

Satisfied customers can help in other ways, too. When they hit a slump, Engler and his reps call on existing clients with whom they have good relationships and ask, "Why do you buy from me?" The answers sometimes surprise them. "It may be a good presentation or a great price, but it also may be the color of my clothes or a great smile," Engler says. Regardless of the reason, Engler says this type of positive feedback inevitably cheers him and his reps up.

Doubt uses motivational books and tapes to renew his enthusiasm. He also attends monthly sales meetings, where he listens to colleagues discuss their successes.

When he was starting out, Doubt turned to older, more experienced coworkers for guidance and reassurance. Talking with successful reps at his company helped him learn their secrets and increase his success rate.

Both Doubt and Engler emphasize that reps in a slump shouldn't take rejection personally. Put things in perspective, they advise. Ask for support and suggestions, and realize that every sales career involves a lot of ups and downs.

Someone once said of the tennis great known for his never-give-up attitude, Jimmy Connors, "He never lost a match—he just ran out of time." It's a subtle concept, so think about it for a minute. Given enough time and enough tries, almost anyone can do almost anything. Of course that doesn't mean that everyone can do everything. But it does mean that with the right attitude, and a willingness to learn from failure, you can add incremental steps toward success until you do get it right, whatever it is you're trying to do—like reaching that prospect who's never in, or closing that account with 10 decision makers.

ADDITIONAL READING

According to Jib Ellison, managing partner in the Trium Group, a leadership consulting firm in San Francisco, it's important to keep failure in the proper perspective. "Failure is nothing more than feedback," he says. "It's simply information you can use to learn from." Ellison speaks from personal experience. Once, when he and his partner began to give their sales presentation to the senior vice president of a Fortune 100 health-care company, they were confident. But by the end of the presentation they knew they had blown it. "We had discussions before the meeting and thought we had a good sense of what the customer wanted," Ellison recalls. They didn't.

Ellison admits that he and his partner had not listened to the customer. "We thought he just wanted to open lines of communication between senior executives, but he wanted to know how to restructure the organization."

Sound familiar? Salespeople experience failure every day: a sale that doesn't go through, customers canceling an order, presentations that don't do the job. What do they do afterward? That's the important question. Ellison looked at where he had made mistakes and then used his know-how and determination to snatch success from the hand of failure. Later that same day, after analyzing the presentation with coworkers, he called the prospect, apologized, and asked for another chance. He got it and landed the sale.

Although it may be difficult to realize at first, many times failure can be a blessing in disguise. Nadir Anise, an attorney in Boca Raton, FL, who provides marketing expertise to the legal profession, notes, "Not closing a deal is not a failure. In fact, it can open up new doors. In the future they may need your services."

1. LEARN FROM FAILURES

Before you can learn from failure, you must know how you view failure in the first place. Are you one of those people who won't even acknowledge the word "failure"? Or do you accept that it's there, but then deal with it in a positive manner? Stephan Schiffman, president of DEI Management Group Inc., a sales-training firm in New York, says, "Failure does exist. It hurts when it happens, it's personal, and it is OK to be angry and feel humiliated when a sale falls through."

Either way, it's important to look back for insight to be better able to move forward. "You can't change what's already taken place," says Stephanie Speisman, president of Strategies for Change, Potomac, MD, which provides personal success coaching. "You can be responsible for what takes place from this moment on."

Rod Walsh, co-owner of Semper Fi Consulting in Sherman Oaks, CA, agrees. "If you're turned down, find out why someone else got the order. If you question your lost sales opportunities, you'll do better the next time."

To learn why you failed, stand back and look objectively at what happened and why. Talk to others. "When I fail, I get information about why the failure occurred. I ask the prospect to help me," says Jerome Colletti, president of Colletti–Fiss LLC, a sales consulting firm in Scottsdale, AZ. And don't be afraid to ask the tough questions. Gene Bledsoe, managing partner at the Casal Group, a marketing consulting firm in Dallas, recommends, "After every sales call, it's a great habit to analyze that call, see what worked, what didn't work. Analyze your plan going in. What did you hope to accomplish? Did you accomplish your plan? Analyze each step."

It's pointless focusing on what might have been. Instead, think of ways you'll do better next time. Dennis LaRosee, senior vice president at Praendex Inc., a training and consulting firm in Wellesley Hills, MA, offers two suggestions after a failure: First, take responsibility for what occurred at the sales call or presentation. Second, think of two or three alternative scenarios that might have worked better. Even if you don't have the opportunity to resell to that prospect, thinking of alternate scenarios helps you deal with future difficult sales calls.

2. HAVE A MENTOR

Selling is not a profession for hermits. Bouncing back from failure is easier when you have help. "Go outside yourself and get input from a customer, your boss, or your colleagues," recommends Colletti. The process demands the support of sales managers. "I think the number one responsibility of frontline sales managers is to help their people be successful," Colletti says. "Ask your salespeople, 'How can I help you do better next week?'"

Salespeople aren't the only ones who need someone to talk to. Managers know that objectively viewing their own work is difficult. Knowing everything about sales is impossible. So both sales managers and experienced salespeople should find a coach they trust. "I think it's important to have a good mentor to help you through the slumps, to give you a pep talk, or to offer some tips or pointers," says Michael Angier, president of Success Networks International, a motivational organization in South Burlington, VT.

3. ATTITUDE MATTERS

Recognize that your attitude colors your view of failure as much as the truth can. "Perception will always win over reality," says Bob Davies, president of Lake Forest, California-based High Performance Training Inc., a performance-coaching company. "Salespeople start out with good intentions," Davies explains, "but are rarely trained to deal with their own fears. Over time, as they experience more and more rejection, they start associating prospecting with pain, and fear takes over their selling. This just makes failure all the more likely."

Associating prospecting with failure and failure with pain means you won't do much prospecting and won't be good at it when you do. You must decide how you want to view failure and prospecting. Viewing them as learning experiences necessary for your improvement makes them part of your road to success, not steps toward failure.

At the same time, don't brush failure under the carpet. Salespeople, who are an optimistic bunch, occasionally refuse to acknowledge their failures. This just encourages the behavior to occur over and over again. "We often don't like to call things that are negative, 'negative,'" notes Stephen Goldstein, host of the television program *The Business Exchange* in Miami, FL. "People have to recognize that they failed. If you don't admit to failure, you won't make the changes you need to make."

4. DON'T TRY TO AVOID FAILURE

Trying to avoid failure is a fool's game. Fred Magee, president of Equal 5 Ltd., a consulting firm in Warwick, NY, researched failure in information technology departments and found that more than 80 percent of all new IT systems initiatives failed to meet one or more predefined goals. "Businesses define failure in such narrow terms that they throw out the successes along with the failures," says Magee. "They say, 'If we have not achieved this metric or this goal by this date, we've failed.'" This can mean lost sales. For example, management may tell a salesperson to generate x amount in dollar sales, without recognizing the value of a small sale that opens the door to a large company with big sales potential.

Failure isn't necessarily bad. You learn from mistakes, maybe more than in any other way. Skiers say if you don't fall, you can't ever get better. You need to push yourself or you'll never improve.

Don't fear failure. After all, what is the worst thing that can happen if you fail? Will you lose the sale? Your job? Chances are, the worst scenario is that you've invested time that will not result in an immediate payoff, and your ego will be a bit bruised. In the end, you will still be as good a salesperson as you've ever been—and as good a person.

5. DON'T GIVE UP

In sales, the lack of persistence is perhaps the biggest cause of failure. Anise tells the story of a salesperson who tried to sell him advertising space. After a couple of meetings, Anise realized that he didn't need what the salesperson was offering at that time. Every few months the salesperson would call and Anise would say he wasn't interested. "This was one of the most persistent people I have ever met," Anise recalls. Then, close to three years later, when the salesperson called again, Anise was ready to buy. In fact, he gave the salesperson considerable business. The lesson? "Don't give up after you hear no," Anise advises.

6. SEE THE BIG PICTURE

Going into a sales call with narrow perceptions of your customer's needs is a journey likely to culminate in a dead end. If you've made that mistake, Magee recommends next time working as many channels of opportunity as you can, both before and after the sale. See the big picture. Consider your pitch, your offer, your product, and your timing. Be creative.

What might customers need from you that they haven't considered? Would coming back at the beginning of a prospect's budget period improve your chances of landing a sale? Very few salespeople ever have the luxury of knowing all the factors influencing a decision maker and the outcome of a sale. You need to do some exploring. And stay in touch—even if you don't get the sale.

7. THINK POSITIVELY

Write down a list of your strengths and your successes, Speisman advises. Then after a lost sale or a presentation that didn't win the client, read these lists and remind yourself that you have not failed but are merely going through one of life's learning experiences.

Reward yourself. Don't forget those important incentives. Give yourself something desirable when you succeed, to help you over those times when you don't. And do not wait until you win a big sale before giving yourself something nice. Think up incentives for each sales stage to give you a boost during each step of the journey as you move along toward your final goal.

Failure is part of sales—part of life. Whether it is crippling or empowering is up to you. "The only one who ever put a label of failure on you is yourself," notes Omar Periu, CEO of Omar Periu International in Boca Raton, FL. "I find that most people who go to sleep with a negative hangover wake up with one. Avoid putting yourself down. Use positive affirmation, self-talk, meditation."

Closing

A HANDS-ON GUIDE FOR MANAGERS

TRAINING GUIDE TIME REQUIRED: 60 MINUTES

CLOSE MORE SALES

Most traditional courses in closing business emphasize the ABC (Always Be Closing) strategy. Old techniques advise salespeople to constantly and repeatedly ask for the business, in order to give the customer multiple points at which to say yes. Over the years, closes have been categorized—the Ben Franklin close, the Yes Set close, and many others.

But times have changed, or at least sales practices have shifted, and customers don't like being hammered to buy. The ABC strategy, says Linda Richardson, president of Richardson, creates a sense of pressure, which inevitably creates resistance to the sale because the customer doesn't want to feel that the salesperson is more interested in the sale than in meeting the customer's needs. If customers succumb to pressure and are disappointed, they inevitably resent the salesperson and often find a way to get out of the deal and not to do business

> **Old techniques advise salespeople to constantly and repeatedly ask for the business, in order to give the customer multiple points at which to say yes.**

with that salesperson again. If a company wants a long-term relationship with a customer, high-pressure closes and the ABC strategy are likely to do more harm than good.

That being said, the old ABC strategy has one benefit—it encourages otherwise reluctant salespeople to actually attempt to close. There are many salespeople who don't close to avoid rejection, being pushy, or closing down what they want to believe is a viable opportunity. However, the primary reason most salespeople resist closing is that they haven't gotten feedback from the client about whether it's safe to close. Absent that essential information, closing becomes a "moment of truth" rather than the natural extension of a productive conversation with the customer.

Salespeople can close more business and build stronger customer relationships if they follow an "Always Be Checking to Close" strategy. By treating closing as a process that happens throughout the dialogue with the customer, salespeople gain the confidence to close and thus increase their close ratio. By asking for feedback on what they present to clients, salespeople have a better idea of how the client is likely to respond when it finally comes time to close.

Richardson suggests these five steps:

Step 1: Cultivate the Right Mind-Set

Great closers believe that the clock has only one time—right now. If they get a lead, they're on that lead immediately, and they follow up flawlessly. If you want to close, you've also got to torque up your sense of persistence. If there are three salespeople competing for the same business, the better closer is on top of the opportunity at the start and in follow-up; for example, sending a tailored follow-up letter or e-mail to the customer within one day of the meeting. Closers are vigilant and inexhaustible in their follow-up. They're good at dialogue and possess the skill and confidence to know how and when to ask for the sale. More important, they realize that it's almost always a mistake to close a sale that, in the long run, does not meet the customer's needs and will alienate the customer and damage the relationship or the company's reputation.

Step 2: Set the Objective for the Customer Meeting

Whenever you call on a customer, have an objective that is specific, measurable, and appropriately aggressive. Specific objectives aren't feel-good goals, such as, "I will get closer to the customer." They're goals that can be easily assessed and measured, such as, "I will get a list of the key decision makers," or, "I will ask for the business." Objectives should be aggressive, but appropriate to the stage of the sales cycle. For example, on a first sales call for a complex multimillion dollar deal with multiple decision makers, it would be overly aggressive to set an objective such as, "I will close the deal today." Setting objectives doesn't mean that you can't be flexible and adjust the goal while you're in the meeting. But a great closer always has a direction and understands where the meeting needs to go in order to maintain momentum and win the deal.

Step 3: Constantly Check to See if You're on Target

Throughout the meeting, keep the customer involved. During the meeting you will, of course, identify the customer's objectives, strategy, decision process, time frames, and so on and position your ideas, products, or solutions to satisfy those needs. That's the customer-focused sales process. However, you must also ask "checking" questions to get feedback from the client about what you've said throughout the call. Asking open-ended, nonleading checking questions allows you to gauge how the customer is responding and to adjust your solution accordingly. Most important, this checking process will give you the information you need to confidently close.

Effective checking does not involve leading questions, such as, "Does that make sense to you?" or, "Do you agree?" With leading questions, customers will often take the easy way out and nod along, without really agreeing. Instead, ask checking questions such as, "How does that sound?" or, "What do you think?" Unlike leading questions, checking questions encourage the customer to provide you with frank, vital information.

INEFFECTIVE:

Salesperson: We have a first-rate delivery capability in all key markets. (The salesperson did not check after expressing this view.)

Client: How do you handle invoicing? (The conversation has moved on, and the salesperson has no idea whether the customer agrees or disagrees with the "first-rate delivery" assertion.)

EFFECTIVE:

Salesperson: We have a first-rate delivery capability in all key markets. How do you think that might be useful?

Client: I'm concerned you can't meet our global needs.

Salesperson: I understand how important global capabilities are to you. Why do you feel we may not be able to meet them?

TIPS ON CLOSING

QUICK TIP

Explain that the key concepts are to treat closing as a process, not an event, and to create a dialogue that gets feedback through checking.

As the manager, if you treat role-playing as serious, so will your sales team. Most salespeople crave feedback that will help them close.

When you role-play the close, let the salespeople give one another feedback and then give you feedback. Ask each salesperson to give one strength and one area for improvement when he or she gives feedback.

Drive home the idea that salespeople should end every call with an action step that moves the sales forward.

Client: We want feet on the street, and you don't have international offices.

Salesperson: It is important to have people where you need them. For that reason, we have partnerships with the top companies in regions where we don't have our own offices. Would that address your concern?

Client: It might, providing you can invoice centrally. (The salesperson is learning what the client thinks and repositioning his company's capability in order to build toward the eventual close.)

Every time you position your products and services, you must check to get feedback. The best part about constantly checking is that if you do it correctly, the client will often preemptively close the sale for you by saying, "So, when do we start?" However, if the customer does not preemptively close, then you MUST move to close or you will lose ground and possibly the entire deal.

Step 4: Make a Final Check for Understanding

You've positioned your products or services so that the customer understands how they meet his or her needs up to now. You've used checking to get feedback to make sure there is agreement and understanding. Now comes the mechanics of the close. First, give the customer a concise, powerful summary that reiterates the benefits of your products or services. Once you've done this, make one final check—not for understanding but for agreement.

SALES REPS' FREQUENTLY ASKED QUESTIONS ON CLOSING AND ANSWERS TO TWO OF THE MOST COMMON CLOSING QUESTIONS

Q: When should I use "trick" closes?

A: Never. Trick closes create a high-pressure sales environment, hurt your credibility, won't work with savvy customers, and can offend customers by implying that they are too naïve to see through an obvious attempt to manipulate. Trick closes tend to block sales rather than close them. Avoid the following:

☑ **ASSUMPTIVE CLOSE:** The assumptive close is when the salesperson asks a question which, when the customer answers it, commits the customer to the sale. For example, "Shall we start Tuesday or Wednesday?"

☑ **FLY-FISHING CLOSE:** The fly-fishing close is when the salesperson promises the customers a special offer, such as a 15 percent discount, that's valid only if the customer buys now.

☑ **PUPPY-DOG CLOSE:** In the puppy-dog close, the salesperson offers a free trial, after which the product can be returned. The salesperson is, of course, gambling that the customer will either become attached to the product or, worst case, forget to return it.

☑ **REVERSE CLOSE:** With the reverse close, the salesperson asks a question that elicits a "no" response, but which is actually a "yes" to the close. For example, "Is there any reason, if we gave you the product at this price, that you wouldn't do business with our company?"

It is the intent that makes these closes so destructive. If a free trial is appropriate (as it is with many products), then you should not hesitate to offer it. Similarly, discounts are fine so long as they're not being used as a way to pressure the customer to buy quickly.

Q: How can I avoid being pushy?

A: Treat closing as a process. Start before you meet with your customer by setting your objective for the call. Your objective is the action step or the next step you will ask for at the end of the call.

☑ Always maintain momentum at the end of each call by having the next step specifically in place or by asking for the business.

☑ Always check for feedback throughout the call, to gauge how you are doing.

☑ Always end every letter, phone call, and meeting by saying you hope to work with the customer, to plant the seed.

☑ Always keep the action step in your court. It is your job to follow up.

Salesperson: Our worldwide service capability will allow your employees access anywhere they travel, at a cost that's significantly less than you're spending today. How does that meet your objective?

The purpose of this final check is to seek a green light to go for the close. The final check also gives the customer the opportunity to surface any final objections that might interfere with your close. If a final objection surfaces, handle it, and then restate the final check.

QUICK TIPS

Here are the key questions that your team members should be asking themselves:

QUICK TIP

1. How would I rate myself as a closer?

2. Am I cultivating the right attitude to close business on a daily basis?

3. Am I dependent upon high-pressure sales techniques?

4. Have I ever delayed closing because I wanted to enjoy the fantasy of getting the business?

5. What would it be worth to me if I could easily and simply close more business?

Step 5: Ask for the Business

Now it's time to be direct and to ask for the business or next step. This must be done confidently and clearly.

Salesperson: We are ready to start. Will you give us the go-ahead?

If the customer declines, acknowledge that fact to the customer and then find out why. As appropriate, make a second effort. Regardless of whether you actually closed, end the meeting with confidence, energy, and rapport to make a positive last impression. Thank the client for the business or reinforce the desire to work with the client. Follow up immediately.

LINDA RICHARDSON was interviewed for this article. She is president and CEO of Richardson, a seminar and e-learning sales-training firm that employs 110 professionals worldwide. Her customers include KPMG, FedEx, GlaxoSmithKline, Tiffany & Co., Dell Computer, Kinko's, Cisco, and JPMorgan Chase. She's the author of nine books, including *The Sales Success Handbook—20 Lessons to Open and Close Sales Now* (McGraw Hill). Her company is located at 1818 Market St., Suite 2800, Philadelphia, PA 19103. Telephone: 215-940-9255. Web: www.richardson.com.

SALES MANAGER'S MEETING GUIDE

Use the following 12 practical steps to help you and your team learn how to close more effectively. This sales meeting should take no longer than an hour.

1. Three days prior to the meeting, send a message to all team members asking them to write a description of one of their customers. This description should include the name of the customer organization, the name and title of the key decision maker, and a sentence or two about the customer's needs. This task should take no more than five minutes for the salesperson to complete.

2. Review the responses and select the one that most closely resembles the type of customer that is a priority for your firm. Ask the salesperson who described that customer to role-play the customer during the sales meeting. Emphasize that this will be an important team-building exercise and that you will greatly appreciate the extra effort.

3. Prior to the meeting, make handout copies of the five-step process described in the article for each participant.

4. Open the meeting by explaining the rules. Explain that the objective is to provide a framework for closing—whether asking for the next step or asking for the business. Explain that the secondary objective is to increase the team's confidence and improve its close ratio. Distribute the handout.

5. Have all participants read the handout on the five-step process for effective closing. Conduct a brief discussion of the concept to help ensure that the participants are willing to learn to close in the manner described.

6. Have the salesperson playing the "customer" briefly describe the sales opportunity. Have each participant select a strategic objective and write it on a worksheet. Ask for a volunteer to make a sales call on the "customer." Have the volunteer state his or her objective. Ask the group and the "customer" to critique (and tighten) the objective so it is measurable within a time frame.

7. Ask the volunteer to position a feature and benefit tailored to the needs of the "customer," and to state it as if the volunteer were speaking to the real-world customer. It is likely the volunteer will not check for feedback, i.e., "How does that sound to you?" or, "How would that work here?" Explain how checking will help adjust the solution and close the business. Repeat until the checking process seems to proceed naturally out of the conversation.

8. Ask the volunteer to close with a summary, a final check, and then by asking for the next step or by asking for the business (depending on the objective). Have the group and the "customer" evaluate the attempt to close and refine these elements to make them more effective.

9. Ask participants to form two-person teams to practice closing on each other, based on the work that they completed prior to the meeting. Have the participants complete worksheets based upon their performance with their teammates.

10. Summarize the five-step closing process and encourage participants to self-evaluate their closing performance during their next few customer visits.

11. Have participants assess where they are in the sales cycle with their five top prospects. Get commitment from them to use the process with these customers and closes (i.e., for the next specific step to maintain the momentum or ask for the business).

12. One week after the meeting, follow up with your team to debrief the impact of setting an action objective, checking, and closing. Share success stories among the group at the next sales meeting.

HOW TO TAKE THE SALE FROM LEVEL ONE TO THE FINAL STEP—THE CLOSE

ADDITIONAL READING

Despite major advancements in the psychology of buying and the emergence of such approaches as "consultative selling" and "question-based selling," many salespeople still rely on outdated techniques to try to convince their prospects to buy things they don't want for more than they can comfortably pay.

Why?

The answer is simple: Some salespeople still view closing as a stage in an adversarial relationship, separate from the rest of the sales cycle. Closing becomes something they have to force upon their prospects or face the possibility of failure. The focus of the relationship is on how to get the customer to sign on the dotted line, no matter what.

But salespeople force a close at the risk of alienating their prospects. "I think buyers have become a little too sophisticated for that," says Mike Norcia, senior account executive for Caltronics, an office equipment company in California. As a result, the most successful salespeople know there is another, better way to look at closing. Here's what the pros tell us:

☑ **CLOSE WHEN THE CUSTOMER IS READY.** Probably the best answer to the question, "When do I close?" is, "When your customer is ready to." No matter how great your gift of

---

EXPERT ADVICE: CATCH THE SIGNAL

EXPERT ADVICE

"If you're skilled at reading your prospect's verbal and nonverbal signals, you'll have a pretty good idea of how he or she feels about you and your product before you ask," says Linda Richardson, founder and CEO of sales training and consulting firm Richardson and author of *The Sales Success Handbook* (McGraw-Hill). "Customers do give closing signals," she says. Here's what to look for:

Positive nonverbal signs:

☑ Arms wide open means the prospect is receptive to you.

☑ Looking intently at you means he or she is listening to you.

☑ Legs crossed toward you means engagement.

☑ Leaning toward you means the customer is with you.

Positive verbal signs:

☑ The customer asks about pricing.

☑ The prospect visualizes him- or herself using the product.

☑ He or she compliments the product.

"All of these are indicators," says Richardson. "That's the time to check in and go for the close."

gab, you can't make buyers buy any sooner than they want to—at least, not without some pretty nasty results. Depending on prospects' own internal timeline and needs, they may be prepared to move forward sooner or later. It's up to you to determine where they are and how ready they are, based on their responses to your questions.

☑ **CLOSE WHEN YOU UNDERSTAND THE PROSPECT.** Many newer salespeople think mainly about their needs—in other words, the need to make the sale—rather than the needs of the customer. This is a big mistake, says John Sable, vice president of Sales for B2B lead generation firm InTouch. The only way to know when your customers are ready to buy is by listening to them. "You have to be open to understanding what their need really is. You have to keep the perspective that it's absolutely about the clients' needs first. The sale is the by-product of a dialogue," he explains.

☑ **CLOSE CONSTANTLY.** "Closing is not an event; it's a process," says Sable. Closing doesn't occur just at the end of the sales cycle, but throughout the relationship with your customers, as you identify and meet their wants and needs. You should be closing all the time on smaller points as you narrow the field for your customer. If you wait for a moment in time where he or she is "ready," you're looking at closing the wrong way.

☑ **CLOSE ONE STEP AT A TIME.** View the journey to the sale as a trip you're taking together, and you're the tour guide. "The actual moment you make the sale may be anticlimactic—just the next step in the process," says Norcia. "Don't ask for the whole deal right off the bat; ask for the next step," he recommends. Sable agrees: "You have to get a whole bunch of small yeses before you get the big yes."

☑ **CLOSE WHEN YOU NEED AN ANSWER.** Sometimes it's tough to tell just where your prospects are in their buying cycle. "If you feel you've got a good understanding of their business and needs, and you've positioned your solution accordingly, don't be afraid to ask for the next level of commitment," advises Norcia. "If you put customers on the spot, they'll have to either move forward or tell you why they don't want to," he explains. "They're normally pretty transparent at that point as to what their next step will be," he says.

☑ **CLOSE WHEN YOU'RE DONE TALKING.** "Closing" doesn't mean "talking." You should say just enough to keep the prospect talking, and no more. "The key is to not overtalk," says Norcia. "If they're in the game and you've overtalked, they start to fade out. If you overtalk, they will get to the point where they just want you to leave." If you find yourself talking and talking, it may be time to ask the prospect to take the next step.

Determining that your prospect is ready to move forward doesn't mean much if you let the moment pass without taking advantage of it. No matter how prepared your customer is, it's up to you to ask for the next step. Norcia recalls a time early in his career when he'd met with a prospect and gone through his spiel. The prospect kept asking, "So, what else does it do?" Norcia responded each time with another list of features. "He must have asked me that 10 times," he says. Finally, Norcia realized, "he was just waiting for me to say, 'Let's do this.'" That episode taught Norcia an important lesson: "Even if you're not the slickest guy in the world, the guy who asks for the order is going to make more sales."

WHEN PROSPECTS BEG FOR A CLOSE

QUICK
TIP

1. **TERMS OF SALE QUESTIONS.** Here the prospect is trying to determine the total cost of your proposed solution.

   Question: Is delivery included in the price?

   Don't Say: Yes

   Do Say: That depends on how you want it shipped. Would you prefer overnight, which is $50 extra, or standard UPS, which is only $10? How would you like us to ship it?

2. **NARROWING INTEREST.** The prospect is figuring out which product matches his or her needs.

   Question: Does it come in light blue?

   Don't Say: Yes.

   Do Say: Would you like it in light blue?

3. **PROTECTION CONCERN.** The prospect is wondering about coverage in a worst-case scenario.

Question: If the car breaks down during the warranty period, will you provide me with a loaner until its fixed?

Don't Say: Yes.

Do Say: If I can get approval for a loaner for you in that case, would we have a deal?

4. **SEEING IS BELIEVING.** The prospect needs visual proof that your product can do what you say it does.

Question: I'd like to be able to see for myself that this crane can lift a 600-pound load at 28-foot reach.

Don't Say: Sure. I'll set up a demonstration with our operator as soon as possible.

Do Say: Is it critical for you that the crane be able to lift that load? (wait for "yes"). If our machine can handle that load at that distance, will you buy it?

5. **YOUR EAGERNESS IS SHOWING.** The prospect is already mentally taking ownership of the product.

Question: How soon can you deliver it?

Don't Say: In about two weeks.

Do Say: How soon would you like to take delivery?

6. **VALIDATION SEARCH.** The prospect wants references who can verify what you're saying.

Question: Do you know of anyone who has bought this spreader with the eight-foot extension?

Don't Say: Yes, I can give you the names of three satisfied customers.

Do Say: I can provide you with the names of three customers who will confirm that our spreader can handle this type of job. Do you think that after this we can move forward with this plan?

7. **TELL ME AGAIN . . .** The prospect wants to revisit a detail you've already discussed.

Question: Can you refresh my memory about how the service contract works?

Don't Say: Sure . . .

Do Say: It sounds like you're definitely interested in this solution. Are there any other remaining questions besides the service contract?

Picture this. You want to sell a portable HIV test to the Florida Department of Health to use in its field offices. Rather than closing one decision maker, you have to convince an entire committee that your product is the best choice.

ADDITIONAL READING

You find yourself in front of a project manager who wanted the test, a budget analyst with concerns about costs, a lab director needing to compare the accuracy of the test with other current tests, and a field coordinator interested in finding out if the new test is easier to use than a traditional blood test.

Now what? How do you get all these different people to agree? Emanuel Amatrudo, a sales manager for Parsippany, New Jersey-based Innovex, a contract sales organization, knows what it takes.

Research and asking questions are Amatrudo's keys to success. Before meeting with the department's committee, he and his reps followed a plan: First, request a list of all committee members' names and titles. Then anticipate what each participant might ask. If possible, call individual committee members to learn about their concerns.

Amatrudo advises asking questions during individual meetings and committee sessions. For example, a lab specialist and member of the Florida Department of Health committee wanted to know how well the product worked. Could it detect virus levels as effectively as traditional blood sampling? Before answering, Amatrudo's rep asked, "What is it that you believe your current product isn't providing for you? If you could select your ideal product, what would you want it to be or do for you?

"Focus on why you are there," urges Amatrudo. "Your committee summary should address each member's concerns, showing how your product is the solution to their problems—the inevitable choice."

Before concluding his meeting with the committee, Amatrudo says, "If there is a question or concern that I haven't addressed, ask it now." He also adds, "Is there any reason why my product or service wouldn't be a benefit to you?" If the committee members start comparing other products, he acknowledges their strengths but emphasizes the unique value of his product, his company, and his sales team's training service.

Before approaching a committee, Amy Aycock, national account manager for strategic accounts for Islandia, New York-based Computer Associates International, starts by asking herself three questions: Do I understand each committee member's role or position in the purchasing process? Am I closing the right person—the one with the authority to make a decision? How well do I understand the approval process and time frames required to complete an order?

She then meets with all committee members individually to learn their hidden objections. What is a personal and professional benefit her product or service can offer each individual? What problems does that person have that she can solve? What will happen if those problems aren't solved?

Aycock's success relies on building relationships and finding an advocate on the committee who wants what she offers. This person sees her product or service as offering a personal and professional benefit. At one company, Aycock recalls, her advocate was a key decision maker who would get a bonus and more time at home if her proposal was accepted.

The advocate also can be an internal coach who helps you understand the corporate culture, the status of your proposal, and who needs to be won over. Aycock recalls, "I was trying to close a 10-person committee. Five people wanted a different solution from mine. My advocate told me three people were concerned about implementation. So I brought in an implementation consultant from my company to address their concerns and show how they could implement my solution within their time limit."

Not doing your homework can cost you the sale. Amatrudo remembers when he sold insurance. "I made a presentation to a small company in Manhattan about changing its health insurance benefits, but I wasn't prepared. I didn't find out who would be at the meeting, why they wanted to change their health insurance, or what they were looking for. I just went in, did my presentation, and recommended they switch to my company. When the company's health-care analyst pointed out that my program cost more and delivered less service than their present program, the meeting was over and I had lost the sale."

Amatrudo learned his lesson. "After licking my wounds, I went to another company on the other side of Manhattan. I asked all the questions I should have asked the last time and used the answers to close that company. It remained one of my accounts for five years."

FIVE STEPS TO CLOSING A COMMITTEE

Speaker and trainer Robert Ayrer emphasizes the ABCs of closing: Always Be Closing. He defines closing as achieving your sales objective as opposed to getting the order and fleeing. "You don't get a buy decision from a committee," says Ayrer. "Purchasing agents only make sourcing decisions. Your goal is to create customers, not make sales. The sale isn't made until you deliver the promised product or service and the customer pays you."

Any committee member can say no and kill your proposal, but you won't generally get everyone to agree on a yes decision.

Ayrer recommends a five-step strategy for closing a committee:

STEP 1: HAVE A CLEAR STRATEGY AND DOABLE OBJECTIVE. What issues will affect the company's decision? Who will be involved in the decision? You won't get an order from a committee. The best you can expect is to advance the sale.

STEP 2: KNOW EACH COMMITTEE MEMBER'S NAME, ROLE, AND RELATION TO WHAT YOU ARE SELLING. How will each one be affected?

STEP 3: CULTIVATE YOUR CHAMPION. Look for the person with the most to gain by using what you sell.

STEP 4: USE YOUR CHAMPION TO HELP YOU DESIGN A STRATEGY AND PRESENTATION THAT MEETS EVERY COMMITTEE MEMBER'S NEEDS. All members will get what they want, and you will avoid any noes.

STEP 5: GET YOUR CHAMPION EMPOWERED TO WORK OUT THE DETAILS. After asking the committee, "Does that answer all of your questions and concerns?" continue with, "If so, can we agree that I can get together with [give your champion's name] and work out the details of the implementation schedule, financing, maintenance contract, and any other areas of concern?"

ROBERT AYRER is with REA Performance Consultants in Huntington Beach, CA, and works with manufacturers and distributors involved in business-to-business selling. Visit www.improvingsales.com or e-mail perform@improvingsales.com.

ADDITIONAL READING

You've worked hard with a prospect, and now it's time to give the presentation that will win the sale. What will be your pièce de résistance? The close. "When you close, it's time to let customers know how you can serve them—not sell to them.

"If you have been good at your job of presenting, so that customers see you as offering a service that will meet their needs, you don't need a closing line at all—the client will ask you for the business," says Harlan Porter, sales associate with Len Dudas Motors in Stevens Point, WI. "It is important to remember that when you are closing, you are not just selling the product; you are asking for the customer's trust, and you are selling your whole company."

> "If you have been good at your job of presenting, so that customers see you as offering a service that will meet their needs, you don't need a closing line at all—the client will ask you for the business."

In sales, the most common close traditionally has been to end a presentation by asking for the business. However, the most effective closing lines are those that flow naturally from the presentation and address each individual customer's needs. "The most useful closing lines I know are not really set lines," Porter says. "Every situation is different, and I want to say something that is personal to the customer."

From the beginning, create the right mood to encourage customers to buy. "In building toward the closing, it's important to set up a positive atmosphere," Porter advises. "Learn about their needs, and then set up a series of questions that will elicit 'yes' answers."

In fact, knowing what's important to customers cannot be stressed enough, Porter says. "If image is important to a business and I am selling Cadillacs, I might ask, 'When you are interviewing a power client and you want to take them out to dinner, a sign of success would be taking them to that dinner in a Cadillac, right?'"

In his closings Porter uses key words that convey a sense of urgency and strike a chord with issues that customers found particularly interesting during the presentation. "If safety is what was important to them, then safety is what should be stressed in the closing," he says.

Building trust and learning customers' needs is even more challenging when selling over the telephone. Peter G. Smith, an inside phone-sales representative for Rush Computer Rentals in Laurel, MD, creates trust with his voice, using the right tone and pace. Delivery of the entire conversation, from the initial questions to the close, is important. Smith emphasizes, "I want to appear unhurried and calm."

Smith also says that a good close flows from knowledge of the customer's needs. In Smith's business the customer, which can be a three-person firm or a corporation the size of TRW, often calls with an urgent need—(x) Number of computers or a server by the next day, for instance. "It is my job to weed out their needs from their wants," he explains. "Most of the time I deal with short-fuse issues—a product they need right away and they must make a decision quickly. It is my job to know what we have and discern what they need, so I can make a good match for them."

Callers may ask for equipment and configurations that Smith does not have available. However, he probes and discovers whether another system or configuration will really do the job for them. "I have to determine if we have what they ask for, or if an alternative solution will actually meet their needs and make the customers feel at ease."

In all cases, the closing line must be phrased in terms of the customers' needs and delivered in terms the customers understand. "My closing line needs to be direct —I must ask if they want to place the order and ask in a way that coincides with their way of speaking and doing business. For example, if that firm operates with purchase orders, I might ask if they want me to follow up with their accounting office. If they use corporate charge cards, I might say, 'Do you want me to put that on your corporate charge today?'"

THE TITAN PRINCIPLE

EXPERT ADVICE

A good close may get customers to finally agree to buy, but all of the work beforehand makes that magic moment possible. "Sales is a process, not a single action," says Ron Karr, president of Karr Associates in Fort Lee, NJ. "There are several of what I call minor closes in each part of the selling process— things that seal your ability to influence the customer. Each sale, no matter how big or small, is the sum total of all of the minor closes you've made along the way. Getting to the ultimate closing line that solidifies the agreement to buy is a part of the process, the result of positioning yourself with the right strategy from the beginning."

"It's important to see the closing as a natural part of the sales process," Karr says. Each step during the process builds another layer of trust into the relationship between the buyer and the salesperson. "The closing line is much more than a single question," he emphasizes. "The process of selling the close actually begins as soon as you say hello to potential buyers. You need to gain their trust so that you can explain your product and service and then agree on it. It's a part of a tactical approach—a process that ends with an agreement to buy."

Structuring the process begins with a good first impression and salespeople ready to listen to customers and discover what they need. "Purchases involve change," says Karr. "The role of the salesperson is to make that process of change easier. Ask questions about the customers' goals and challenges. Become a resource even before you speak about the services you have to offer. Gain their trust. Concentrate more on positioning yourself as a valued resource than on describing features. Spend more time on qualifying than on explaining features. Then you can show how certain features meet their specific needs."

"Nevertheless, while explaining all of the features is 'the obvious thing' during a presentation, a 'features' presentation is not enough," Karr points out. "People do not want you to sell to them. They want help in buying. The Internet is a great leveler. It provides easy access to information about a number of products and gives them the opportunity to shut out a hard sell."

"In the closing, include material covered in the presentation, especially issues that are important to the customer," advises Karr. "If you rely on material that you just covered, you will be following a logical step and your close will be a part of a natural conversation."

Karr, author of *The Titan Principle: The Number One Secret to Sales Success* (Chandler House Press), explains, "My Titan Principle is that the business goes to individuals and organizations that give customers what they need, the way they want it. When salespeople become a resource, they are selling outcomes, not products or services. That approach shows how what they are offering meets the customer's goals."

"It's about winning the war, not just one battle. The closing line presents a solution to their needs, makes this change one that furthers their goals. In addition, your work with them will make the transition period smooth. All of this information builds to the agreement process, which is more than a single closing line."

The sales process that relies on larger issues will often bring an invitation to sell from the customer. In other words, Karr says, "My favorite closing line is none at all—it is a request to buy, from the customers. This happens when you have presented a solution to their needs so that they want to purchase. You have shown that what you offer is what is missing; it's what is needed for them to achieve their goals and will allow them to reach the next higher level in their business. That is a good closing."

RON KARR is a professional consultant, speaker, and president of New Jersey-based Karr Associates. For more information, call 1-800-423-5277 or e-mail ron@ronkarr.com.

Another key to a winning close is silence—giving the customer time to think things over. After Porter concludes the closing and asks for the business, he simply says nothing. "I keep quiet. Even if it is three minutes or more, I've learned to be comfortable," he says. "This is the time that gives the customer the opportunity to respond."

Tom McCartney, sales manager for RW Mercer Company in Jackson, MI, agrees. "While I leave it up to each of the 14 people on my staff to determine their own style of closing, I do advise them to be explicit about asking for the sale and then to end the sales presentation with a moment of silence." McCartney notes that the quiet interlude not only allows the customer to think about what was said, but also leaves the next move up to the customer. "You don't want to oversell, but of course, we don't want them to leave the meeting without an indication of the success of their bid," McCartney points out.

Porter admits that he has "enormous return clientele." What's his secret? "Don't promise more than you and your company can deliver," he advises. "I often walk a customer through the service department before the close. I often say outright, and certainly want to convey to each buyer, that their buying experience is just the beginning of their relationship with me."

CLOSING TIPS

QUICK TIP

Following are a few out-of-the-ordinary strategies you can use to persuade customers to put pen to paper:

1. Looking for one phrase to reassure customers that you will always do right by them? Try this: "I will spend your money as if it were my own."

2. As you close, hold up a $50 bill, tear it in half and give one half to the customer. Then hold up the remaining half and say, "If you can find a better value for your money, I'll give you the other half."

3. Put it in writing. Print up a list of services you can personally guarantee to the customer: "I will return all phone calls the same business day," "I will always treat your time as a precious commodity," for example. Offer this sheet to the customer in exchange for the business.

Attitude Motivation

 **A HANDS-ON GUIDE FOR MANAGERS**

TRAINING GUIDE TIME REQUIRED: 20 MINUTES

DEVELOP A POSITIVE ATTITUDE

Most sales professionals understand that a positive attitude—comprising optimism, expectancy, and enthusiasm—is a key element, perhaps *the* key element, of top sales performance. Despite knowing this, most sales professionals find it extraordinarily difficult to approach work with a positive attitude each and every day. This is because they wrongly believe that one's attitude is the result of external circumstances rather than something that is under their own control.

Attitude is not the result of what happens in the world but how one decides to interpret what happens in the world. Take the weather, for example. In the United States, many people feel depressed when it's raining and uplifted when it's sunny. In the Middle East, many people feel the exact opposite—a cooling rain is an excuse to have a picnic under a tree. Similarly, many adults grumble when it snows while most children are delighted. This illustrates that one's attitude toward the weather is essentially arbitrary. It's not the weather but the interpretation of what the weather means that creates the attitude.

> **In short, attitude is the mental filter through which one sees the world. Some see the world through a filter of optimism . . . Others see the world through a filter of pessimism.**

Arguing that children like snow because they don't have to go to school is missing the point. A snowbound child could just as easily mope around inside and complain about not being able to play croquet because it's snowing. Similarly, a sales rep making a sales call while it's snowing could grouse about the extra drive time or could look forward to the appreciation a customer might feel because the sales rep was committed enough to fight the weather to make the meeting.

In short, attitude is the mental filter through which one sees the world. Some see the world through a filter of optimism: no matter what happens they always make lemonade from the lemons. Every truly great sales professional thinks this way. Others see the world through a filter of pessimism: no matter what happens, they always find the cloud and not the silver lining. People who think this way are usually terrible at sales.

Most sales reps, however, don't belong to either extreme. Instead, most sales reps (indeed, most people) have a variable filter that creates resourceful attitudes and nonresourceful ones based upon arbitrary interpretations of events. The challenge is to trade their variable and out-of-control mental filter for a consciously optimistic filter. This will consistently create the attitude that results in top sales performance. The rest of this chapter examines four methods for accomplishing this feat.

Method 1: Redefine the Meaning of External Events

Sales reps who have trouble maintaining a positive attitude are almost always letting arbitrary external events automatically trigger bad feelings. For example, a sales rep might become annoyed and defensive prior to a customer call simply by running into a series of red lights during the drive. To that sales rep, the red lights mean that it's an unlucky day. As a result, the sales rep walks into the customer meeting feeling depressed and defensive.

To get a different result, you must modify your interpretation of external events that formerly triggered your bad attitude. Once those events have a different meaning, they won't be able to trigger a bad attitude. For example, the sales rep above might see a series of red lights as an indication of how smart it was to leave early for the call. Or, if the sales rep is late because of the delays, the red lights can be an opportunity to collect thoughts and decide upon a damage-control strategy.

Many sales professionals view so-called failures—lost sales, missed calls, bad prospects—as triggers for bad attitude. However, it's also possible to view failures as learning experiences that point out the adjustments you must make in order to be more successful. Rather than become irritated at a failure, it makes more sense to consider that, if you never failed, it would mean that you were taking no risks. Even the best sales rep doesn't close every sale. If you make it your business to learn from every setback and stay focused on your end result, failure simply becomes a way station on the road to success.

Method 2: Start Each Day with at Least 15 Minutes of Positive Input

It's easier to achieve and maintain a positive attitude if you have a library of positive thoughts in your head. Starting each day reading, or listening, helps ensure that you have such a library to draw upon. Consider reading an inspirational book right after you wake

SALES REPS' FREQUENTLY ASKED QUESTIONS

Q: What if I just don't feel all that great today? Should I just fake it?

A: Your attitude is largely based upon your focus. Regardless of what's going on in your life, it's possible for you to focus on something positive, which motivates you to achieve your goals. Unless something really disastrous happens to you (news of a major illness or death in the family) or you suffer from clinical depression, the statement, "I don't feel terrific," is simply another way of saying, "I'm too lazy to get myself into a good mood."

Q: My boss/spouse/friend/relative really needs to know about this. How can I get them to change?

A: Mark Twain said it best: "Nothing needs reforming more than somebody else's bad habits." The truth is you really can't get somebody else to change. The best you can do is hold yourself to such a high standard that those around you notice how you've changed for the better. Once you've become a role model, you can answer questions about how you've managed this new level of personal success.

Q: I know successful people who aren't positive all the time and who often mistreat the people around them. How do you explain their success?

A: Successful people—even if they seem obnoxious or negative at times—have a positive attitude about their own abilities. In other words, an obnoxious but successful sales manager is usually convinced that he or she will be successful in sales. They are positive about that. However, being successful in sales does not guarantee that you'll have superior people skills, or that you'll be well liked. Of course, these people would probably be even more successful if they weren't obnoxious to those around them.

up. You might also want to spend your commute time listening to motivational tapes rather than the news. Set a target of at least 15 minutes a day. If you commit more time than this, you'll get more benefits.

Along these lines, don't forget that music is a time-honored way to manage your moods and attitudes. Consider investing in CDs of music that you find motivating and energizing. Use music to pump yourself up right before your big meetings or to cool you down when things get challenging.

**QUICK
TIP**

QUICK TIPS FOR YOUR TRAINING SESSION

If team members aren't getting the best results or have been discouraged by repeated failures, suggest that they ask themselves the following questions:

1. **DO I HAVE AN UNREALISTIC TIMETABLE?** Success is usually achieved one step at a time. Be patient with yourself, and resist the temptation to compare your progress to that of others.

2. **AM I TRULY COMMITTED?** Be willing to do whatever it takes (within legal and ethical bounds) to banish any thought of giving up before you accomplish your objective.

3. **DO I HAVE TOO MANY DISCOURAGING INFLUENCES?** Surround yourself with people who support and believe in you. If you spend time with people who are highly critical or who are doing very little in their own lives, your energy and enthusiasm will be drained.

4. **AM I PREPARING TO SUCCEED?** Are you taking steps to learn everything you can about accomplishing your goal? Are you reading books, listening to tapes, taking courses, and networking with highly successful people in your field? Do you need a mentor or a coach?

5. **AM I TRULY WILLING TO FAIL?** In most cases, you will encounter setbacks before you finally succeed. When you are not afraid to fail, you're well on the way to success—view failure as an unavoidable component in your quest.

Method 3: Reduce Your Exposure to Broadcast News Media

Our mass media culture bombards us with highly emotional messages that are intended to lead us to buy a particular product. Such mental manipulation is fairly obvious when it comes to television commercials (e.g., using sex to sell beer), but there are more subtle influences that can be highly toxic to your overall attitude about life. In particular, overexposure to the news media can be a real killer of a positive attitude.

Thirty years ago, news programs primarily provided people with information intended to help them understand the issues of the day. Today, most news broadcasts consist of "infotainment" specifically crafted to support commercial messages. Much of today's news programming consists of if-it-bleeds-it-leads stories followed by commercials offering some form of security or comfort. The idea is to amp up your fear, anger, or frustration

SALES MANAGER'S MEETING GUIDE

Below are 12 practical steps to improve your team's ability to cultivate
a positive attitude that will result in better sales. This sales meeting should
take about 20 minutes.

1. One month before this training session, make a commitment—and keep it—to follow the four methods described in the article. Maintain a positive attitude for most of the month. This is important because unless you're a positive role model, any attempt on your part to encourage a positive attitude in your sales team will probably fail.

2. Explain to team members that the meeting is going to be about attitude. Tell them that there won't be any grading of performance and that the exercise is entirely for their own private benefit. However, suggest that they take this information seriously, because it will be important to their long-term success in sales.

3. Spend five minutes explaining the basic principles of attitude and how important attitude is to sales success. Illustrate this point with anecdotes from your own experience and observation.

4. Have the team take out writing materials. Ask members to rate their attitude on a scale of 1 to 10 (1 is extremely negative, and 10 is extremely positive). They should base their score on how the majority of the people in their life would rate them. Then ask the team members to estimate where their level of attitude would have to be in order for them to become top sales performers.

5. Explain how most people use events to trigger a poor attitude and how it's possible to redefine the meaning of events. Have each team member write down a daily event that tends to trigger a bad attitude. Then have them write a new meaning for (or new interpretation of) that event that will not trigger the bad attitude. Offer to help anyone who has problems with this step.

6. Have the team members list all the mass media they hear and see during a typical day. (This should include television programs, radio shows, newspapers, magazines, training materials, motivational tapes, etc.)

7. After they complete this, have them imagine that they've just experienced each of these media. Have them put an up arrow beside media experiences that make them feel positive, a down arrow next to experiences that make them feel negative, and a straight arrow next to neutral experiences.

8. Ask the team members to estimate the amount (on a scale of 1 to 10) their average attitude would change if they eliminated negative media inputs.

9. Have the team members list 10 friends and colleagues with whom they spend time every week. Have them imagine that they've spent time with each of these people. Have them mark an arrow (up, down, or straight) next to each person's name, depending on the impact that person has on the team member's attitude.

10. Ask the team members to estimate the amount (on a scale of 1 to 10) their average attitude would change if they spent half as much time with the people who earned a down arrow and twice as much time with the people who earned an up arrow.

11. Explain how following the four methods to achieving a better attitude has positively influenced your own life over the past month. Point out that everyone is different, and everyone must make his or her own decisions about how much or how little time to spend on maintaining a positive attitude.

12. Reassure the team members that they're not going to be judged on how they maintain a positive attitude, but suggest that they take active steps to follow the four methods and close the meeting.

and then suggest an action such as buying comfort food that promises to relieve the pressure.

This constant flow of negative imagery and commentary not only can destroy a positive attitude, but also it can actively create a negative attitude about life and the world. Therefore, if you want to maintain a positive mood, you should consider reducing, or even eliminating, your exposure to broadcast news programming.

Method 4: Avoid People Who Have a Contagious Negative Attitude

Spending time with people who have a negative view of life makes it difficult for you to maintain a positive attitude. You probably have one or more friends, relatives, or acquaintances who make you feel tired and drained. They always seem to have something sour to say; criticisms come to their lips far more quickly than compliments. If you tell them of a success that you've had, their congratulations ring hollow. You sense that they'd just as soon see you fail. What a drag (literally)!

Such people are toxic to your attitude (and to your success in sales) because if they're not actively tearing down your enthusiasm, they're trying to make you think the same way about the world as they do. If you want to maintain a positive attitude, you should consider sharply limiting your daily exposure to such people. Don't show up at the daily "water-cooler complain-fest." Don't go to lunch with the grouse-and-grumble crowd. If you can't avoid these people, don't get drawn into lengthy gripe sessions. Limit your conversation to business issues you need to address and change the subject to a positive topic as soon as possible.

JEFF KELLER was interviewed for this article. Jeff Keller is the author of the best-selling book *Attitude is Everything: Change Your Attitude . . . and You Change Your Life* (International Network Training Institute). Using speeches, seminars, writing, audio programs, and video programs, Keller helps organizations develop achievers by providing specific techniques to foster a more positive, winning attitude. His clients include Allstate Insurance, Merck & Co., Snap-on Inc., Super 8 Motels, and JPMorgan Chase. He may be reached at Attitude is Everything Inc., PO Box 310 East Norwich, NY 11732-0310. Telephone: 1-800-790-5333. Fax: 516-922-7385. Web: www.attitudeiseverything.com.

ADDITIONAL
READING

HOW TO ESTABLISH A CLEAR PATH TO YOUR DESTINATION BY ASKING YOURSELF, WHERE DO I WANT TO GO?

Tryon Edwards said, "Thoughts lead on to purposes; purposes go forth into action; actions form habits; habits decide character; and character fixes destiny."

Recently, while conducting a sales seminar, I asked, "How many of you have written out your goals?" The results were stunning. Of 123 salespeople present, only three admitted to writing down their goals. I find that alarming.

Proper goal setting and good execution of those goals automatically solve many important problems for salespeople. Once goals have been set, the salesperson can translate them into positive action. Then the salesperson automatically becomes well organized by doing things in the order of their importance. Finally, that salesperson develops good working habits and becomes self-disciplined.

> **Proper goal setting and good execution of those goals automatically solve many important problems for salespeople. Once goals have been set, the salesperson can translate them into positive action.**

Goal-minded salespeople never take their minds off of long-range goals, because the penalty—short-term frustrations—can wipe out a haphazard plan. It's simple to set goals and establish a positive track to run on. Yet, in my opinion, 95 percent of salespeople work without any plan to follow. They are merely going this way one day and that way the next day, with no exact target in mind. This is nothing less than sheer folly, since it's as impossible to hit a target you have never seen as it is to return from somewhere you have never been.

William Jennings Bryan commented about goals and destiny by saying, "Destiny is not a matter of chance, it is a matter of choice; it is not a thing to be waited for, it is a thing to be achieved."

Salespeople who have no specific goals that they are interested in and committed to achieving go around in circles feeling lost and professionally purposeless. People who say that life is not worthwhile are really saying that they have no worthwhile goals. Goals should be realistic, personal, and worthy. They should justify the effort it takes to achieve them. They should stand for something worth working for. You should feel proud when you have accomplished them.

To accurately and honestly determine your present situation, know exactly where you now stand, where you want to go, and what you can realistically expect in the future. This does not take into account what you might win in a lottery, where you thought you would be by this time last year, or what you vaguely think you're really worth if only prospects would pay attention to you. Look at yourself honestly and squarely. Ask yourself:

- ☑ What do I want to do and what do I want to be?
- ☑ Do I want a promotion?
- ☑ How far do I want to grow?
- ☑ What are my resources?
- ☑ What are my strengths and where are my weaknesses?
- ☑ How much money do I want to make?
- ☑ What do I have to do to get there?
- ☑ What do I want to provide my family—home, education, car, vacation, insurance?

Make a complete list of the facts and then study it.

To set and define your realistic, worthy goals, use crystallized thinking. Looking at your list, decide your overall major goal. Aim high, have great expectations, but know that every journey begins with a single step, and you will arrive only by putting one foot in front of the other.

The very minute you write out your goals, dedicate yourself to their successful attainment. Imagine yourself succeeding, thus crowding out negative, fearful thoughts. If such thoughts do come into your consciousness, do not try to squelch them, but examine where they come from, deal with them, and then discard them as useless in your overall plan. Don't take negative thoughts personally. Dress and act the part of the successful salesperson you really want to be. Always work and live by faith and be persistent. Persistence by its very nature develops purpose, direction, and courage.

To develop a complete plan of specific activities, determine how you are going to accomplish your major and sustaining goals. Develop a plan of specific activities—what has to be done and how you are going to do it. The more specific you make this stage, the more likely you are to meet your goals. If every point is clearly defined on an hourly, daily, and weekly basis, you geometrically increase your success ratio. Major goals are accomplished by completing the sustaining goals one at a time. Your selling day will be one of organized activity. Visualize in your mind the successful completion of every sustaining goal.

Go at every activity without giving thought to the possibility of defeat. Concentrate on your strengths and not on your weaknesses. Be determined to follow through on every point in your goal achievement plan. You will develop even more self-confidence in your abilities, and following your plan will help you to conquer obstacles and circumstances that might get in your way. Because a heartfelt, burning desire is the most powerful motivator there is, develop your own burning desire.

> **Timetables and deadlines are very important to achieving goals. When do you want to achieve your goals? . . . Write down the actual dates your want these goals to be a reality. Every date should be specific, nothing general, nothing fuzzy.**

Timetables and deadlines are very important to achieving goals. When do you want to achieve your goals? Don't use terms like "a long time," "shortly," "about two years," "sometime in the future," or "possibly six months." Write down the actual dates you want these goals to be a reality. Every date should be specific, nothing general, nothing fuzzy. This stops procrastination and provides you with checkpoints along your path.

Think about what you are really doing when you write out your goals. You are turning intentions into commitments, commitments into involvements, involvements into positive actions. Goals prevent drifting. Remember—where there is no purpose, no progress follows.

To set and achieve your goals, I suggest developing a complete goal blueprint. Since everyone's circumstances are different, use the form here as a guide. Take time right now to build yourself a complete goal outline. Set down your major goal, 10 to 15 sustaining goals, and from 5 to 15 specific activities you must accomplish to reach each sustaining goal.

Major Goal

I will do an outstanding job for the next calendar year by increasing my sales commission or achieving a promotion to (title), so that my total income will be (X). Then, each year thereafter, I will increase my income to (X) over the previous year. This will enable me to purchase (item) by (date), (item) by (date), (item) by (date).

Sustaining Goal #1

To maintain an adequate number of bona fide prospects to keep me busy selling productively all day, every day. Specific activities to do daily, weekly, and monthly include:

1. Devote a minimum of four hours per week to productive prospecting.

2. Develop and maintain close contact with productive centers of influence.

3. Get leads from every person I sell to.

4. Get favorable PR by speaking to one service club or company meeting per month.

5. Prospect at least two hours per week using the telephone.

6. Use the telephone, or use person-to-person contact, to call on five present customers each month and ask each for names of prospects.

Sustaining Goal #2

Make (X) number of face-to-face presentations monthly. Specific activities to do daily, weekly, and monthly include:

1. Fill each day with (X) number of productive appointments.

2. Fill each week with (X) number of productive appointments.

3. Be in the field making calls for (X) number of hours daily, weekly.

4. Do necessary paperwork during nonproductive calling hours.

5. Have available a more-than-adequate number of bona fide prospects each day.

6. Each day make alternate cold calls, to fill in any open time.

7. Make (X) number of face-to-face presentations daily, weekly.

Sustaining Goal #3

Increase the ratio of sales closings. Specific activities to do daily, weekly, and monthly include:

1. Analyze each attempt to sell.

2. Read a book on selling (X) number of minutes per day.

3. Listen to tapes or CDs in between calls.

4. Review and study company sales-training methods (X) number of times weekly.

5. Set up a definite self-improvement program.

Sustaining Goal #4

Make the most productive use of my time. Specific activities to do daily, weekly, and monthly include:

1. Every evening, plan for the best use of time the next day.

2. Phone to firm up all appointments each day.

3. Visit less and spend more time selling on each interview.

4. Permit no nonproductive time during prime selling hours.

5. Daily, weekly, and monthly do things in the order of their importance.

6. Arrange appointments according to their geographical locations.

Sustaining Goal #5

Maintain a positive, enthusiastic attitude. Specific activities to do daily, weekly, and monthly include:

1. Give myself (X) number of pep talks daily.

2. Read one good book on self-improvement every month.

3. Listen daily to inspirational tapes.

4. Keep my mind on the importance of achieving my goals.

5. Be an example of an enthusiastic person.

6. Review my goals daily.

To complete a goal blueprint like this for yourself requires concentrated thought and the effort of writing it down. In the same way that sales calls yield better results when you are prepared—knowing the buyer and the company, knowing the competition and the value of your product—your goal-setting program will prove its worth if you'll give it a chance. Anything that produces real results is worth the effort you put into it.

HOW TO BE INSPIRED AND STAY MOTIVATED THROUGHOUT YOUR CAREER

ADDITIONAL
READING

Every salesperson has motivational hot buttons. What are yours? Fancy cars, more vacation time, winning sales contests, recognition from management and your peers—or simply the personal satisfaction of a job well done?

You might look to your organization and sales manager to keep you going full steam ahead. Perhaps you are a self-motivator.

"What motivates me is attaining a level of professionalism and a belief in my product and my product's ability to help my clients," says Bill Berenz, account executive at the *Milwaukee Journal Sentinel.* "I get pumped up by helping my clients be successful."

> **"What motivates me is attaining a level of professionalism and a belief in my product and my product's ability to help my clients."**

Or does money make your world go around? Berenz believes that once a salesperson achieves a certain level of success, money—although a very attractive carrot—plays a less important motivational role. "When I started out, money was important, but once I hit my financial goals, I was motivated more by learning as much as I could about the newspaper, marketing, and advertising businesses so I could advance my career," he explains. "When the money starts coming in, motivating factors change."

Consequently, companies should design different motivation "platforms" that take into account the diversity of a sales staff. "Salespeople are at different stages in their careers," Berenz says, "and platforms are the monetary or other compensation factors offered to keep all the diverse types of salespeople motivated."

"You may have people who have been with a company for 25 years and have more vacation time than they know what to do with. Then you have someone like me, who has only two weeks vacation. Winning a trip with additional days off is a key motivating factor for me."

No matter where you are in your career development, there are limitless ways to keep the adrenaline flowing. "If you're stuck in traffic crawling around at 20 miles an hour, listen to a tape and think about how you can apply what you're hearing to your next sales call and what that means in terms of reaching your goals," advises Berenz. "Don't dwell on a bad situation you might be in. Be positive."

Don't overlook the importance of visual images to inspire you. "Surround yourself with things that remind you of your goals," Berenz adds. "For example, in my home office

SKILL SET: MOTIVATE YOURSELF

1. Set moderate, attainable goals. By the yard it's hard; by the inch it's a cinch.

2. Focus on goals. Keep reminders handy of what you're working for.

3. Track your progress continuously. Evaluate and reflect on how you're doing.

4. Reward yourself for reaching goals, even small ones. Get in the success mode.

5. Grow professionally and utilize what you learn.

6. Be your own personal corporation.

7. Don't allow yourself to be a victim. The only person who can make you have a bad day is you.

I have a 40-pound muskie mounted on one wall and a six-point, whitetail buck on another. I have goals—to catch a 45-pound muskie and shoot a 12-point buck—and seeing those two reminds me of them.

"The same thing is true for business goals. If you have a short-term goal of buying a new boat, keep a picture of it where you can refer to it to keep you on track."

Stephen Noel, vice president and sales director for Pella Products of Omaha and Lincoln, NE, believes that creating an infrastructure and climate for sales success goes a long way in motivating salespeople. "We're of the opinion that if you give salespeople a working environment that helps them succeed, that, in and of itself, is a motivating factor," he says. "That means putting in place processes and procedures, along with information and sales tools, that make their job easier and more productive."

> **"When our salespeople get a job or land a target, we try to give them high praise. I know from experience that they take this to heart."**

Noel also believes that while money is a significant motivator, other components come into play. Positive reinforcement, recognition, and incentives often beat out money as motivators. "People like a pat on the back and an encouraging word on a job well done," he explains. "When our salespeople get a job or land a target, we try to give them high praise. I know from experience that they take this to heart."

"We have a year-end awards dinner where we recognize salespeople not only for volume, but also for consistency and years of service. We reward not only the race horses, but the plow horses as well."

Material rewards also work. "We supply our salespeople with company vehicles," says Noel. "Beginning salespeople start out in a Chevy S10 pickup truck. Once they hit a certain sales goal, we give them an extended-cab S10. Then they can graduate into a full-size pickup. They see their peers driving around in a brand-new full-size pickup, and that's an incentive for them to go to a higher level."

Even though Noel's salespeople are company employees, he encourages them to view themselves as their own personal corporation. "When I was a salesperson, I viewed myself as my own business. I was a selling agent for Pella Products of Omaha and Lincoln," he says. "I tell my people to think like an owner, to think outside the box of just selling. I tell them to ask themselves, 'What would I do in this situation if this were my own company?' If you give them the freedom to invent themselves and take charge of their own futures, that's motivating."

In order to foster that attitude, Noel moved all his outside sales reps out of his retail stores and into home offices so they can better plan their time and not have to go to the

EXPERT ADVICE: JUST REWARDS

EXPERT ADVICE

"If everybody came to work and did their best every day, we wouldn't need supervisors or managers," says author and consultant Dr. Aubrey Daniels. "The fact is, managers are needed to create an environment that brings out the best in people."

Says Daniels, managers should first set parameters for success. "People should know not only the results that are expected of them, but the behaviors necessary to create these results," he says. "Managers need to manage both the behaviors and the results."

In what other ways can managers keep salespeople motivated? They should provide positive reinforcement and have a good attitude. "For example, a new salesperson breaks a tough account that nobody else has ever been able to sell," Daniels explains. "The salesperson calls his boss, all excited, and the manager hardly acknowledges it. A little positive reinforcement is all that is needed to make that salesperson's day and keep him pumped up."

Daniels says that if the sales manager just asks, "How did you do that?" he will seem more positive and reinforcing. "It's all about expressing an interest and giving people an opportunity to relive the accomplishment. Salespeople thrive on it."

While it's important for salespeople to reward themselves and be rewarded for their accomplishments, it's a mistake to reward yourself for the wrong reasons. "Don't hesitate to reward yourself for the right behavior," says Daniels. "When you make a sale, eat a candy bar, take a break, something. But don't reward yourself for the wrong behavior. The worst time to take a break is when things aren't going well. Stick with it until you're successful and then reward yourself.

"Success motivates you for further success."

DR. AUBREY DANIELS is president of Aubrey Daniels and Associates Inc. and author of *Bringing Out the Best in People* (McGraw-Hill Professional Publishing). For more information, call 678/904-6140, or visit www.aubreydanils.com.

office late at night to handle paperwork. "We don't force our salespeople to make any kind of call reports," he explains. "I've never had a salesperson who liked doing them or was really honest about putting anything on them that was worth a darn."

"If salespeople hit a certain sales volume, we give them a sales assistant to provide clerical support, and that frees them up to go out and sell more. We actually have a salesperson who has moved up to two assistants."

No salesperson has a great day every day, and when salespeople get "down," Noel suggests they should realize that they're not victims. "Salespeople can't allow other people to make them feel like victims, because that's not going to get them anywhere. I have a quote on attitude on my desk that I refer to all the time, and the last line is, 'I'm convinced that life is 10 percent what happens to me and 90 percent how I react to it.'"

ARE YOU ON THE HIGHLY MOTIVATED PATH FOR LONG-TERM SUCCESS?

On the following quiz, rate yourself on a scale of 1 to 5 (1 is for almost never; 5 is for almost always).

____**1.** I seize opportunities for personal development and to educate myself about developments in my industry.

____**2.** I read books and listen to tapes that will increase my motivation and help me accomplish my short- and long-term goals.

____**3.** In my sales career, I view myself as the sole proprietor of my own personal corporation and take responsibility for its growth and development.

____**4.** At regular intervals I assess my progress and reevaluate my future plans to reflect any recent developments.

____**5.** I have a strategy for bouncing back from rejection that works to keep me from letting short-term disappointments derail my long-term goals.

____**6.** I reward myself for accomplishments, improvements, and giving extra effort but don't reward myself for negative behaviors.

____ Now add up your score:

5–10: The wheels have come off your motivational train. Sit down and develop a new plan for success that includes achievable short-term goals to get you back on the right track.

11–17: Your motivation fluctuates like the tides. Figure out where your motivational hot buttons lie and then look for ways to hit them more frequently.

18–24: You're doing a better-than-average job staying motivated but could be doing more. Evaluate what's happening when you find yourself in a downward spiral, and then develop strategies to pull yourself out more quickly.

25–30: You're on target for a highly motivated career. Keep up the good work, but watch out that you don't become complacent.

ADDITIONAL READING

STAYING POSITIVE NO MATTER WHAT IS HAPPENING WITH YOUR SALES

Anybody can have a bad day. It might start out when you get to the office and find a note on your desk saying a long-time customer canceled an order. Then shipping calls and says they are running three days behind on deliveries. You are a half-hour late for an appointment because you get stuck in traffic. The prospect you thought was "in the bag" is stalling, and another is beating you up on terms.

After only five minutes at the office you may be asking yourself, "Why am I doing this?"

While the rewards of a sales career can be great, the profession is not for the fainthearted. It takes a resilient ego to handle all the rejection and problems that make up a salesperson's day and still stay pumped up.

"I tell my staff that today's a new day and yesterday died last night," says Jeffrey Roub, territory sales manager for the California State Automobile Association. "After all, Babe Ruth hit a lot of home runs, but he also struck out. You've got to swing the bat."

EXPERT ADVICE

EXPERT ADVICE: ACCENTUATE THE POSITIVE

Consultant Joyce Weiss advises unmotivated salespeople to get out of their comfort zones and reevaluate the way they do business.

"When things aren't going well, salespeople can either continue to do things the same way and dry up like a dinosaur or force themselves out of their safe little boxes and do things differently," says Weiss. "It's easy to blame the marketplace or the economy but you have to stop whining, look in the mirror, and force yourself to squarely address the problem and brainstorm for solutions."

Weiss has a number of tips for salespeople in a motivational slump.

1. Tap your networking relationships. Build a mutual support team to talk to them, either by phone or e-mail. Who else better understands what you're going through than your sales peers?

2. Make a commitment to lifelong learning by attending seminars and reading sales and motivational material. Learning builds confidence, and confidence builds a good self-image.

3. Reflect on where you are and where you want to be. Identify your strengths and continuously remind yourself of them. Don't be so hard on yourself, because the world already is and you don't have to help the process. Be your own positive coach, not a negative influence.

4. Put some fun in your life. Don't take things so seriously. Keep a fun journal of humorous items you've read, or even cartoons, and refer to it when things go south.

5. Keep up the enthusiasm and just don't allow yourself to get motivationally down. If you're really depressed, phone your favorite customer and just chat. It will make the customer feel good, and it's positive reinforcement for you.

Remember the quote from Ralph Waldo Emerson: "Standing in our own sunshine causes most of the shadows in our life."

JOYCE WEISS, MA, The Corporate Energizer, is a certified speaker, consultant, and author of *Full Speed Ahead: Become Driven by Change*. For more information, call 1-800-713-1926 or visit her Website at www.JoyceWeiss.com.

Roub is a firm believer in salespeople using motivational material to keep them in the right frame of mind. To that end, he sends out an e-mail newsletter every day to his 12 salespeople. "Topics range from working smarter to attitude and motivation, closing and follow-through techniques, and sales tips of the day," says Roub. "I concentrate on sales fundamentals because, in many cases, I feel salespeople don't revisit sales basics as often as they should."

Roub encourages salespeople to talk to their managers when they're feeling down or when things just don't seem to be going their way. "My job is to do everything I can do to help my people reach their goals, and I encourage my people to tell me how I can help," says Roub. "It may be a matter of actually going step by step through a difficult sales scenario, identifying what went wrong and how we can improve the next time through. It could be the salesperson needs more training, sales and motivational materials, or even additional sales leads. We try to continually reenergize our salespeople."

Ellen Burach, sales consultant for US Home Corporation, draws on the positive feedback she receives from satisfied customers to keep her up to speed. "Basically, I stay motivated by the positive feedback I receive from the people I work with, because I'm involved with my customers," says Burach. "It's the thank-you cards. I need that positive feedback, and my buyers give it to me."

SKILL SET

1. Recognize that everyone goes through periodic motivational slumps. You can't be "up" all the time. Even Superman had his bad days.

2. Remember that prospects are not saying no to you, they are saying no to what you have to offer at the time you're offering it. Today's "no" may be tomorrow's "yes."

3. Use sales and motivational books, tapes, and seminars to boost your confidence.

4. Build a peer support team. Other people have run into the same hurdles you have, and they can offer comfort and insight.

5. Look to your sales manager to help you get back on top of your game. Your manager is paid to help you become more successful.

6. Truthfully analyze why you're in a down mode and take steps to get out of the rut, even if it means changing the way you do business. Take control of your actions.

7. Resolve to have some fun in your life.

"Sure, I do get beat up, and sometimes that's hard to accept," says Burach. "But the other side of that is when I see them smiling after a closing and they know they made the right decision and I helped them. I feel so good."

"I think about all the people I've helped and the positive things I've accomplished," says Burach. "Sometimes I feel like I sell water in the desert . . . I'm really doing a service. And the more I give, the more I receive."

> **"I think about all the people I've helped and the positive things I've accomplished. Sometimes I feel like I sell water in the desert . . . I'm really doing a service. And the more I give, the more I receive."**

Burach also feels that reading sales and motivational material helps when you're in a down mood. "I'm an avid reader of motivational books, and I write down quotes in a journal that I read every morning," says Burach. "I also carry in my wallet an obituary of someone I knew personally. When I'm having a bad day, I take it out and read it, and I don't feel so bad anymore. Every new day is a gift.

"It's OK to have problems because if I had no problems, I'd have no customers," says Burach.

Psychology

A HANDS-ON GUIDE
FOR MANAGERS

TRAINING GUIDE TIME REQUIRED: 50 MINUTES

THE PSYCHOLOGY OF SELLING

There are two elements to the psychology of selling: the psychology of the salesperson and the psychology of the customer. The most effective sales professionals are those who can bring these two elements together.

Step 1: Achieve Congruence among Your Core Beliefs

Most sales training deals with the mechanics and techniques of the sales process, such as identifying needs or handling objections. While such things are important, they are seldom effective unless the salesperson is psychologically prepared to sell. The foundation of this psychological preparation is achieving congruence among the following core beliefs:

1. What are my basic values about people and life?
2. What do I think selling is all about?
3. Do I believe that I can take the necessary steps?
4. How committed am I to taking these actions?
5. Do I believe in the product or service I'm selling?

When these core beliefs are incongruent, low sales productivity inevitably results. Salespeople who lack congruence find it extraordinarily difficult to perform the basic mechanics of selling. Worse, most customers can easily tell when a salesperson is conflicted, and, sensing something is wrong, become far less likely to buy.

For example, salespeople who believe it's a sin to tell a lie will likely flub a presentation if they feel they must misrepresent a product in order to close business. Similarly, salespeople who believe life is all about helping others will subtly avoid closing business if they also believe that selling means convincing people to buy something they don't need.

Many organizations have sales cultures that create incongruity between core beliefs. For example, imagine a car dealership where the entire emphasis is on closing a deal quickly rather than, say, making a customer happy. The salesperson most likely to prosper in that environment would be one who basically doesn't care much about customer satisfaction. Many salespeople working in that environment are likely to be incongruent, and thus ineffective. Furthermore, salespeople who deeply feel the difference between their own personal values and the values of the organizational culture are likely to succumb to a variety of stress-related illnesses, including alcoholism, drug usage, and depression. Not surprisingly, organizations that encourage high-pressure sales tactics often have high turnover rates—another major productivity killer.

In order to become fully productive, salespeople and sales managers alike must explicitly articulate those five core beliefs and then modify any beliefs that are incongruent. This must take place on two levels—both in the belief system of the individual salesperson and in the culture of the sales organization.

For example, an honest salesperson who, for one reason or another, believes at heart that selling is "inherently deceptive" must be convinced to view selling in a more positive way, such as a process of educating the customer to the customer's ultimate benefit. Similarly, if the salespeople in an organization feel that they lack basic selling skills, the sales manager must find a way, either through training or mentoring, to help the salespeople become more confident, thereby bringing their core beliefs closer to congruence.

FREQUENTLY ASKED QUESTIONS

SALES REPS' FREQUENTLY ASKED QUESTIONS

Q: Isn't it possible to simulate congruence, even if you don't feel it?

A: Yes, indeed. Many salespeople work hard to create a false sense of congruence even when they don't believe in the product or service that they're selling. Such behavior, however, always takes its toll on the salesperson, in the form of lower productivity and poor customer relations.

Q: What do I do if I don't really believe in the product or service that I'm selling?

A: There is no easy fix for this problem. While it's sometimes a hard rule to accept, if you truly believe that what you're selling is substandard, you owe it to yourself and to your employer to seek employment elsewhere.

Q: How can I use my knowledge of sales psychology to manipulate people into buying more?

A: If you go into a sales situation with the idea that your job is to manipulate people, the customer will likely sense this and resist the sale. A better option is to approach the customer with an honest desire to help.

Step 2: Identify Your Customer's Behavior Styles®

It's a truism that building strong customer relationships results in better sales performance. However, many salespeople lack the tools to understand the psychology driving the behavior of each individual customer. The following conceptual map provides an easily understood method for categorizing customer Behavior Styles, so that a salesperson can more easily build a strong relationship.

The model has two axes, each of which represents a polarity of human behavior. The up-down axis describes a customer's tolerance to risk. Risk takers typically have a high need for recognition, while those who are risk averse generally have a high need for security. The right-left axis describes a customer's view of how work should be approached— either as a set of goals to be achieved or a set of processes to be followed. The four quadrants represent the four basic customer Behavior Styles:

1. **DOER** (results-oriented, needs recognition). This customer tends to make decisions quickly, prefers brief presentations, and deeply resents any person who wastes time.	2. **TALKER** (process-oriented, needs recognition). This customer desires social approval and thus will avoid making a decision.
3. **CONTROLLER** (results-oriented, needs security). This customer will be highly logical and analytical and will generally look for what's wrong with any situation or plan.	4. **SUPPORTER** (process-oriented, needs security). This customer seldom looks at the bottom line, but is more concerned with getting a job done and is usually not a decision maker.

Customers tend to have a primary and secondary behavior style, and those styles tend to be in contiguous quadrants. For example, a CEO might be a Doer when dealing with underlings but a Talker when dealing with fellow CEOs. Similarly, a bank manager might be a Controller when it comes to writing loans, but a Supporter when it comes to working with top management on strategic issues. However, it's very unusual to find a customer who is a Doer for one activity and a Supporter in others, because the two Behavior Styles are too disparate. Similarly, a Controller will almost never behave like a Talker (or vice versa) and, when in the same room together, they may find it difficult to communicate with one another or come to agreement on any important issue.

Salespeople, when interacting with a customer contact, should watch (and listen) carefully for clues about the customer's primary and secondary Behavior Styles. A Doer, for example, will often wear flashy or distinctive clothing and is likely to communicate in short bursts. Similarly, a Supporter will tend to dress conservatively and use catchphrases like "the way things are done here" and "the powers that be."

QUICK TIPS FOR YOUR TRAINING SESSION

QUICK TIP

1. Make it clear that the psychology of selling is a profound subject and that a 50-minute meeting can only be a brief introduction to the subject matter.

2. If the first part of the meeting turns into a lively discussion about congruity between values and beliefs, postpone the training on Behavior Styles to a later meeting.

3. Resolving incongruities between values and beliefs about selling can have a massive positive impact on the overall productivity of a sales group.

4. If some team members indicate a lack of confidence in their ability to sell, be certain to schedule additional training sessions in sales techniques.

Step 3: From a State of Congruence, Adapt to the Customer's Behavior Style

Once you've determined the customer's primary and secondary Behavior Styles, you can reach a higher level of rapport by taking on some of the attributes of those Behavior Styles. For example, when selling to a Doer, speak quickly and get right to the point. By contrast, when selling to a Supporter, take the time to explain, in detail, how what you're selling fits into the status quo.

Salespeople who attempt to do this quickly learn that they're more comfortable selling to customers with one or two of the four Behavior Styles. This is because salespeople, like customers, also have their own natural Behavior Styles. That's why salespeople who (successfully) call at the CEO level often seem to have the air of authority that one normally associates with a top executive. Similarly, salespeople who target their activities to engineers (typically Controllers) are generally the most effective when they can slip easily into an analytical mind-set.

This is not to say that salespeople can only sell effectively to customers who share a similar Behavior Style. In fact, a top salesperson can not only intuitively sense the customer's Behavior Style, but also can find the corresponding behavior in his or her own character that best matches the customer's. In short, even the most action-oriented Doer has the potential to reach rapport with a Supporter, providing the Doer can empathize and respect the fact that every Behavior Style has its strengths and weaknesses.

RON WILLINGHAM was interviewed for this article. His sales training courses have reached more than 1.5 million graduates worldwide and more than 2,000 companies. He is also the author of eight books, including *Integrity Selling for the 21st Century* (Doubleday). His company, Integrity Systems Inc. is located at 1850 North Central Avenue, suite 1000, Phoenix, AZ 85004. Telephone: 1-800-896-9090. Web: www.integritysystems.com.   •

SALES MANAGER'S MEETING GUIDE

Below are 10 practical steps to whet your sales team's interest in the psychology of selling. This sales meeting should take about 50 minutes.

1. Before the meeting, draw a diagram of the four-quadrant Behavior Styles model on the whiteboard. Be certain that a flip-chart is available for recording the statements of the team members.

2. Open the meeting with a brief statement that the group is going to work on sales psychology, which is the foundation for achieving higher sales. Request that team members participate to the fullest and make it clear that the session is intended to be enjoyable and helpful.

3. Review the four-quadrant model of customer Behavior Styles and explain the characteristics of each.

4. Going around the room, ask each team member to name his or her three most important customer contacts. Put the name of each team member on the top of a flip-chart page and list the three names after it, leaving space between each name.

5. Have team members identify the primary and secondary Behavior Styles of their most important customers. Add that information to each flip chart and tape the chart to the wall.

6. When you've gone around the room, ask each team member to characterize his or her own Behavior Style. Make it clear that no specific Behavior Style is better or worse when it comes to sales activities. Add that Behavior Style to the bottom of each flip-chart page.

7. Ask team members to share their experiences selling to those three customers taking into account the similarity (and dissimilarity) of the team member's Behavior Styles to that of the customer contact.

8. In cases where a team member with one Behavior Style has been successful in selling to a customer with a different Behavior Style, ask the team member to recall anything that he or she did in order to build rapport.

9. Have team members, as a group or individually, devise strategies for building a better rapport with the customer contacts, based upon this understanding of Behavior Styles.

10. Close the meeting with a request that the team members report back to you on the effectiveness of those rapport-building strategies after they have worked with Behavior Styles.

QUICK TIP

QUICK TIPS FOR YOUR NEXT SALES MEETING

Top salespeople share four specific characteristics. Have your salespeople
ask themselves the following questions:

1. **DO I HAVE GOAL CLARITY?** Top salespeople have clear, specific, written-down statements of what they want to happen.

2. **DO I HAVE A HIGH DRIVE FOR ACHIEVEMENT?** Top salespeople are completely committed to take the necessary steps to build strong customer relationships.

3. **DO I HAVE HEALTHY EMOTIONAL INTELLIGENCE?** Top salespeople have the ability to understand and control their own emotions.

4. **DO I HAVE EXCELLENT SOCIAL SKILLS?** Top salespeople have the ability to achieve rapport with a wide variety of customers.

ARE YOUR INSECURITIES KNOCKING YOU OUT OF A SALE?

ADDITIONAL
READING

You don't have to be perfect to be successful. In fact, it's how you live with the knowledge that no person or product is perfect that can determine the difference between winning or losing the sale.

Consider three salesmen we got to know during a recent training session—Bill, Hank, and Tom.

Bill's the kind of guy most people like. He's a good listener and intelligent. His sense of humor keeps everyone around him smiling. As a salesman, however, Bill struggles to be average. He does wonderfully well when he has an agreement from his buyers, but whenever he comes up against an objection, he becomes insecure. Oh, you can tell he's insecure all right, and so can his buyers: Bill "moves away."

Hank, on the other hand, is usually aloof and distant. He is all nuts and bolts. He can quote you every detail about his products, and his expertise is unquestionable.

Like Bill, Hank is an average salesman. Again, like Bill, Hank becomes insecure whenever he is questioned by a buyer. But Hank differs from Bill in the way he shows his insecurity. You see, Hank "moves against."

Finally, there's Tom—ambitious, young, and proud. No one in the office can understand why Tom's sales record isn't better. Boiling with enthusiasm at weekly sales meetings, Tom seems to cool down in front of buyers. His problem, unfortunately, is the insecurity he feels whenever the outcome of a sale is in doubt. When Tom feels insecure, he "moves toward."

It was psychiatrist Karen Horney, some half century ago, who first described the "neurotic" trends of "moving away from, moving against, and moving toward people." It was she who said that all three trends were responses to insecurity. All three responses, she said, could get in the way of successful, satisfying living. So, too, can they get in the way of successful selling.

> It was psychiatrist Karen Horney, some half century ago, who first described the "neurotic" trends of "moving away from, moving against, and moving toward people. . . ." all three trends were responses to insecurity.

THREE INSECURE SALESMEN

Bill, Hank, and Tom could be successful, even outstanding, salesmen. Yet each is hampered by insecurity. Oddly enough, it isn't their faults that do them in, but the shifts they make in themselves to cover up their faults.

Reading Bill's body language, we see that Bill moves away. He leans back in his chair, diverts his eyes from the buyer's, and becomes uncharacteristically bland. Hank, on the other hand, "moves against." He leans forward, frequently slaps the table top, stares his buyer down, and clenches his fists. His usually aloof posture becomes intimidating and aggressive. And Tom, who "moves toward," leans forward, nods incessantly, grins with vacant eyes, and seems like a frightened puppy dog hoping to please his master.

What it is important to remember is that none of them is reacting to the buyer. Each is reacting to his own internal insecurity. Sure, the buyers may be offering objections or asking questions, but neither the objections not the questions kill the sale. It's the way Bill, Hank, and Tom react to objections and the way each feels insecure and reacts to that internal feeling that kills the sale.

It's as if they are so afraid of doing something wrong, of being imperfect, that they allow those fears to cloud their judgment and dilute their ability to make the sale. Unfortunately, Bill, Hank, and Tom are not unique.

In the years we've been training salespeople, we have met thousands of Bills, Hanks, and Toms. These thousands of salesmen and saleswomen allow their own insecurities to prevent them from being successful. They hear an objection or receive a question from a buyer and get sidetracked off the road to success and become hopelessly entangled in a net of cover-ups and diversions.

BLINDED BY INADEQUACIES

They forget to read their buyers and, instead, become obsessed with reading themselves. By turning their vision inward, they find every fault and inadequacy they possess. To make it worse, when they discover their own faults, they seem to do their very best to expose these faults to the buyer. They move recklessly "toward," "away from," or "against" their customers.

Funny thing about security: it's not how much you have that matters, but rather how much you can do without! The weakest among us aren't those who are loaded with insecurity. Instead, the weakest are those who cannot tolerate even the slightest bit of self-doubt. Yet, who is really ever without doubt? Didn't Picasso wonder, at first, if his revolutionary style of painting would be successful? Didn't Alexander Graham Bell think, even for a moment, that the telephone would never work—would never be what he hoped it would be?

> Proceeding in the face of doubt is what separates the successful from the beaten, the winners from the losers.

All great men and women have doubts, as do all great salespeople. There always is something that cannot be controlled, that may go wrong, that can spoil even the best plans for success. Proceeding in the face of doubt is what separates the successful from the beaten, the winners from the losers.

OUR GUIDING FICTIONS

It has to do with expectations, with what psychologist Alfred Adler called "guiding fictions." We all have them. They are the notions we develop about how we are supposed to behave and how the world works. Since we form them as children, more often that not our guiding fictions are inaccurate. Yet, we tenaciously hold onto them, even as adults, when experience should have taught us better.

It's a guiding fiction, for example, to think that everyone should like you. Of course, that's impossible, yet many people spend all their days trying to please each and every person around them, trying to be liked at all costs. So many guiding fictions exist that they all cannot be enumerated. All the false "shoulds" and "oughts" that any of us have are guiding fictions.

In sales, there are a few important guiding fictions worth addressing. There's the "I should never be proven wrong by a customer" guiding fiction and the "I shouldn't let the customer think I'm dumb" guiding fiction. There are the "If I don't make the sale, I'm bad" and "Good salespeople never lose" guiding fictions. Just think of the many ways salespeople set themselves up for feelings of failure and insecurity, and chances are you can find a guiding fiction at work preventing their success.

Remember Bill, the salesman who "moves away" from his buyers each time they object to his product? Bill's guiding fiction is that if he "presents the product right, no one should object." Of course, when Bill gets an objection, he feels a failure, he feels insecure. That's when he tries to hide his feelings by moving safely away from his buyers. His withdrawal is his way of protecting himself.

Then there was Hank who "moved against" his customers whenever they questioned his facts and figures. Guess what Hank's guiding fiction is? That's right, Hank thinks that to be successful he should always be seen as intelligent. When he gets questions from buyers, Hank feels stupid and insecure. His angry "moving against" customers is Hank's way of covering up his insecurity.

Finally, there's Tom, who believes he must always be in command to be successful. When a customer doubts Tom, he feels weak and unsure of himself. His "moving toward" his buyers is his way of hiding his feelings and of trying to regain his customers' favor.

Each of these hard-working salespeople lets his own false notions of himself prevent his real talents from showing. All stop reacting to their buyers and start reacting to themselves. All start reading their inner language of insecurity. The moment they turn inward, they face much more than a cantankerous buyer. Each battles himself, and regardless of how hard anyone tries to win that battle, there can be no winner.

WHAT ARE YOUR GUIDING FICTIONS?

Think for a moment about what you believe concerning your success as a salesperson. What do you think you "ought" or "should" be to achieve sales success? Must you be an expert? Must you be liked by all your buyers? Must you always be in charge?

Increasing your awareness of what goes on inside you is the first decisive step toward sales success. With nothing to hide from yourself, you will have no need to "move toward, away from, or against."

Salespeople become their own worst enemies when they are sidetracked by their guiding fictions and turn their attention to themselves and away from their buyers.

ADDITIONAL READING

Consider the case of Steve Robinson. Bob Tiller listens attentively to Steve Robinson's presentation. He seems impressed as the young salesman asks about his needs and interests. Robinson appears effective and confident, but the minute Tiller interrupts to say that he has another appointment waiting, Robinson falls apart.

Suddenly his mind is racing . . . he silently blames himself for mistiming his presentation and for wasting his morning without a sale.

Robinson stops reading Tiller's buying signals and begins reading his own expressions of insecurity. His cross-armed, fidgeting, eye-darting body language communicates his feelings to his buyer. Before long, Robinson is out the door and out of a sale.

Robinson's guiding fiction has become the major obstacle on the way to a sale. We all have guiding fictions—unrealistic expectations we have acquired during childhood. In Robinson's case, whenever he runs into trouble during a sale, he starts comparing himself with what he thinks he ought to be. (In this situation, a better planner.) Of course, he then feels inadequate and insecure.

Successful selling calls for confidence. Anything that detracts from your belief in yourself is sure to ruin the sale. Sitting before a buyer is not the time to dig into your personality, looking for faults and inadequacies.

FILTERING OUT FICTIONS

Like Robinson, many salespeople are plagued by their own guiding fictions. They fail to concentrate on their buyers during the sale and end up self-conscious, insecure, and unable to get the order. They fail to filter out their fictions.

Did you ever notice how easy it is at a noisy party to concentrate on the people who interest you? Successful perception depends on what you can ignore as well as what you can see or hear. People who can ignore what is unimportant to them have a real edge.

Filtering out information is vital to successful living. Scientists estimate that the human eye can handle about 5 million bits of information per second. According to a scientific study, however, the brain can only process approximately 500 bits per second. This may help explain why our perception needs to be guided.

In selling, learning to focus your attention on the buyer is essential. Every time you meet a prospect, you must determine what is and isn't vital to your sales success.

Perhaps the greatest distractions to success come from within the salesperson, however, not from the buyer. Your inner feelings, triggered by your guiding fictions, can be

> In selling, learning to focus your attention on the buyer is essential. Every time you meet a prospect, you must determine what is and isn't vital to your sales success.

the greatest obstacles to sales success. When your buyer frowns, interrupts, or objects to your major product feature, these messages can quickly prompt your guiding fiction to become the dominant theme in your mind. The key is to quiet or neutralize your guiding fictions. Before we can accomplish this task, we first have to become aware of what they are.

FIND YOUR FICTIONS

Which of the guiding fictions listed below belong to you? Which of these "shoulds" and "oughts" do you secretly use to measure your own success or failure? How are they getting in the way of your success as a salesperson?

- ☑ I should always be in charge during the sale and never let the buyer control the decision.
- ☑ Buyers should always like me. We should be friends as well as business partners.
- ☑ When I don't get the order, it's because I've made some mistake.
- ☑ Customer objections are a sign that I haven't presented my product well enough.
- ☑ In order to become a good salesperson, I have to overcome my insecurities.

On the surface, each guiding fiction above seems to be true. Some of them echo the shoulds and oughts we learned as children. As adults, these guiding fictions often give us the illusion of security. We believe that if we can always please others and never make mistakes, we can control our lives and achieve all that we wish. Neither assumption is true.

We cannot control the customer's decision; we can only influence it. Everyone can't like us, nor do we have to like everyone. Friends are those who like us as we are, not as we think we ought to be. We can't expect perfection in everything we do, but we can try to view mistakes as opportunities for learning—not as sources of shame. We can't completely overcome our insecurities, but we can learn how to manage ourselves.

Become aware of what guiding fictions are operating during your sales calls. It's the first step to neutralizing your guiding fictions. To silence them is to accept your adulthood and reality. Remember that no buyer can do or say anything to defeat you, unless you give him or her the tools to do so.

It was Eleanor Roosevelt who said, "No one can make you feel inferior, unless you agree with him." Take her advice. Silence your fictions, and you'll silence your insecurities.

WHY WISDOM IS WEAK AND STUPIDITY IS STRONG AND WHAT YOU CAN DO ABOUT IT

Every day, salespeople everywhere are waging war—with themselves. They want to do better, make more calls, improve their closing ratios, but for many professionals something always seems to thwart their best-laid plans. Sometimes it's just a matter of bad timing or competitive forces that are beyond their control. But, according to consultant Pete Greider and clinical psychologist Dr. Steven Levinson in their book *Following Through: A Revolutionary New Model for Finishing Whatever You Start* (Kensington Books), the problem is inside the salesperson. Here's how Greider and Levinson explain how salespeople shoot themselves in the foot by failing to follow through with their positive plans for improvement.

Everyone has a weak but smart force Greider and Levinson call The Wise One that urges you to do what's best for yourself and your sales. Everyone also has another side, say the authors, a stupid but very strong force known as Thor that tempts you with more appealing options—leaving work at the stroke of five to catch your favorite sitcom instead of making the extra cold calls you said you would or staying in bed for an extra hour of sleep instead of keeping your vow to get an early start on the selling day. To win the war, you must control Thor—or at least get him out of the way, according to Greider and Levinson. Instead of relying on self-discipline or willpower, Greider explains exactly how you can follow through to get the job done. His three-step plan works by creating compelling reasons, leading the horse to water, and striking while the iron is hot.

WEAK WILL

As a psychologist in a cardiac rehabilitation unit, Dr. Levinson noted that some recovering heart attack victims followed diet and exercise orders initially, then abandoned their lifestyle changes after a few weeks, failing to follow through even when their lives depended on it, while other patients maintained their discipline. In looking for rational reasons for this seemingly irrational behavior, Greider noted that even when patients desperately wanted to follow through, willpower may have waned when they needed it most.

"How many salespeople are out there who really, really want to increase their income and their

> "How many salespeople are out there who really, really want to increase their income and their performance, for all kinds of reasons, but year after year they don't follow through?"

performance, for all kinds of reasons, but year after year they don't follow through?" he asks. "We're saying that the reason is that they're looking in the wrong place for the solution. The wrong place, essentially, is willpower and self-discipline. They don't work." Sure, you might enjoy the occasional triumph of will, but as a follow-through tool it's unreliable, and consistent success demands consistent follow-through.

INNER CHILD

Few people always feel like doing the right thing, and there's good reason. As Greider explains it, "We all have a split personality. Our every move is guided by two inner systems—one primitive, one state-of-the-art. The two systems do not speak the same language or communicate with one another, and while the state-of-the-art system guides us to do the logical thing for long-term benefit, the primitive one leads us into temptation by pressuring us to do what we most want to do right now."

"The best metaphor for this is a car with two steering wheels and two drivers," he says. "On the left you have a 98-pound weakling who is smart, called The Wise One. The Wise One figures out what to do for long-term benefit and steers the car in that direction. But there's another driver on the right, very strong, but not very smart. We call that driver Thor. And Thor has no destination at all. He's like a three-year-old child—totally into the moment, totally into his physical needs, his five senses, and very persistent and powerful when he wants something. When The Wise One says 'Improve your closing skills' or 'Read your new sales literature' and Thor says 'I want to go to the movies,' Thor wins even though he's stupid, because he's stronger."

POWERFUL PAIR

Lest you think that Thor is evil and determined to foil your every attempt at success, Greider emphasizes that he really isn't good or bad but simply self-absorbed. When you can't overpower him, you can outsmart him. If you know how to use his power, the same Thor that keeps you from getting anything done one day can drive you to new heights of productivity the next.

"If you set things up right," says Greider, "Thor will help you be a peak performer. And that's what's so exciting about how these strategies work. When you do set your environment up the right way, you'll find Thor yelling and pushing to get you to do what's right, and you achieve incredible things."

To hit on just the right solutions, keep it simple and stupid. You may have to do some silly things to make Thor cooperate, but not following through on tasks that will make you successful is equally absurd.

"The solution is to take a simple action so that Thor and The Wise One are both steering in the same direction at the same time. So in other words, you feel like doing what you know is best. They become a team so you have the power of Thor and the brains of The Wise One working together."

SMART STRATEGIES

Greider offers several strategies to help you make Thor your follow-through friend. The first, creating compelling reasons, shows that using the "wrong" reasons to follow through works better than using the right ones. For example, motivating yourself to work late because you want a raise in three months is like talking to the wrong decision maker on a sales call. You're trying to appeal to a force that has intelligence but no power. The Wise One wants the raise but Thor wants to go home now, and Thor is the one with the decision-making muscle. To create compelling reasons that will spur you to action, Greider advises considering less logical but more powerful motivators.

> "Compelling reasons are immediate, certain, and personal, whereas the right reasons tend to be logical and long term, but they have very little immediate impact."

"The idea here is that there's a big difference between the right reasons for doing something and the truly compelling reasons," he says. "Compelling reasons are immediate, certain, and personal, whereas the right reasons tend to be logical and long term, but they have very little immediate impact."

Greider illustrates his point with the story of salesperson who called him about a year ago, after hearing him speak. For years, the salesperson failed to follow through on his resolution to get up at 5:15 in the morning to study technical material. The salesperson, who had two very young children, had great logical reasons for getting up to study, but he failed until he created a truly compelling reason for himself. He decided to set one alarm clock in his bedroom for 5:12, and another one in the kids' room for 5:15. When the alarm went off in his room, he would have a compelling reason to get up immediately—to go to his children's room and turn off the second alarm clock before it went off at 5:15 and woke them up. "One he set up a compelling reason that made him feel like doing the right thing, he didn't have to rely on willpower anymore," Greider says.

Greider recommends creating your own compelling reasons by reviewing "when you've been highly motivated in the past. Write down times in your life when you've been really into following through. Next to those instances, write down what was motivating you at the time. It will often be something kind of silly, but that'll give you some clues." In other words, if last quarter you were really motivated to put in extra hours so you could outsell another saleperson on your team, you can use that knowledge to create a compelling reason to follow through now.

While creating compelling reasons helps you use the wrong reasons to do the right thing, "leading the horse to water" lowers your resistance to following through by reducing the amount of effort involved. To lead the horse to water, simply tell yourself that you don't have to complete the task—you only have to get started on it.

EASY DOES IT

"The idea with this one is that every intention has an easy part and a hard part," Greider says. "Normally we think of the hard part. Leading the horse to water says that all you have to do is the easy part, and then you can stop. This sets Thor out of the way and in fact, doing the easy part often helps you build up enough momentum to do the hard part as well. You can use this for cleaning up your office, for example. Tell yourself, 'I only have to spend five minutes cleaning up my office, and if I want to stop then, I can.' Thor won't object to a five-minute job, because that's easy. But very often, that 5 minutes will turn into 20 or 30, and by the time you really want to stop, you've made a big dent in the job or finished it completely."

Greider's third strategy gets you to strike while the iron is hot so you can take full advantage of the fleeting moments when you feel inspired to move mountains. An uplifting speech or an inspiring passage from a book can put you in a motivated mood, but Greider points out that moods inevitably swing, and you have to take action when you do feel like it to help you follow through when you don't.

"When you're inspired to set something in place, take action immediately so that when the inspiration fades, you still follow through. Strike while the iron is hot instead of thinking that your supermotivated mood will last—because it won't. Thor is a three-year-old, and three-year-olds are jumping from one thing to another all day long." When the spirit is willing but the two-part mind rebels, alternatives to willpower can overcome even the most stubborn inner child. Since sales success depends on consistent follow-through, taming Thor, and getting him to work with, instead of against, The Wise One puts any salesperson in top-scoring position.

Emotional Intelligence

A HANDS-ON GUIDE FOR MANAGERS

TRAINING GUIDE TIME REQUIRED: 55 MINUTES

USE EMOTIONAL INTELLIGENCE TO IMPROVE SALES

What Is EQ?

EQ (emotional quotient, aka emotional intelligence) is the ability to use your street smarts to deal effectively with other people, their feelings, and your own feelings. In sales situations, EQ is the ability to use emotions (your own and others') to produce mutually beneficial sales.

EQ differs from IQ (intelligence quotient) in two important ways.

First, unlike IQ, which is genetically determined and cannot be changed, there are numerous studies demonstrating that EQ can be increased through a combination of awareness and training. Second, while many people assume that a high IQ leads to success, EQ is a much better predictor of success, especially in sales, where personal interaction plays such an important role.

EQ is measured using five basic "scales" which are defined by 15 "subscales." The conceptual framework appears in Table 15.1.

The five subscales that are the most important in sales situations are: assertiveness, emotional self-awareness, empathy, problem solving, and happiness. Sales reps who learn to pay attention to these five subscales are highly likely to see an increase in their sales effectiveness.

Assertiveness

This aspect of EQ helps the sales rep to move a sales situation forward without offending or frustrating the customer. Assertiveness can be seen as located halfway between passivity and aggressiveness. For example, suppose you are trying to close, but the customer is delaying the final decision. There are at least three possible responses:

1. **PASSIVE:** "Could you give me a call when you've made a decision?"

Table 15.1	
SCALE	**SUBSCALES**
1. Intrapersonal	1. Self-regard 2. Emotional self-awareness 3. Assertiveness 4. Independence 5. Self-actualization
2. Interpersonal	6. Empathy 7. Interpersonal relationships 8. Social responsibility
3. Adaptability	9. Reality testing 10. Flexibility 11. Problem solving
4. General mood	12. Optimism 13. Happiness
5. Stress management	14. Stress tolerance 15. Impulse control

2. **ASSERTIVE:** "Can you give me a specific time and date when you'll make you final decision?"

3. **AGGRESSIVE:** "If you don't buy right now, the offer is off the table."

The first response is almost guaranteed to fail, while the third response, if it succeeds, will probably make the customer feel pressured and resentful. The middle approach, by contrast, sets up the specific conditions for the close without forcing the customer's pace.

Emotional Self-Awareness

This helps the sales rep to identify his or her own emotions and then use those emotions to build a stronger customer relationship. Using emotional self-awareness in a sales situation is a three-step process:

1. Examine your internal processes to identify the emotions you're feeling.

2. Based on your experience, predict how those emotions will affect your sales effort.

3. Compensate for negative emotions that might hinder the sale, and expand positive emotions that might help the sale.

For example, if you're furious that your first customer in the morning stood you up, you might take a break before your second meeting in order to recover your temper. Alternatively, you might, as an icebreaker, tell the second customer that you're having a tough day and why. (Obviously, whether this kind of self-revelation is appropriate depends upon your relationship with the second customer.) Regardless of what action you take, you must ensure that your emotions help rather than hinder your sales effort.

SALES REPS' FREQUENTLY ASKED QUESTIONS

FREQUENTLY
ASKED
QUESTIONS

Q: How is EQ different from dozens of self-assessment methodologies that have come and gone over the years?

A: Unlike self-assessment quizzes, which typically reflect the quiz writer's opinions, EQ is based upon clinical studies with thousands of subjects. Independent psychologists and scientists have repeatedly verified this research.

Q: Isn't EQ, like IQ, just genetics and, thus, impossible to change?

A: Not at all. While some people seem to have been born with a higher EQ than other people, there's clinical evidence that EQ, unlike IQ, can be raised through awareness and behavioral changes.

Q: Won't changing my EQ just teach me to be fake when I'm dealing with my customers?

A: No. We all have multiple dimensions to our personality, which we use in different ways and at different times. EQ allows you to select from your own range of emotions and behaviors in order to sell more effectively.

Empathy

This helps sales reps adapt their behavior to the customer's unique moods and emotions. Empathy begins with effective listening and effective observation. However, simply "knowing" what the customer might be feeling is not enough. To be empathetic, a sales rep must actually be able to feel what the customer is likely

> **To be empathetic, a sales rep must actually be able to feel what the customer is likely to be feeling.**

to be feeling. For example, suppose, during a sales call, you discover that the customer's firm just announced major layoffs. There are at least three possible responses:

1. Proceed with the sales call as if nothing had changed. (After all, it's not your problem.)

2. Find out whether the customer will have buying authority after the layoffs are complete.

3. Take a moment to imagine the sense of fear and confusion that's an inevitable result of layoff announcements and, depending on the situation and your reading of the customer, decide whether the customer would prefer to commiserate and complain or alternatively to be distracted from the entire situation.

Clearly the third response is most likely to build a stronger customer relationship.

Problem Solving

This helps the sales rep create new ways to satisfy the customer's needs. These needs might be business-oriented, such as a large company's need for transportation, or emotional, such as an individual customer's need to be convinced that your company is reputable and reliable. Problem solving is a three-step process:

1. See the customer situation as it really is. Don't try to solve a problem before you fully understand it.

2. Help the customer visualize how he or she would like the situation to be.

3. Devise a way to move the customer from the way things are today to the way the customer would like them to be.

QUICK
TIP

QUICK TIPS

These EQ elements are very important for sales reps:

☑ **ASSERTIVENESS:** Ability to express feelings, beliefs, and thoughts openly.

☑ **EMOTIONAL SELF-AWARENESS:** Ability to recognize and understand what you are feeling and why.

☑ **EMPATHY:** Ability to understand and appreciate the feelings of others.

☑ **PROBLEM SOLVING:** Ability to identify problems and generate effective solutions.

☑ **HAPPINESS:** Ability to enjoy oneself and others and to feel satisfied with one's life.

While the above might seem a bit obvious, many sales reps are under the mistaken (and sometimes fatal) impression that they are merely a conduit for products or services. Effective sales reps realize that they are selling a solution that satisfies a need, which means that selling must involve a large amount of problem solving.

Happiness

This helps the sales rep maintain a sense of balance when things go awry. One way to look at happiness is as a reflection of the unspoken rules that sales reps use to interpret the meaning of events. For example, imagine two sales reps with two different rule sets (see Table 15.2).

Note that both sets of rules are arbitrary, emotional responses to identical events. From an entirely objective viewpoint, neither set of rules is strictly realistic. However, sales rep number two is far more likely to be happy than sales rep number one. Because of this, sales rep number two will consistently be more effective in sales situations, because he or she will be better able to feel and communicate enthusiasm and energy.

IMPROVING EQ

EQ can be enhanced in two ways. First, simply becoming aware of the EQ concept can help sales reps change their thoughts and behaviors, thereby increasing their EQ. Second, EQ can be enhanced through training, either online or in a classroom setting.

Table 15.2		
EVENT	SALES REP ONE'S RULES	SALES REP TWO'S RULES
The first call of the day goes poorly.	A bad first call means that I'm off my game and will have a bad day.	Every sales call is different, so the next will probably be better.
A customer changes an order at the last minute.	Customers who change orders can't be trusted.	Customers who change orders are more likely to be satisfied.
A big sales win comes seemingly "out of nowhere."	Even a blind pig finds an acorn once in a while.	An unexpected win means that I'm essentially a lucky person.

In most cases, participants in an EQ course start by taking a test to measure their current EQ levels. Sales reps then observe (or participate in) a series of interactions that illustrate the way sales reps with differing EQ capabilities handle common sales situations. After the training is complete, the EQ is remeasured in order to determine if it has changed. EQ trainers often have participants devise a follow-up action plan detailing specific steps that participants plan to take in order to continually improve their EQ capabilities.

Ultimately, however, the best measurement for EQ training is whether sales reps can sell more effectively. In most organizations, sales reps see a sharp increase in sales and in customer satisfaction immediately subsequent to EQ training. That uptick in sales is often followed by a period of gradual, additional improvement.

QUICK TIPS FOR YOUR TRAINING SESSION

QUICK
TIP

☑ Real EQ training is conducted by clinical psychologists and usually involves scientific measurement testing.

☑ This session can give your team only a taste of the potential of the EQ concept.

☑ The most important part of the training session is not the role-play but the discussion about what happened during the role-play.

☑ Don't let the mechanics of the session get in the way of the discussion.

☑ If a role-player experiences a problem with the acting element of the role-play, interrupt the training and, without comment or censure, assign a different volunteer. Act as if this is part of the training.

☑ During the discussions, keep the focus on the five key elements of EQ and how they influence the mock sales call.

ROB SCHER and **DR. JENNIFER WALDECK** were interviewed for this article. They are (respectively) the president and the director of curriculum development at the Scher Group, a full-service performance improvement company with clients in the automotive industry, real estate, property management, manufacturing, and behavioral health. Address: 650 Mondial Parkway Streetsboro, OH 44241. Telephone: 330-422-2028. Web: www.schergroup.com.

SALES MANAGER'S MEETING GUIDE

The following is a 10-step guide to making your sales team more aware
of EQ, resulting in better customer relations and higher sales. This training
session will take approximately 55 minutes.

1. Prior to the meeting, prepare a short set of slides based upon the material in this module. Be sure to include the material listed in the "Quick Tips" segment of this training module.

2. Still prior to the meeting, write the following captions on five sheets of paper, one caption per page: "Layoffs were just announced," "Your aunt has been in a car accident," "Your spouse just won the lottery," "Your MD called about the tests," and "You're probably going to be promoted." Put each piece of paper in an envelope and seal it. Mix up the envelopes.

3. Open the meeting by explaining that the team will be learning about EQ and how it influences sales situations. Explain that the team will be doing some role-playing and critiquing of each other's performance. Ask team members to participate to the fullest, and make it clear that you consider active participation in these training sessions to be an important part of their job evaluations.

4. Review the overall concept of EQ and the five most important EQ elements with the team. If necessary, provide examples from your own experience to illustrate these five elements. Briefly review the other 10 elements of EQ. Check with the team members to confirm that they believe an increase in EQ would be of benefit.

5. Have the team members mentally select a customer who represents a selling challenge. Set a time limit of five minutes and have each sales rep write a description of that customer containing everything that the rep can remember, including the customer's age, appearance, background, experience, work environment, etc.

6. Ask for two volunteers. Tell the first volunteer to describe his or her difficult customer to the entire team. Then ask the first volunteer to "become" the difficult customer. Tell the other volunteer that he or she will be making a sales call to that difficult customer.

7. After three minutes of this sales call, announce a halt and declare to the team that the phone has just rung in the customer's office. Select one of your prepared envelopes at random and hand it to the customer. Explain that the envelope contains the gist of the phone conversation the customer just had and that the customer should act as he or she believes the real-life customer would react. State that there are two important rules: first, the customer cannot end the sales call and, second, the customer cannot tell the sales rep the contents of the envelope.

8. Let the role-play continue for another three minutes, and then tell the sales rep that he or she now needs to wind up the meeting.

9. Have the customer reveal the contents of the envelope to the entire team. Take five minutes to discuss how the sales rep reacted to the situation and how, using EQ, that reaction might have been more effective.

10. Repeat steps 6 through 9 until you've gone through all the envelopes.

The company explored the normal failure routes: Perhaps products lacked competitiveness. Maybe the advisors couldn't explain the product adequately. But none of the standard areas revealed an answer. Instead, focus feedback groups indicated a need for better client relationships. Poor customer service swept substantial profits off the table like crumbs at a banquet.

ADDITIONAL READING

"The problem was a lack of coping skills, relationship-building habits, and empathetic listening among our sales force," explains Pam Smith, program manager for the emotional competence program at American Express Financial Advisors University in Minnesota. "Our team scratched their heads—this was more than any one item we could hang our hats on."

Yet they all had to admit that something was needed. That something was called "emotional intelligence," a phrase coined three years later by Harvard visiting faculty member, psychologist and author Daniel Goleman, whose book *Emotional Intelligence* (Bantam) shot to the top of the *New York Times* best-seller list and stuck around for 18 months. According to AEFA's Smith, "Our response [to the book] was: 'So that's what you call our program!'"

Yes, emotional intelligence, a highfalutin term that's really quite simple, means "the ability to monitor one's own and others' emotions, to discriminate among them, and to use the information to guide one's thinking and actions."

Once you know what it means and how to apply it, you can jump from average performer to sales superstar. AEFA did.

By investing one year, five psychologists, and millions of dollars in developing an internal training program, then rolling it out to field leaders in 1994, the company achieved impressive results. Participating regions enjoyed 11 percent greater sales. Advisors under managers who took the program grew their businesses by 18.1 percent compared to the 16.2 percent under the untrained managers. And in a company with more than 10,000 personal financial advisors, who manage more than $232 billion in assets, every iota magnified to a pretty payoff.

> Emotional intelligence: "the ability to monitor one's own and others' emotions, to discriminate among them, and to use the information to guide one's thinking and actions."

SECOND THAT EMOTION

Thanks to publicity after the book appeared, information on emotional intelligence has exploded among business leaders, so your company doesn't need to spend big bucks to follow AEFA's lead. In fact, AEFA now takes its training program on the road to interested companies.

One reason for the interest in emotional intelligence is the changing marketplace. The New Economy is exploding with emerging companies that have unknown track records. Consequently, first impressions—primarily made through salespeople—are more important than ever. "Billboards tout hundreds of dot-com companies whose names are unfamiliar. Customers don't remember logos or catch phrases—the New Economy is built on relationships," says Esther Orioli, CEO of San Francisco-based Q-Metrics, which offers EI mapping and consulting services. "People don't bring us in because they want employees to feel better. They're losing clients, they can't attract the best talent, or there's a low level of trust among the main players in the organization. So they don't have new products in the pipeline. Relationships dictate who owns the future."

Orioli keeps good company. When the U.S. Air Force relied on emotional intelligence to predict recruiter success, it saved $3 million a year by avoiding poor hires. Salespeople selected for emotional competencies at L'Oreal outsold their colleagues by $91,370 each, for a net revenue increase of $2,558,360. Met Life proudly proclaims that new salespeople who scored high on its learned-optimism test sell 37 percent more life insurance in their first two years. The Consortium for Research on Emotional Intelligence in Organizations cites 15 such startling examples. Even Enterprise Car Rental posts emotional intelligence information and self-tests at its Web site for wannabe sales players.

DEFINING EI

Like Hydra's head, however, the surplus of data about emotional intelligence also spawns a tangle of myths. According to experts, here are some of the things emotional intelligence is not:

1. Touchy-feely New Age babble about crying and being demonstrative in public.

2. Something women automatically excel at more than men.

3. A brand-spanking-new concept never before introduced or used in the business world.

4. A single trait—which is why EI fathers Goleman and Dr. Richard Boyatzis, chair of the organizational department in the Weatherhead School of Management at Cleveland's Case Western Reserve University, say they now refuse to refer to this concept with the popular one-size-fits-all EI acronym.

"People most commonly mistake emotional intelligence for being nice," says Goleman. "Emotionally intelligent leaders can be very firm, very directive when necessary. Or, empathic when that makes sense. The key lies in having a repertoire of relating styles and knowing when to use which."

The secret also lies in the ability to manage your own reactions as well as others' emotions. So when emotionally savvy sales stars feel pressure about their quotas, they continue to keep lunch appointments, refuse to snap at interruptions, and focus their office time on the strategy to meet their goals. In other words, they manage performance anxiety, according to Mary Fontaine, senior vice president and general manager at Hay/McBer in Boston. "An emotionally poor salesperson who freezes at conflict, procrastinates about calling irate customers because the idea is too painful—and the business link deteriorates with each passing hour." she explains. The emotionally gifted person sucks it up, phones the client, and deescalates the anger.

You can spot the highs and lows by simple observation. Stars aren't afraid to express their feelings, yet they don't let such negative emotions as guilt, embarrassment, or obligation rule them. They read nonverbal cues well, express optimism, and act independently with confidence. On the other hand, employees needing work refuse responsibility for their feelings, blaming others instead. Often they can't explain why they feel as they do without finger-pointing. They let things build up until they explode over a minor technicality. And they cling tightly to their beliefs even in light of new facts.

> "An emotionally poor salesperson who freezes at conflict, procrastinates about calling irate customers because the idea is too painful—and the business link deteriorates with each passing hour."

"Emotional intelligence is what we used to call character," Fontaine says, "Think of it as a two-by-two table: top left is 'Self,' top right is 'Others,' row one is 'Awareness' and row two is 'Management.' This trait is about covering all the combinations in the square." When seeking role models, former President Bill Clinton shows what to avoid: He rocks one-on-one in persuasion and empathy but flounders at impulse control.

That's one reason why Goleman insists that salespeople need strengths in at least six specific competencies:

1. **PERSUASION AND INFLUENCE:** Establish credibility, address the customer's issues and concerns, listen well, and understand how a customer sees the situation before matching product to need.

2. **DRIVE TO ACHIEVE:** Continually try to do things better to meet an internal standard of excellence.

3. **INITIATIVE:** Refuse to give up easily, and seize opportunity.

4. **EMPATHY:** Sense other people's attitudes and feelings, and know how they react to your message.

5. **CUSTOMER SERVICE:** Make the extra effort to meet customer needs, and follow up on contacts.

6. **SELF-CONFIDENCE:** Know strengths and remain optimistic about abilities.

In statistical weight, number one, persuasion/influence, is twice as important as numbers two and three, says Goleman, while drive to achieve and initiative rank equally. Both carry more importance than the remaining three traits.

KNOW YOURSELF

> **"Unless the employee shows enthusiasm for the possibilities, don't waste your time or the company's money on any development activity."**

"We all know you can do sales tasks up the wazoo and it won't make you great," says Boyatzis. "Typical sales training topics only bring you up to mediocre." So after dispensing product knowledge, spin techniques, and objection-handling skills, savvy sales leaders introduce an ongoing awareness of emotional intelligence components. "Inner motivation is essential—you can send them to a workshop, and they still won't get it," he adds. "Unless the employee shows enthusiasm for the possibilities, don't waste your time or the company's money on any developmental activity."

Start with the best practice guidelines Goleman and Dr. Cary Cherniss of Rutgers University developed for the consortium: formally assess individuals, preferably using a 360-degree feedback system. Goleman himself created one that Hay/McBer applies to its clients. Dr. Rich Handley, founder of EQ University in Texas, offers the Bar-On test to match participants against norms in their gender and age groups across North America. Q-Metrics provides a validated mapping program. At the least, provide feedback through a videotaped session of employees' interactions.

"There's a glaring problem when you ask employees to figure out where they stand on their own," Goleman points out. "The first component of emotional intelligence is self-awareness. If you lack that, you're blind to the main things you need to work on." In fact, his research shows that star performers in any field tend to overestimate their abilities versus how others rate them on only one of 20 competencies. Average performers overrate themselves on four or more competencies.

AEFA devotes two days to self-awareness, with a strong emphasis on self-talk. "Messages rattle around in our brains all day, and most of them are restrictive," Smith says. Your mission: Tag and bag that negative self-talk, replacing it with more upbeat conversation. AEFA leans on sensory walks to open these subconscious channels. Often the participants stroll through an ordinary parking lot, describing the different things they pick up with their senses. Other experts swear by journalizing, mapping, and yoga. No matter the method, focus on pinning down words that complete such phrases as "I am afraid . . ." "I appreciate . . ." and "I feel confused about . . . ."

A word of warning is necessary: Understand the difference between feelings and thoughts disguised as feelings. The disguised thoughts will finish the sentence "I feel like . . ." with a label (a moron, a doormat, a million bucks), a judgment (you were wrong, I should win), or a behavior (slapping someone, crawling under the covers) rather than an honest-to-God emotion. You're on the right track when you express emotions with such adjectives as comfortable, free, independent, worthy, resentful, pessimistic, nervous, or empty.

Fontaine advocates setting aside time each day for quiet reflection. "It's hard to manage yourself if you don't know what's happening to you. You don't need to be 100 percent accurate, but do make an effort to name your thoughts," she explains. You want to head off a brain hijack, where emotions overtake you. "Emotionally intelligent doesn't mean people never get angry. But they use strategies to manage it," she says.

Follow this exercise with interpersonal effectiveness training. In Smith's world, this breaks down into building relationships through skillful self-disclosure and learning how to respect boundaries. AEFA shows the comedic scene from the film *Planes, Trains and Automobiles* in which John Candy removes his sock near Steve Martin. Half the group watches to log the ways Candy violates his partner's personal space; the other half studies Martin's cues that this behavior pushes his buttons.

Finally, effective emotional intelligence programs touch on how to achieve optimal performance. For instance, EI neophytes often immediately jump to problem-solving or selling mode when a customer demands satisfaction. Emotionally intelligent salespeople

EXPERT ADVICE

LOOK OUT BELOW

Introducing emotional intelligence to your sales team carries dangerous baggage, say the experts. Stow these natural impulses:

1. **EXCLUDE YOURSELF.** Most senior levels need to understand, appreciate, and do their own development before it makes sense to cascade it through the organization. In fact, at nearly $1,500 per person, AEFA reserves the Cadillac five-day version of its EI training for senior levels, where it offers the most trickle-down impact.

2. **SHIP EMPLOYEES TO A TRAINING SESSION TO FIX THEM.** "Mandatory attendance makes a poor motivator for self-awareness," says Pam Smith, manager of the emotional intelligence program at American Express Financial Advisors University.

3. **ENCOURAGE EMPLOYEES TO ADDRESS EVERY VULNERABILITY OFF THE BAT.** "The best results occur when salespeople choose to first improve an area where they already experience decent success," says Esther Orioli, president and CEO of Q-Metrics. "The assessment feedback is predominately a tool," she stresses. "First, choose to change something that appeals to you. If you've never been good at making sustained, effective change, don't pick the worst thing you've waited all your life to fix."

4. **EXPECT IMMEDIATE RESULTS.** Reading the literature and attending a seminar represents the beginning. "True change takes months—plus support group feedback," says Mary Fontaine, Hay/McBer's senior vice president and general manager.

5. **CONFUSE TESTING RESULTS WITH THE GOSPEL TRUTH.** A coach should probe why a salesperson answers questions with, "I see things others don't see." A religious explanation separates the inspirational from those not grounded in reality.

6. **LABEL PEOPLE BY THEIR TEST RESULTS.** "Take the hubbub about IQ, for example," says Dr. Richard Handley, founder of EQ University. "Its highest correlation to success is approximately 12 percent. Yet look how our society has used this test to base decisions on and exclude people—when it fails as a good predictor, anyway." Instead, consider emotional intelligence to be a training subject that clarifies and points toward improvement, rather than a fence to protect your territory.

validate the customers' feelings, distract them, and then move on to selling when the customers can join them on the journey. "The rule should be to practice sharing a person's feelings before you present. You get much further if the person feels heard and empathized with," Fontaine assures.

Here's where deep breaths, paraphrasing, and such intensity-breaking speeches as, "Boy, it sounds like you're having a terrible day," and, "Could you hold one second? I really want to get something for you," do the most good. But without the self-awareness base, these sentences ring hollow. "You'll find pieces of EI in many sales training programs. But a formal EI program integrates it so that you're not just learning stock answers," Fontaine says. "Without the EI emphasis, oftentimes

> "The rule should be to practice sharing a person's feelings before you present. You get much farther if the person feels heard and empathized with."

people can't sustain the rote behavior; under stress, they can't manage themselves, and they revert to old habits. Then the self-talk chimes in, 'See, that was useless. I'm not a good listener.'"

That's not to suggest you can't rely on standard training programs to teach interpersonal skills, Boyatzis says. Even churches and temples offer great awareness exercises in marriage encounter sessions. The key lies in identifying in advance why employees attend and what emotional gain they can expect.

"No doubt readers are saying, 'So what's new here?'" Boyatzis acknowledges. Referring to Goleman's six competencies, he explains, "We're saying instead of worrying about every cognitive capability—including initiative, empathy, and networking—we now know which of them add value, so you can focus on the high-leverage ones." Just-in-time delivery of that training on an individual basis demonstrates the sales leader's own emotional intelligence growth.

As for AEFA, leaders there expect emotional intelligence recognition to ensure their future. "We're all going through substantial changes in the way we do business," Smith admits. "It's critical for us to better manage change and to minimize the depth and duration of down time. And EI encompasses just that: Can you and will you do what you need to do to meet your objectives? You can have the best and brightest in technology and academics, but if they can't martial those skills through their emotions, you have nothing."

Will you soon list emotional intelligence among such catch phrases as "swimming with sharks"? Psychologist and author Daniel Goleman shudders at the mention. After all, in one department's pilot program he discovered that after one year of coaching and on-the-job practice in self-selected emotional competencies, the results raised eyebrows. Salespeople previously in the 50th percentile improved by 15 percent. Those in the 70th percentile jumped 21 percent. And the 90th percentile rockets shot up an additional 24 percent.

So after 500 studies spanning hundreds of organizations, the emotional intelligence guru now says that when you weigh technical and purely cognitive abilities against emotional-intelligence skills, EI ranks twice as important as everything on the other side of the teeter-totter combined.

But this cheese doesn't stand alone. Consider what Dr. Richard Handley, founder of EQ University (an online testing, training, and coaching option for smaller businesses) honed in on in his course development research:

1. Hiring based on emotional intelligence fit to the sales job decreased one company's turnover. It previously lost 25 percent of all salespeople hired during their first year, at a cost in lost-training and employment fees of $3 million per year. After the program, first-year losses due to sales "failure" decreased by 92 percent. Not to mention that these veterans produced 2.7 times more money than average employees. "In the past, machinery was an organization's most important asset. The company could tell you to the dollar how much money they invested in equipment. Emotional intelligence indicators point to the red ink when auditing human beings," Handley says.

2. Emotional intelligence increases with age. Handley's highest group was 40- to 49-year-olds. He lacked sufficient numbers above age 50 to form conclusions in that category.

> "By locating an area of drag—often an emotional intelligence incompetence—you effect the same performance increase more cost effectively."

"To speed up, whether we're talking about a company or a plane, you make one of two choices: reduce the drag or increase the thrust," says this expert in business administration and licensed mental-health practitioner. In sales, a bigger engine means increasing sales output by hiring more staff as the thrust. But this option burns more fuel because it costs additional money to pay those bodies. "By locating an area of drag—often an emotional intelligence incompetence—you effect the same performance increase more cost effectively," he points out.

CREDITS

The following pieces were originally published in *Selling Power*.

Chapter 1

"How to Earn Customer Referrals" by Geoffrey James
"See New Faces, Win New Opportunities" by Lain Ehmann
"Six New Ways to Meet Hard-to-Reach Prospects" by William F. Kendy
"Leapfrog Your Competition" by Lain Ehmann
"Lead On" by William F. Kendy

Chapter 2

"What Is Sales Process" by Geoffrey James
"16 Ways to Increase Your Sales" by John R. Graham
"Process Is a Snap" by Henry Canaday

Chapter 3

"Building Relationships with Strategic Accounts" by Geoffrey James
"Get More Out of Your Best Accounts" by Carolee Boyles
"How to Master Major Account Sales" by Joe White
"Use the Right Tools" by Joe White

Chapter 4

"Gain Access to Decision Makers" by Geoffrey James
"Warm Calling Gets Appointments" by Graham Roberts-Phelps
"Get Your Foot in the Door" by John Fellows
"Don't Dis Appointments" by Ray Dreyfack

Chapter 5

"How to Build Report" by Geoffrey James
"Establishing a Relationship" by Renee Houston Zemanski
"Be Fast, Be Friendly, Be Cool" by Betsy Wiesendanger

Chapter 6

"Persuasive Presentations" by Geoffrey James
"Prepare for the Unknown" by Gina Rollins
"The Wow Factor" by Allison Smith
"Perfect Your Process" by William F. Kendy

Chapter 7

"The Mystery of Effective Proposals" by Geoffrey James
"How to Win Customers with Unbeatable Written Proposals" by William F. Kendy
"The Proposal Trap" by William F. Kendy

Chapter 8

"Consultative Selling Strategies" by Geoffrey James
"Differentiate Your Products and Boost Your Sales" by William F. Kendy
"Become a Business Asset to Your Prospects" by Joan Leotta

Chapter 9

"How to Handle Objections" by Geoffrey James
"No Price Too High" by Malcolm Fleschner
"Price Negotiating for Winners" by Andrea J. Moses

Chapter 10

"The Art of Sales Negotiation" by Geoffrey James
"Sharpen Your Sales Negotiation Skills" by Thomas P. Reilly
"The Fine Art of Handling Chiselers" by Renee Houston Zemanski

Chapter 11

"The Role of Rejection in Sales Success" by Geoffrey James
"How to Deal with Rejection" by William F. Kendy
"Positive Realism" by Steve Atlas
"Quick Recovery" by Alan S. Horowitz

Chapter 12

"Close More Sales" by Geoffrey James
"Is It Time to Close?" by Lain Ehmann
"Using the Right Techniques to Close a Committee" by Steve Atlas
"Effortless Closing" by Joan Leotta

Chapter 13

"Develop a Positive Attitude" by Geoffrey James
"Clear the Track" by Grant Gard
"What Gets You Going?" by William F. Kendy
"Self-Motivation" by William F. Kendy

Chapter 14

"The Psychology of Selling" by Geoffrey James
"The Psychology of Successful Selling—Part 1" by Dr. Charles Larson
"The Psychology of Successful Selling—Part 2" by Dr. Charles Larson
"Trick Psychology" by Dana Ray

Chapter 15

"Use Emotional Intelligence to Improve Sales" by Geoffrey James
"Create a Sales Edge by Using the Six Competencies of Emotional Intelligence" by
    Julie Sturgeon
"Fad Fodder?" by Julie Sturgeon

INDEX

ABOUT THE AUTHOR

© Hisham Bharoocha

A dual citizen of both Austria and the United States, Gerhard Gschwandtner is the founder and publisher of *Selling Power*, the leading magazine for sales professionals worldwide, with a circulation of 165,000 subscribers in 67 countries.

He began his career in his native Austria in the sales training and marketing departments of a large construction equipment company. In 1972 he moved to the United States to become the company's North American Sales Training Director, later moving into the position of Marketing Manager.

In 1977 he became an independent sales training consultant and in 1979 created an audiovisual sales training course called "The Languages of Selling." Marketed to sales managers at Fortune 500 companies, the course taught nonverbal communication in sales together with professional selling skills.

In 1981 Gerhard launched *Personal Selling Power*, a tabloid format newsletter directed to sales managers. Over the years the tabloid grew in subscriptions, size, and frequency. The name was changed to *Selling Power*, and in magazine format it became the leader in the professional sales field. Every year *Selling Power* publishes the Selling Power 500, a listing of the largest sales forces in America. The company publishes books, sales training posters, and audio and video products for the professional sales market.

Gerhard Gschwandtner has become America's leading expert on selling and sales management. He conducts webinars for such companies as SAP. His company has recently launched a new conference division which sponsors and conducts by-invitation-only leadership conferences directed toward companies with high sales volume and large sales forces.

For more information on *Selling Power*, its products and services, please visit www.sellingpower.com.

Subscribe to *Selling Power* today and close more sales tomorrow!

GET 10 ISSUES – INCLUDING THE SALES MANAGER'S SOURCE BOOK.

In every issue of *Selling Power* magazine you'll find:

■ **A Sales Manager's Training Guide** with a one-hour sales training workshop complete with exercises and step-by-step instructions. Get a new guide in every issue! Created by proven industry experts who get $10,000 or more for a keynote speech or a training session.

■ **Best-practices reports** that show you how to win in today's tough market. Valuable tips and techniques for opening more doors and closing more sales.

■ **How-to stories** that help you speed up your sales cycle with innovative technology solutions, so you'll stay on the leading edge and avoid the "bleeding edge."

■ **Tested motivation ideas** so you and your team can remain focused, stay enthusiastic and prevail in the face of adversity.

Plus, you can sign up for five online SellingPower.com newsletters absolutely FREE.

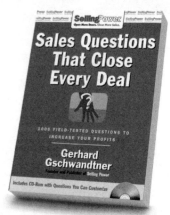

for any Sales Career

201 Super Sales Tips

The Pocket Sales Mentor

The Pocket Guide to Selling Greatness

The Ultimate Sales Training Workshop

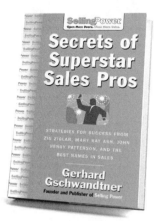

Secrets of Superstar Sales Pros

The Art of Nonverbal Selling